Palgrave Studies in Music and Literature

Series Editors
Paul Lumsden
City Centre Campus
MacEwan University
Edmonton, AB, Canada

Marco Katz Montiel
Edmonton, AB, Canada

This leading-edge series joins two disciplines in an exploration of how music and literature confront each other as dissonant antagonists while also functioning as consonant companions. By establishing a critical connection between literature and music, this series highlights the interaction between what we read and hear. Investigating the influence music has on narrative through history, theory, culture, or global perspectives provides a concrete framework for a seemingly abstract arena. Titles in the series, both monographs and edited volumes, explore musical encounters in novels and poetry, considerations of the ways in which narratives appropriate musical structures, examinations of musical form and function, and studies of interactions with sound.

More information about this series at
http://www.palgrave.com/gp/series/15596

Susan Reid

D.H. Lawrence, Music and Modernism

palgrave
macmillan

Susan Reid
University of Northampton
Northampton, Northamptonshire, UK

Palgrave Studies in Music and Literature
ISBN 978-3-030-04998-0   ISBN 978-3-030-04999-7   (eBook)
https://doi.org/10.1007/978-3-030-04999-7

Library of Congress Control Number: 2018965174

Cover credit: Photo 12 / Alamy Stock Photo

This Palgrave Macmillan imprint is published by the registered company Springer Nature Switzerland AG
The registered company address is: Gewerbestrasse 11, 6330 Cham, Switzerland

For Niall, Aidan, and Emily

ACKNOWLEDGEMENTS

The impetus for this book was provided by the 2014 biennial award to a newly published scholar in Lawrence Studies from the D.H. Lawrence Society of North America (DHLSNA) for my essay "'The Insidious Mastery of Song': D.H. Lawrence, Music and Modernism" (published in the *Journal of D.H. Lawrence Studies*, 2011). This honour was a motivating factor in writing up years of research, and I hope this book goes some way towards repaying the considerable efforts of the DHLSNA to foster Lawrence scholarship. I am particularly grateful to Holly Laird, then DHLSNA President, for her subsequent mentorship and astute comments on several draft chapters and conference papers.

The encouragement and critical skills of Howard J. Booth were crucial to the submission of my book proposal, and he has also generously read or heard most of the draft contents: his wise comments have resulted in a better book. I have learned much from Paul Poplawski and thank him more than I can say for his rigorous comments on an early draft of one chapter and an entire draft of the book. There are few trail-blazers in Lawrence and music, so I value the friendship of Bethan Jones and Fiona Richards, whose musical talents and writings I admire. My thanks to Bethan for her helpful reading of a draft chapter and to Fiona for her encouraging comments about my draft book proposal. Any remaining errors are, as the saying goes, entirely my own.

The research for this book began with two invitations to talk on the neglected topic of Lawrence and music. The first was from Delia da Sousa Correa, an exemplary scholar of literature and music, whose ongoing fellowship is warmly appreciated. The second came from the D.H. Lawrence

Society of Great Britain, to whom I am indebted for welcoming me as a postgraduate student in 2006 and for subsequent support: especially Malcolm Gray, Andrew Harrison, Sean Matthews, John Worthen, and friends who sadly are no longer with us, Ron Faulks, Rosemary Howard, Leslie Parkes, and Peter Preston.

The staff of Manuscripts and Special Collections at the University of Nottingham have been repeatedly helpful in retrieving items, catalogued and uncatalogued, from the archives, and in providing images of the *David* manuscript included in Chap. 7.

Terry Gifford generously shared his findings of songs transcribed by Lawrence that he tracked down many years ago at the Harry Ransom Center at the University of Texas at Austin.

I am grateful to the staff of the Anthony Burgess Foundation, Manchester, for tracking down materials relating to Anthony Burgess's song settings of four D.H. Lawrence poems, and to Andrew Biswell for his insights.

Quotations from the letters and works of D.H. Lawrence are reproduced with the permission of Paper Lion Ltd, acting on behalf of the Estate of Frieda Lawrence Ravagli.

With the permission of the *Journal of D.H. Lawrence Studies*, some initial thoughts about Lawrence's early poems set out in my exploratory essay "'The Insidious Mastery of Song': D.H. Lawrence, Music and Modernism" (*JDHLS* vol. 2.3, 2011) have been significantly expanded in parts of Chaps. 1 and 2.

I warmly thank Ginette Roy and the supportive network of scholars who regularly attend the annual international D.H. Lawrence conference at Université Paris Nanterre, not least Ginette's co-organiser Cornélius Crowley, who also shared with me his detailed notes on my reading of "Piano". There are a host of scholars, Lawrentian and otherwise, whose sagacity and humour I enjoy in equal measure: Michael Bell, Elise Brault-Dreux, Shirley Bricout, Catherine Brown, Nick Ceramella, Jane Costin, Keith Cushman, Fiona Fleming, Lee M. Jenkins, Jonathan Long, Brigitte Macadré-Nguyên, Stefania Michelucci, Christopher Pollnitz, Marina Ragachewskaya, Chris Ringrose, Neil Roberts, Judith Ruderman, Betsy Sargent, Joseph Shafer, Margaret Storch, Andrew Thacker, Jeff Wallace, and Janet Wilson.

Most of all, I am indebted to my family and friends for their endless support and encouragement; to Emily for her invaluable help with the index and proofreading, and wisdom beyond her years; and to Niall, Aidan, and Emily for their love and belief.

Contents

ABBREVIATIONS

LETTERS OF D.H. LAWRENCE

1L   *The Letters of D.H. Lawrence Volume I: September 1901–May 1913*. Ed. James T. Boulton. Cambridge: Cambridge University Press, 1979.

2L   *The Letters of D.H. Lawrence Volume II: June 1913–October 1916*. Eds George J. Zytaruk and James T. Boulton. Cambridge: Cambridge University Press, 1981.

3L   *The Letters of D.H. Lawrence Volume III: October 1916–June 1921*. Eds James T. Boulton and Andrew Robertson. Cambridge: Cambridge University Press, 1984.

4L   *The Letters of D.H. Lawrence Volume IV: June 1921–March 1924*. Eds Warren Roberts, James T. Boulton and Elizabeth Mansfield. Cambridge: Cambridge University Press, 1987.

5L   *The Letters of D.H. Lawrence Volume V: March 1924–March 1927*. Eds James T. Boulton and Lindeth Vasey. Cambridge: Cambridge University Press, 1989.

6L   *The Letters of D.H. Lawrence Volume VI: March 1927–November 1928*. Eds James T. Boulton and Margaret H. Boulton with Gerald M. Lacy. Cambridge: Cambridge University Press, 1991.

7L   *The Letters of D.H. Lawrence Volume VII: November 1928–February 1930*. Eds Keith Sagar and James T. Boulton. Cambridge: Cambridge University Press, 1993.

8L   *The Letters of D.H. Lawrence Volume VIII: Previously Uncollected Letters and General Index*. Ed. James T. Boulton. Cambridge: Cambridge University Press, 2000.

WORKS OF D.H. LAWRENCE

AR   *Aaron's Rod*. Ed. Mara Kalnins. Cambridge: Cambridge University Press, 1988.

CP   *Complete Poems*. Eds Vivian de Sola Pinto and Warren Roberts. Harmondsworth: Penguin 1993.

EME   *England, My England and Other Stories*. Ed. Bruce Steele. Cambridge: Cambridge University Press, 1990.

FWL   *The First 'Women in Love'*. Eds John Worthen and Lindeth Vasey. Cambridge: Cambridge University Press, 1998.

IR   *Introductions and Reviews*. Eds N.H. Reeve and John Worthen. Cambridge: Cambridge University Press, 2005.

K   *Kangaroo*. Ed. Bruce Steele. Cambridge: Cambridge University Press, 1994.

LAH   *Love Among the Haystacks and Other Stories*. Ed. John Worthen. Cambridge: Cambridge University Press, 1987.

LCL   *Lady Chatterley's Lover and A Propos of 'Lady Chatterley's Lover'*. Ed. Michael Squires. Cambridge: Cambridge University Press, 1993.

LEA   *Late Essays and Articles*. Ed. James T. Boulton. Cambridge: Cambridge University Press, 2004.

LG   *The Lost Girl*. Ed. John Worthen. Cambridge: Cambridge University Press, 1981.

MM   *Mornings in Mexico and Other Essays*. Ed. Virginia Crosswhite Hyde. Cambridge: Cambridge University Press, 2009.

MN   *Mr Noon*. Ed. Lindeth Vasey. Cambridge: Cambridge University Press, 1984.

Plays   *The Plays*. Eds Hans-Wilhelm Schwarze and John Worthen. Cambridge: Cambridge University Press, 1999.

PO   *The Prussian Officer and Other Stories*. Ed. John Worthen. Cambridge: Cambridge University Press, 1983.

Poems   *D.H. Lawrence: The Poems, Volumes I and II*. Ed. Christopher Pollnitz. Cambridge: Cambridge University Press, 2013.
          D.H. Lawrence: The Poems, Volume III: Uncollected Poems and Early Versions. Ed. Christopher Pollnitz. Cambridge: Cambridge University Press, 2018.

PS   *The Plumed Serpent*. Ed. L.D. Clark. Cambridge: Cambridge University Press, 1987.

Q   *Quetzalcoatl*. Ed. Louis L. Martz. New York: New Directions, 1998.

R   *The Rainbow*. Ed. Mark Kinkead-Weekes. Cambridge: Cambridge University Press, 1989.

SCAL   *Studies in Classic American Literature*. Eds Ezra Greenspan, Lindeth Vasey, and John Worthen. Cambridge: Cambridge University Press, 2003.

LIST OF FIGURES

CHAPTER 1

Introduction: "Words Writ to the Music"

Absolute music is not intended to have any relation to ideas, I think. It has no more meaning than the wind round the house, or the cries of sea gulls over the low surf. Who knows what thought, or meaning, or ideas are behind a larkie's singing – there ain't any; ... and there isn't thought behind music, but the music is behind the thought, music behind the idea, music the first wild natural thing, and thought is the words writ to the music, the narrow rows of words with little meanings. There *is* no *meaning* no verbal, ideational meaning to the *Pastoral Symphony* – or any other ... There ain't no meaning, and if there is, there oughtn't to be. All that is sayable, let it be said, and what isn't, you may sing it, or paint it, or act it, or even put it in poetry. (*1L* 100–101)

An informed debate about music and its role in the arts runs through D.H. Lawrence's earliest correspondence and focuses, in this letter of December 1908, on the central question of "absolute music".[1] As the son of a coal-miner from Eastwood, with a teaching certificate from University College Nottingham, Lawrence approached writing from a different perspective than his more privileged contemporaries, but if his views about the relationship between words and music varied from theirs, this was not from a position of ignorance. He engaged with symphonies but found more meaning in song, he could read and write music, and he demonstrated a deep interest in sound and its physical properties. Music was—and remained—a profoundly formative influence on his art, shaped by a love of singing, diverse reading and listening, and an attentive ear.

© The Author(s) 2019
S. Reid, *D.H. Lawrence, Music and Modernism,*
Palgrave Studies in Music and Literature,
https://doi.org/10.1007/978-3-030-04999-7_1

This first book-length study of Lawrence's lifelong engagement with music aims both to survey his extensive musical interests and how they permeate his writing, and to situate Lawrence within a growing body of work on music and modernism.[2] My twin focus is therefore on the music that Lawrence knew and how this influenced his writing, and on contemporary developments in music that parallel his quest for new forms of expression.[3] To enhance these discussions, each chapter ends with recommendations of music that illustrates its main themes.

This introductory chapter begins by explaining the context which prompted Lawrence to write about "absolute music" and why this issue was fundamental to the formation of early modernism. Lawrence had already begun to work out his position in his first essay "Art and the Individual", presented at the Eastwood Debating Society in March 1908, and to experiment with musical patterns in his early poems, notably "A Life History in Harmonies and Discords" (c. 1909). But his breakthrough to a mature style came through explorations of rhythm suggested by the Chladni patterns of sound waves made visible in sand (*2L* 184), illustrated in Fig. 1.1; since the specifically acoustic and musical implications of his oft-quoted analogy have never been fully considered, I set them out here as the basis for recurring discussion in subsequent chapters. Lawrence shared interests in music and sound with other contemporary writers and composers, but there were many ways to be a musical modernist: this book pursues his distinctive approach to writing words to music.

Absolute Music

Following Beethoven (whose Sixth or Pastoral Symphony Lawrence discussed above), orchestral music emerged in the nineteenth century as the pre-eminent form of music and as a model for the other arts: James McNeill Whistler responded in paint with his *Symphony in White, No. 1* (1861–1862) and the poet Stéphane Mallarmé wrote of the need "to find a way of transposing the symphony to the Book" (qtd. Bucknell 2001: 25). Conversely, Richard Wagner, who coined "absolute music" as a pejorative term for music without words or extramusical programme, argued for the continuance of an older concept, largely unquestioned before the Romantic period, which combined the Platonic principles of *harmonia*, meaning "regular, rationally systematized relationships among tones; *rhythmos*, the system of musical time, which in ancient times included dance and organized motion; and *logos*, language as the expression of human reason" (Dahlhaus 1991: 8).

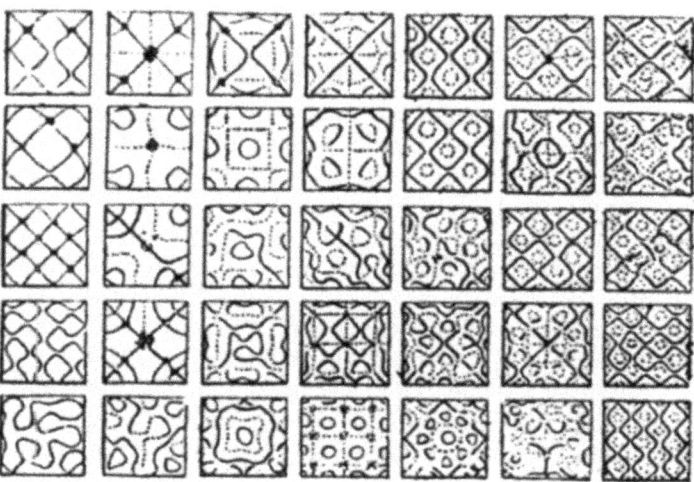

Fig. 1.1 Chladni patterns in sand: *Thought-Forms* (1901), by Annie Besant and C.W. Leadbetter

A growing tension between these three principles had profound effects in shaping various forms of modernism and provides an important context for understanding Lawrence's interest in music and his development as a writer who would come to prefer rhythm over harmony as an organising structure.[4]

Daniel Albright has argued that while there was "one stream of modernism" in which "the arts seem endlessly interpermeable, a set of fluid systems of construing and reinterpreting, in which the quest for meaning engages all our senses at once", there were others that "insist[ed] strongly on the absolute separateness of the artistic media" (Albright 2000: 6–7). Around 1910, even as modernism began to emerge, according to Virginia Woolf's well-known dictum (Woolf 2009: 38), conflicting methodologies became evident. A stream of inter-arts modernism was anticipated by Ezra Pound's claims—in the "Introduction" to his 1910 translation of the Italian troubadour poet Guido Cavalcanti—that music and writing shared an affinity with rhythm (Bucknell 2001: 54). Pound's view was soon echoed in John Middleton Murry's editorial in the first number of *Rhythm*, an "Art, Music, Literature Quarterly", which proclaimed that "the Life of art hang[s] upon seeking new chords to create new harmonies" (Murry 1911: 12). However, Irving Babbitt adopted an opposing stance in *The New Laokoon: An Essay on the Confusion of the Arts* (1910), harking back to Gotthold Ephraim Lessing's old *Laocoön* (1766), a landmark treatise on the separateness of art and poetry, which Babbitt now extended to insist on a domain of absolute music free from the extramusical "programmes" espoused by Berlioz, Liszt, and Wagner.

Lawrence had already begun to formulate his views in "Art and the Individual", a paper that upholds the Romantic concept of the artist, alienated from the everyday world and exempted from the need to be "intelligible", and berates those who find the "music of some of the great Germans ... too vague, confusing, unintelligible" (*STH* 141). In this respect, Lawrence's starting point resembles Pound's attraction to an "older romanticism that sees music as the highest art precisely because it is the least engaged with the material things of the world but expresses a pure subjectivity" (Wilson 2013: 77). For both writers, music offered a means of countering the inherently visual mimesis of nineteenth-century realism, while it also left them searching for ways to recover the materiality of sound in language. Lawrence's first essay thus arrives at "the edge of the great darkness, where no word-lights twinkle" (*STH* 141), a paradoxical position for a writer that contributes to his subsequent struggle against a Romantic tendency towards transcendence of the body and of language.

Lawrence's essay references "the Laocoon" (*STH* 139), an ancient Roman statue that shaped discussions about the beautiful in art from the Renaissance onwards (see Albright 2000: 8–21).[5] Although neither Lessing's *Laocoön* nor Walter Pater's discussion of Lessing in "The School of Giorgione" (1873) are mentioned, there are striking resonances with their ideas about artistic form.[6] Art, Lawrence explains, does not simply arise from "being intelligible" through language:

> the art was more likely to be in the tones, the gestures; and the value of song is its music, and its power to call up new pictures; and the value, the beauty of the tale or the song lies in the emotion which follows the music of the tones, the harmony of looks and gesture, the quivering feelings for which there are no words, and the pictures which were never on the retina, and never will be. (*STH* 140)

The references to "tones" and "harmony" here are redolent of absolute music and its perceived ability to evoke more than words or pictures, and so the essay resonates with Pater's well-known claims that:

Art, then, is always striving to be independent of the mere intelligence, to become a matter of pure perception ...

It is the art of music which most completely realises this artistic ideal, this perfect identification of form and matter, this strange chemistry, uniting, in the integrity of pure light, contrasted elements. In its consummate moments, the end is not distinct from the means, the form from the matter, the subject from the expression; they inhere in and completely saturate each other; and to it, therefore, to the condition of its perfect moments, all the arts may be supposed constantly to tend and aspire. Music, then, not poetry, as is so often supposed, is the true type or measure of consummate art. Therefore each art has its incommunicable element, its untranslatable order of impressions, its unique mode of reaching the imaginative reason, yet the arts may be represented as continually struggling after the law or principle of music, to a condition which music alone completely realises. (Pater 1873: 135)[7]

Pater's theoretical synthesis of content and form is also echoed in Lawrence's conclusion that words must "'pair like lovers, and chime in the ear'; they must 'progress in cosmic fellowship'—they must, in short, have form, style" (*STH* 140).[8] In Lawrence's case, however, there is already a hint of a spatial turn towards the "cosmic" that informs some schools of literary and musical modernism.

A shared discourse of the related purity and autonomy of music is closely related to Eduard Hanslick's *Vom Musikalisch-Schönen* (*On the Musically Beautiful*) (first published in 1854 and running to its tenth edition in 1901).[9] Pater uses the word "pure" twice in the passage quoted above and proceeds to propose an art form with "all impurities being burnt out of it and no taint, no floating particle of anything but its own proper elements allowed to subsist within it" (Pater 1873: 153). Lawrence's invocation of "the music of the tones" resembles Hanslick's assertion that the "content of music is tonally moving forms" (qtd. Bucknell 2001: 33), which is entirely separate from any incidental effects of music, including emotional responses. Lawrence concurs that "the emotion ... follows the music of the tones" rather than representing the essence of the music itself, although this was a contested point during the nineteenth century. Influential assertions by Friedrich Schlegel that music is a "universal language" of feeling (Bonds 2014: 113–114), and by Herbert Spencer that "it is the function of music to facilitate the development of this emotional language" (Spencer 2013: 261), ran counter to the thinking of Hanslick (and also of Arthur Schopenhauer, to whom I return later). In 1905, the music writer Ernest Newman directly disputed Spencer's findings, and although Spencer had influenced Lawrence's religious views, the views of Newman, Hanslick, and Schopenhauer prevailed in "Art and the Individual", which ends by criticising artists "who wallow in emotion" (*STH* 142).[10]

For Hanslick, the essence of music lay in the universal rather than the particular. The Pythagorean/Platonic conception of a "music of the spheres", which flowed through the writings of Boethius (c. 477–524) and circulated widely during the European Renaissance, also informed the first edition of Hanslick's *Vom Musikalisch-Schönen*, which concluded:

> It is not merely and absolutely through its own intrinsic beauty that music affects the listener, but rather at the same time as a sounding image of the great motions of the universe. Through profound and secret connections to nature, the meaning of tones elevates itself high above the tones themselves, allowing us to feel at the same time the infinite in the works of human talent. Just as the elements of music—sound, tone, rhythm, loudness, softness—are found throughout the entire universe, so does one find anew in music the entire universe. (Qtd. Bonds 2014: 184)[11]

Lawrence's 1908 essay places similar emphasis on the ability of "Art" to access secret and elemental connections in its assertion that "It is Art which opens to us the silences, the primordial silences which hold the secret of things, the great purposes, which are themselves silent" (*STH* 140). His threefold repetition of silences/silent evokes an unheard *musica mundana* (music of the world/spheres) that links to allusions in a letter (written in the same year) to a second order of *musica humana* (music of the human body), which sets souls "vibrating" (like a musical instrument) and, in an extended metaphor of a "keyboard", describes the "soul of a man [as] a stubborn and unwieldy instrument" (*1L* 66).[12] In this world scheme, it is not the role of *musica instrumentalis* (instrumental music) to "dress the unutterable experience in the livery of an idea", as Lawrence writes in "Art and the Individual", in which he then proceeds to dismiss programme music as so much noise:

> [People] should know that they are purposely led to the edge of the great darkness, where no word-lights twinkle. They had rather listen to a great din of a battle-piece and exclaim "There, the trumpet sounds charge!, hark, you can tell it's horses galloping!—do you hear the rumble of cannon?—isn't it fine!" The true battle-piece would call up the fury and fear in the hearts of a mass of soldiers, the pain and the primeval lust, without tin-pan clash-of-swords imitation. So Chopin's Funeral March seems far superior to the March in Saul; it has no drum thumping and artifice and extravagance. (*STH* 141)

Lawrence condemns the imitation of ideas in programme music as a "great din" of "rumbl[ing]", "clash[ing]" and "thumping", and asserts his preference for the quieter, self-contained music of Chopin over large-scale, publicly performed productions such as Handel's oratorio *Saul*.[13]

Hanslick mainly invoked Haydn, Mozart, and Beethoven as exemplars of "absolute music", but by the *fin de siècle*, Chopin's piano music stood out as a contrast to the noisy programmatic music of Wagner. Emma Sutton notes, for instance, how "The composers were often identified as representatives of antithetical musical traditions: Wagner associated with the Germanic, and with orchestral and dramatic music on a huge scale, Chopin (celebrated primarily for his brief piano pieces) aligned with the French, the expressive and impressionistic, and with intimate salon performance" (Sutton 2002: 169). Lawrence draws a similar contrast between two musical schools, although if he shows little awareness of Wagner at this time, this is because his musical tastes favoured a parlour repertoire exemplified by Chopin (as discussed in Chap. 2) and ran counter to the theatricalism of Wagner, at least until he started work on his second novel, *The Trespasser* (1912).[14] His initial ambivalence towards Wagner may have been reinforced by Edward Carpenter's article "Music-Drama in the Future" in the *New Age*, which precedes a review cited by Lawrence in "Art and the Individual".[15] Carpenter complains that Wagner was mistaken in "chain[ing] together" words and music "in a kind of forced union", "both endeavouring to express the same or related things" (Carpenter 1908: 312). This, asserts Carpenter, "is the all-too-common mistake of the theorist—of the man who levels his art to an idea", a criticism that resonates with Lawrence's condemnation of the human imperative to reduce art to the "intelligible": to "dress the unutterable experience in the livery of an idea, and prison it with fetters of words" (*STH* 141). Although Lawrence subsequently took a Wagnerian turn in *The Trespasser*, this signalled the beginning of a deepening critique of the cultural codes of Wagnerism, which was closer to Carpenter or Friedrich Nietzsche than his Wagnerite contemporaries, such as Ford Madox Hueffer (later Ford), E.M. Forster or Virginia Woolf.

Emotional Patterns: Words and Music

Towards the end of "Art and the Individual", Lawrence returns to the question of emotion and he condemns the expression of "sentimentality" as "by far the most grievous disease that an artist can contract" (*STH* 142)—akin to what Hanslick called the "decayed aesthetics of feeling" (qtd. Bonds 2014: 9). Lawrence's earliest poems, many of which have musical titles and themes, explore this perceived risk of combining words and music. "The Piano" (c. 1906–1908), an early draft of what would become the much-anthologised "Piano" (1918), explores the ability of song to transcend verbal meaning and transport the listener to another time and space: "To the old Sunday evenings, when darkness wandered outside / And hymns gleamed on our warm lips" (*Poems* 1399).[16] Lawrence's characteristically visceral response to music and its ability to bypass rational thought suggests an answer to the mind-body problem— "A woman is singing me a wild Hungarian air / And her arms, and her bosom, and the whole of her soul is bare"—even as "music's ravaging glamour" threatens to "devour" the poet's senses in an excess of emotion (*Poems* 1400). This threat to selfhood is more explicitly rendered by "the insidious mastery of song" in the poem's final 1918 version, "Piano", analysed at greater length in Chap. 2, but already music presented itself to the young Lawrence as a form of siren song with the potential either to enhance or overwhelm the poet or the individual, as something simultaneously to be desired and resisted.

The profound internal effects of music suggested by "The Piano" can also be interpreted in terms of the following analysis by Lawrence Kramer.

> As the art of the ear more than the eye, music collapses the sense of distance associated with visuality, and more broadly with the whole field of concepts, images and words. The resulting sense of immediacy tends to feel like bodily self-presence, the intimacy of oneself with one's own embodiment. We may know the suspension between autonomy and contingency all around us, but in music we feel it in ourselves. (Kramer 2002: 2–3)

For Kramer, music articulates "one of the core conditions of subjectivity", in which the self is poised between the particular and the universal: "In a sense, the absolutely particular ... seems to merge with the universal. On the other hand, all such experiences occur as parts of particular life histories whose meanings are contingent through and through" (Kramer 2002: 3). If Lawrence's "The Piano" illustrates the risks for the individual self of merging with the universal, then his series of poems called "A Life History in Harmonies and Discords" strives for balance between the particular and the universal, as Lawrence seeks to depersonalise individual experience by tracing impersonal musical patterns.

As John Worthen states, these fragments from Lawrence's 1909 note-book represent "some of his most inventive early poetry" (Worthen 1992: 274).[17] The titles suggest an informed interest in the structure of musical composition, with a sequence of five "Harmony" poems alternating with four poems called "Discord". This structure is used to describe the prog-ress of "A Life", from birth to mature relationship between two people, thus equating life with the harmonies and discords of a series of musical pieces, and in a form that resembles a sort of song cycle. Importantly, these poems describe and work with patterns. Indeed, the final poem begins "I trace a pattern" and for Worthen it is "in a way the most fascinat-ing of all", because the poet "recognises that his job is to find out what the pattern is" and the poem "describes an artist confronting the patterns made by the lives and conflicts of others" (Worthen 1992: 275–276). The unfinished poem runs as follows:

"Last Harmony"

Watch each pair of stepping feet trace a strange design
    With broken curves and faltering lines
I trace a pattern, mine or thine
    Patiently, and over-line

Ah the blindly stepping kindly feet
    Watch them tracing their design
The curves waver and meet and intertwine
    Twisting and tangling mine and thine

With pain did I carefully overline
    What part of my graph was plainly plotted
Where the curves were knotted I must define
    Pains that were clotted over mine

I have come [*Unfinished*] (*Poems* 1429)

The repetition of pattern words is striking: design (twice), curves (three times), line/over-line/overline, feet (twice). For Worthen, this language suggests an "artist (and word-artist) ... bring[ing] out the shape of the pattern he has managed to distinguish", but these words might equally suggest mathematics, dance or music. The puzzling term "overline" means to draw a line above or over text. As an antonym to the more common "underline", which adds emphasis, does overlining imply that emphasis is removed? Overlining, then, is a very different process than tracing; it is a term that is most commonly used in mathematical notation, as a way of grouping symbols together. Its synonyms of overbar or overscore suggest that, in Lawrence's poem, "line" may double as bar or score, which are musical terms, while "overline" also chimes with "overtones", another feature of music, which denotes the pitches in the harmonic series which resonate together above a specific note.[18] Overtones are present when any single note is struck—due to the physics of sound waves—and though to many of us they are barely audible, they have been fundamental to the harmonics of music since Pythagoras.[19] "Last Harmony" thus attempts "the music of the tones" described in his 1908 essay.

For Lawrence, then, there are patterns that transcend individuals, which he describes elsewhere as "involuntary", since "Various folk vibrate to various frequencies, tones, whatever you like" (*1L* 66). But such patterns—or vibrations—are difficult to plot objectively and so "Last Harmony" enacts a painful struggle to join up "broken curves and faltering lines" and to untwist, untangle and unknot "mine" from "thine", which nonetheless is a crucial process for individual and artistic development. At a later point in his literary development, Lawrence articulated what he was "after" to Edward Garnett as "that which is physic—non-human, in humanity" or "the inhuman will" (*2L* 182–183). In some respects, this oft-quoted 1914 letter is a more sophisticated working out of the concerns that Lawrence first raised in "Art and the Individual", which now compound the Futurism of Marinetti and a Schopenhauerian worldview.

In 1914, Lawrence again insists on going "deeper" than the feelings: "I don't care so much about what the woman *feels* ... I only care what the woman *is* – what she *is* – inhumanly, physiologically, materially" (*2L* 183). His aim is to reveal "states of the same single radically-unchanged element ... The ordinary novel would trace the history of the diamond – but I say 'diamond, what! This is carbon.' And my diamond might be coal or soot, and my theme is carbon" (*2L* 183). Lawrence's metaphorical excavation of the diamond for the purposes of breaking it down into its elements is the opposite of the unifying effect that Pater asserts in his claim that it is "the art of music which most completely realises this ... strange chemistry, uniting, in the integrity of pure light, contrasted elements" (quoted above, Pater 1873: 135).[20] Instead, what Lawrence describes as the "rhythmic form" he would develop in *The Rainbow* (1915) signals his move towards a quintessentially modernist concern with rhythm that he shared with Pound and Murry, among others.[21]

Lawrence's idea of rhythmic form specifically engages an acoustic analogy to sound waves made visible by Chladni figures: "Again I say, don't look for the development of the novel to follow the lines of certain characters: the characters fall into the form of some other rhythmic form, like when one draws a fiddle-bow across a fine tray delicately sanded, the sand takes lines unknown" (*2L* 184).[22] His letter describes a technique, discovered by the physicist, musician and pioneer of modern acoustics, Ernst Chladni (1756–1827), which consists of drawing a violin bow over a horizontal piece of metal lightly covered with sand (see Fig. 1.2).[23] The plate is bowed until it reaches resonance, when the vibration causes the sand to move and concentrate along the nodal lines where the surface is still. The patterns formed by these lines are what are now called Chladni figures (see Fig. 1.1).[24] These same figures feature in the first part of Schopenhauer's *The World as Will and Idea* (1819), suggesting, at the very least, that this was a shared influence with Lawrence, along with a Pythagorean emphasis on geometry and numbers which also informed Schopenhauer's theory of music as a "universal language":

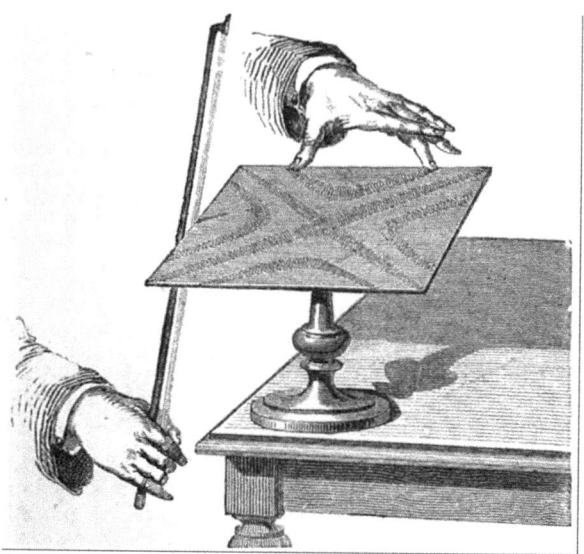

Fig. 1.2 Chladni's sound plate as illustrated in *Thought-Forms* (1901), by Annie Besant and C.W. Leadbetter

Its universality, however, is by no means that empty universality of abstraction, but quite of a different kind, and is united with thorough and distinct definiteness. In this respect it resembles geometrical figures and numbers, which are the universal forms of all possible objects of experience and applicable to them all *à priori*, and yet are not abstract but perceptible and thoroughly determined. (Schopenhauer 1909: 342)

Indeed, Chladni figures are a valuable example of the principle that Schopenhauer describes, since the patterns determined in accordance with variations in the harmonic series are rendered fully perceptible, and in similar ways, Lawrence applies the model of Chladni figures to render his various characters in *The Rainbow* and *Women in Love*, as I will discuss further in Chaps. 4 and 5.

Although the musical implications of Lawrence's analogy with Chladni figures have been neglected by critics, Leo Salter has noted how these patterns provide a structuring device for the interactions between characters:

Lawrence (the fiddler) places [his characters] in various situations to which a limited pattern of reaction was possible. This device operates most obviously when the four major characters are all together (for example, in *Water Party* and *Snowed Up*) but since each of the chapters in *WL* [*Women in Love*] is dominated by interactions between two or more of Ursula, Gudrun, Gerald and Birkin, the image is also a key structural feature. (Salter 2008: 28)

In positing Lawrence as a "fiddler", Salter complements Worthen's analogy of Lawrence as an artist following a pre-existing pattern in "Last Harmony", but he also comments further on Lawrence's struggle for autonomy as an artist since he does not place the lines in the sand himself: "the patterns are created indirectly by the fiddler" and in fact "the nature of the possible patterns is predetermined. However, because of their large number and variation in design there are many possible harmonic patterns which can result". These predetermined patterns have profound implications for the nature of the artistic act—or the action of an individual—which may also illumine the baffling "Moony" chapter of *Women in Love*, in which Birkin's stoning of the moon's reflection causes a "clamorous confusion" of waves on the surface of a pond (*WL* 247), akin to Chladni patterns.[25] Forster's judgement that "Why he [Birkin] throws, what the scene symbolizes, is unimportant" (Forster 1990: 131) attends closely to the wording of this passage, which specifies that Birkin's throwing of the stones, and the resulting rocking and surging of the pond and the obliteration of the moon, is "at random" and "without aim or meaning" (*WL* 247–248). The reader is subsequently warned that "words make no matter, any way" and "What was the good of talking, any way? It must happen beyond the sound of words" (*WL* 250). What happens beyond "the sound of words" is their rhythm—their "pulse" and "return" as depicted by the waves on the pond (*WL* 247)—and what Lawrence himself described in his Foreword to this novel as "continual, slightly modified repetition" (*WL* 486).

Lawrence's deeper engagement with rhythm accompanies a turn away from harmony. The "rocking and crashing … noise" (*WL* 248) resulting from Birkin's stoning of the moon is an assault on harmonics in a similar way that modernist composers pushed tonal relationships to the limit. Lawrence was aware of such developments, for instance, from his attendance at one of the first London performances of Richard Strauss's *Elektra* in 1910 (*IL* 157 n.5; *STH* 147). In the context of "Moony", however, Arnold Schoenberg's *Pierrot Lunaire* (*Moonstruck Pierrot*) (1912) offers a parallel response to a shared heritage of moon symbolism flowing through Beethoven's "Moonlight Sonata", the nocturnes of Chopin, and Debussy's "Clair de lune" into Maeterlinck's play *Pélleas et Mélisande* (1892), which inspired Debussy's moonlit opera of 1902 and Schoenberg's symphonic poem in 1903.[26] The modernist music of Debussy and Schoenberg responded, in different ways, to the challenges of negotiating a post-Romantic legacy that also preoccupied writers like Lawrence, and so these composers inform a series of comparisons throughout this study.[27]

OVERVIEW

This introduction has begun to trace a pattern in Lawrence's aesthetic development from 1908, when he began writing about "Art" in terms of the harmony of tones, through to a rhythmic turn realised in the writing of *The Rainbow* and *Women in Love* (largely completed by 1918). My examples here have suggested how his early experiments with music focused on poetry—the art closest to music through a shared origin in song—and these provide the basis for a more detailed consideration in Chap. 2 This opens by examining Lawrence's early musical influences and how he used the cadences of folk song and hymns in his early poems, while also working through a Romantic legacy of transcendent song. Subsequently, Edward Marsh's criticisms of his rhythms prompted an exploration of "the hidden *emotional* pattern that makes poetry, not the obvious form" (*2L* 104), that marked the beginning of Lawrence's quest for "rhythmic form" sketched above.[28] The evolution of his revised version of "Piano" (1918) suggests Charles Baudelaire, Ernest Dowson, and Thomas Hardy as important forebears in forging a poetics through decadent musicality that would also help to shape a musical prose. In this respect, Lawrence resembles his contemporaries, Pound and W.B. Yeats, in his negotiation of modernism through what Vincent Sherry (2015) has usefully framed as a reinvention of decadence.

Chapters 3, 4 and 5 track the parallel musical development of Lawrence's fiction as he worked through a discourse of literary Wagnerism and leitmotif in his early novels to the realisation of rhythmic forms in *The Rainbow* and *Women in Love*. The shattering violence of the First World War, already underlined by the language in "Moony" of exploding and clamouring, influenced an increasing fragmentation of form in Lawrence's works of the 1920s: these draw increasingly on poetry and song, which are perceived to offer the potential to heal individuals and communities, as I argue in Chaps. 6 and 7.

Discussions of Lawrence and music have been infrequent (see Michelucci and Poplawski 2015: 8–9), but they often turn on the influence of Wagner (notably Blissett 1966; Martin 1982; Oates 1978; Stevens 2014), while overlooking an initial ambivalence in his first novel *The White Peacock* (1911) that draws instead on Bizet's *Carmen*, praised by Nietzsche as "the opposite of Wagner" (Nietzsche 1911: 2). Chapter 3 considers Lawrence's Wagnerian turn in *The Trespasser* as both a response to a cultural phenomenon that was impossible to ignore in early twentieth-century literary circles and a deepening engagement with a discourse of decadence. Piqued by Hueffer's criticisms of his fiction, Lawrence looked closely at the literary form of Gustave Flaubert and Thomas Mann and his resulting critique of leitmotif in his review of "German Books" (1913) bears striking parallels with Nietzsche's attack on Wagnerian decadence in *The Case of Wagner* (1888). A re-reading, in turn, of Lawrence's experiments with leitmotif in *The Trespasser* as an engagement with Wagner's *Tristan und Isolde*, and its iconic "Tristan chord", suggests a counter critique akin to Debussy's opera *Pélleas et Mélisande* (referenced in its opening pages: *T* 52).

Although a debate with Wagnerism persisted throughout much of Lawrence's long fiction, it is muted in *Sons and Lovers* (1913), arguably also his least musical novel in its foregrounding of a visual realism. Chapter 4 considers how—in negotiating a path between realism and romanticism, the material and the spiritual—*The Rainbow* takes an opposite trajectory to Wagner's retreat from the outside world in his final opera, *Parsifal* (1881). The novel's structure of widening circles (akin to sound waves) and acoustic patterns of repetition and stasis at the level of language facilitate a spatial turn "Away from time, always outside of time!" (*R* 187) that parallels musical techniques such as Debussy's *arabesque*. Lawrence's project of reconciling "man's artistic effort and his religious effort" (*STH* 59) emerges as remarkably similar to that of Schoenberg, who aspired in his oratorio *Die Jakobsleiter* (begun in 1912) to create "Perhaps the most glorious work in existence ... Philosophy, religion that are perceived with the artistic senses" (qtd. Auner 2003: 119).

Against the backdrop of the war, the rhythmic form of *Women in Love* becomes "a pulsing, frictional to-and-fro" (Foreword *WL* 486). Chapter 5 maps the oppositional modes of agitation and stillness in this novel against two sound worlds represented by Gerald Crich's Wagnerian concept of harmony and Birkin's formulation of a more ethical polyphony. A ground bass of machine noise—"a music more maddening than the siren's" (*WL* 116)—erupts occasionally into the foreground, as in the Stravinsky-esque episode at the level crossing in "Coal-Dust", and contrasts sharply with the Debussyan stillness sought by Birkin and Ursula in "Excurse". Lawrence's deepening critique of Wagnerism is evidenced by Gerald's characterisation as the doomed victim of an industrial society in love with war and death, which bears comparison with Arnold Bax's use of Wagner's "Sick Tristan" motif in *Tintagel* (1917–1919), also composed during the war. A reassessment of the influence of Lawrence's friendships with the composers Philip Heseltine and Cecil Gray considers how their shared interests in folk songs suggested a counterbalance to the putative stature of Wagnerian opera. This interplay of the local and the universal in music resonates with Gustav Holst's *The Planets Suite* (1918), which also has rich parallels with Birkin's "star equilibrium" as a music of the spheres. Lawrence's polyphonic novel thus corresponds with a diverse range of musical developments.

Chapter 6 traces a further retreat from large-scale musical productions towards the simplicity of song in Lawrence's "little book[s]" of war poems (*3L* 233) and his episodic novel about an itinerant flute player, *Aaron's Rod* (1922). These works register the shattering noise of wartime London in contrast with the pre-war elegies to the centre of Empire and unified aesthetic forms in H.G. Wells's novel *Tono-Bungay* (1909) and Ralph Vaughan Williams's *A London Symphony* (1914). This provides the context for an exploration of Lawrence's outburst of "disgust" at the "sham Egypt" depicted in a performance of *Aïda* in *Aaron's Rod* (*AR* 46), and how this militaristic imperialism is counterpointed by "All of Us" (1916), his "tiny book" of war poems (*3L* 51) based on the songs of the Egyptian fellaheen (labourers). Analysis of the war poems of *Bay* (1920) suggests thematic and structural interests in song and silence that on the one hand resonate with Debussy's muted response to the war and, on the other, with the loose-knit structure and themes of Schubert's *Winterreise*, including the notions of "wintering", journeying and fragmentation that helped to shape *Aaron's Rod* (*3L* 197).

This broadly chronological study culminates with Lawrence's novel *The Plumed Serpent* (1926), which incorporates the text of a cycle of songs and hymns, and his final play *David* (1926), for which he composed ten pieces of music. The intermedial form of these works bears comparison with the quintessentially modernist operas *Le Testament de Villon* (1919–1923) by Pound and *Four Saints in Three Acts* (1927–1928) by Gertrude Stein. Indeed, *The Plumed Serpent*, with its emphasis on costume and staging, as well as songs, flute and drum music and dance, resembles "grand opera", as his friend Witter Bynner observed (Bynner 1953: 218). The scale of *David* is similarly operatic, with its large cast of 58 performers, including soloists, choruses, dancers, and instrumentalists. Chapter 7 considers how the "Songs and Hymns of Quetzalcoatl" (the Aztec god in the form of a plumed serpent who gives the novel its title) and the music for *David* draw on the rhythms of Native American music in ways that contrast markedly with the "American" music of Antonín Dvořák and Aaron Copland and are more comparable with the "Aztec" compositions of Carlos Chávez and the corporealism of Harry Partch. The songs in Lawrence's major works of the 1920s are integral to their form and structure in ways that blur the boundaries between prose and poetry, music and drama. In *The Plumed Serpent* and *David*, Lawrence most closely realises what he described in his letter of 1908 as "words writ to the music" (*IL* 101), but this is not absolute music: it is music with a programme to regenerate the old world.

My concluding chapter begins to explore why Lawrence has been marginalised in studies of what Werner Wolf calls *The Musicalization of Fiction* (1999). During the twentieth century, the symphony emerged as the preeminent musical model for the novel and Lawrence was sidelined as a protagonist of song (Forster 1990: 116; Huxley 1932: xvii). Anthony Burgess is a notable exception, a prolific composer as well as a celebrated writer, who placed Lawrence alongside James Joyce as writers who revelled in the musicality of language. Burgess also paid tribute by setting four Lawrence poems as the song cycle *Man Who Has Come Through*

(1985), which, since it has gone largely unnoticed within Lawrence studies, I describe in my Afterword.

Cumulatively, this study demonstrates the modernist blending of the arts within Lawrence's oeuvre, which contains far more musical references and contexts than can be covered fully in a single volume. Lawrence's relationship with opera, for example, could occupy an entire book, while there is much more that could and should be said about the influences of music hall and jazz music, or parallels with specific composers and other musical writers. Above all, my book intends to suggest areas for further study and a place for Lawrence within the field of music and modernism.

RECOMMENDED LISTENING

Beethoven	Sixth Symphony
Chopin	Piano Sonata No. 2, third movement "Marche funèbre: lento"
Debussy	"Clair de lune", third movement of *Suite bergamesque*
Handel	*Saul*, "The dead march" (Act III, Scene 77)
Schoenberg	*Pierrot Lunaire*
Wagner	Prelude to *Tristan und Isolde*

NOTES

1. See, particularly, Lawrence's letters to Blanche Jennings on various aspects of music and the arts, between July 1908 and January 1910 (in *1L*).
2. See, for instance, comparable surveys of E.M. Forster and music by Michelle Fillion (2010) and of Virginia Woolf and music by Emma Sutton (2013); and more general studies of music and modernism referenced here by Daniel Albright (2000) and Brad Bucknell (2001). For a comprehensive overview of recent literature that I therefore will not replicate here, see Waddell 2017. Several of the works discussed by Waddell are referenced within my following chapters. For a summary of existing critical work on Lawrence and music see Michelucci and Poplawski (2015: 8–9).
3. Modernism in music is defined as breaking "with traditional modes of writing dependent on a diatonic system (rooted in the use of major and minor keys), and challeng[ing] the narrative-like structural coherence which had reached a dramatic culmination in the large-scale post-romantic works of Richard Wagner, Richard Strauss, and Gustav Mahler" (Jones 2003: 267). Beginning in the 1890s, its key figures are Claude Debussy, Arnold Schoenberg, and Igor Stravinsky, although for a much more comprehensive survey see Albright 2004.

4. My study seeks to work with a fluid definition of modernisms in accordance with the suggestion that "modernism should be thought of as an overdetermined, overlapping, and multiply networked range of practices that were always caught up in a dialectical process of affirmation and negation" (Brooker et al. 2010: 10). Nonetheless, like Vincent Sherry, I use "modernism" as a singular term, "not as a gesture of constriction" but as the expression of "sensibility, temperament, disposition, attitude, outlook – a range that indexes the extensive import of the special awareness we designate as 'modernism'" (Sherry 2017: 19–20).

5. In summary, Lessing noted that the sculpture of a man being squeezed to death by a snake is not depicted as screaming, partly because of the obligation to be beautiful, but also because "the visual arts must never depict a moment of climax". Poetry, on the other hand, can portray the full drama because it is a medium that operates in time, while "painting and sculpture must observe the decorum of space" (Albright 2000: 9).

6. James T. Boulton notes that Lawrence's "interest may have derived from Garnett's 4000-word extract from Lessing's *Laocoön* illustrated by a picture of the sculpture" (*1L* 5). His brother Ernest owned the 20-volume edition of Richard Garnett's *The International Library of Famous Literature* (1899), which was a much-prized resource for the family and particularly for Lawrence.

7. Lawrence may well have read this by January 1914, when he refers again to "the Laocoon" and to Pater in a letter which describes his struggle with a new style of writing as he completes 340 pages of what would become *The Rainbow* (*2L* 137–138).

8. Lawrence seems to be quoting Henry Bryan Binns (see *STH* 274 n.140:25).

9. The first English translation was in 1891 (Bonds 2014: 7).

10. Spencer's influence on Lawrence is disclosed in a letter of October 1907, to Reverend Robert Reid, which states that reading Spencer, among others, "has seriously modified my religious beliefs" (*1L* 36–37). Spencer's views on music were disputed by Ernest Newman in *Musical Studies* (1905). In his letter of December 1908, Lawrence told Blanche that he "snatched at Ernest Newman" (*1L* 100), but we do not know exactly what he had read.

11. This passage was excised from the second edition, perhaps, as Bonds suggests, because Hanslick realised that he had moved beyond music in itself as a self-contained absolute into something that relied on a relationship with the universe, although what then was lacking in subsequent editions was any "explanation at all of just how music might relate to anything beyond itself" (Bonds 2014: 190).

12. For a brief account of Boethius's threefold classification of music, see Bonds 2014: 32.

13. Chopin was part of the repertoire of Lawrence's sister Ada, who recalls that "Bert brought me Chopin waltzes, music by Tschaikowsky and Brahms" (Lawrence and Gelder 1966: 52).

14. Lawrence's letter of 15 December 1908 mentions *Tannhäuser* and *Lohengrin*, but as the editor notes "Helen Corke asserts that, in 1909, DHL's 'only experience of Wagner's music had been a performance, in Nottingham theatre, of *Tannhäuser*, when he reacted against the stridency of the Venusberg music'" (*1L* 99 n.3).

15. A review by F.S. Flint of the prose poems of Henry Bryan Binns in the *New Age* (15 August 1908) is the likely source for Lawrence's quotation of Binns in his essay (*STH* 274 n.140:25). The title of his essay and its opening paragraph also reflect Lawrence's interest in the *New Age*, a paper which Jessie Chambers records that "Lawrence took regularly for a time" (*STH* 271 n.135:2).

16. As this book went to press Volume III of the Cambridge Edition of *The Poems* had just been published: this presents three variants of "The Piano". The version discussed here is "The Piano [1]" (*Poems* 1399–1400).

17. The poem-sequence was first printed in full in Appendix III of Worthen 1992: 495–499, and is now collected for the first time in *Poems* 1425–1429.

18. For a definition see http://dictionary.onmusic.org/terms/2459-overtone

19. "Pythagoras's discovery of the relationship between number and sound … demonstrated an even broader connection between the worlds of the visible and the invisible" (Bonds 2014: 23).

20. Lawrence had recently been reading Pater (*2L* 138).

21. E.M. Forster discussed "Pattern and rhythm" in the final chapter of *Aspects of the Novel* (1927), and Virginia Woolf described herself as writing "to a rhythm and not a plot" (Nicolson 1978: 204).

22. Lawrence's concern with vibrations is also quintessentially modernist, deriving from a combination of interests in music, science, and theosophy. See Enns and Trower (2013) for a study of what they call *Vibratory Modernism*, in which an essay by Sausman (2013) briefly discusses Lawrence.

23. For a discussion of this letter and its sources see Kinkead-Weekes 1996: 121–126. C.P. Ravilious (1973) was the first to decipher the metaphor of the fiddler and the sandbox and Thomas Gibbons (1988) conjectured that Lawrence may have encountered the Chladni experiments by reading *Thought-Forms* (1901), by C.W. Leadbetter and Annie Besant. Figures 1.1 and 1.2 use the illustrations given in that book, but Chladni patterns were widely referenced in other books that Lawrence read, including Schopenhauer 1909: 347. For Lawrence's reading of Schopenhauer see Worthen 1992: 174.

24. Video demonstrations are also widely available on YouTube. See, for example: https://www.youtube.com/watch?v=9uEeADQN8Jo

25. For a succinct reading of the "Moony" chapter, including an acknowledgement of occult sources, see Kinkead-Weekes 1996: 393–394. Critical interpretations of "Moony" usually focus on the visual aspects, see, particularly, Stewart 1999: 84–88.

26. Schoenberg's settings of 21 poems from a series by Albert Giraud "rang[e] in style from ironic echoes of romantic lieder, salon and cabaret music, by way of Schoenberg's own recently evolved expressionistic atonality, to an intricately constructivist mode of counterpoint" (Northcott 2012: 9). For brief remarks about how Lawrence's writing compares with Schoenberg, see Krockel 2007: 107, 161.

27. Music also had the advantage of freedom from the realism and naturalism that had dominated the visual and literary arts in the second half of the nineteenth century (Dahlhaus 1989: 5–7).

28. A large volume of criticism addresses Lawrence's experiments with rhythm and language—see particularly the studies by Balbert (1974) and Ingram (1990) and the section "Bibliography 93: Lawrence and Language" in Poplawski (1996: 574–578). My intention throughout this book is not to elide this valuable work but to draw attention to the relatively neglected acoustic and musical dimensions of Lawrence's oeuvre.

REFERENCES

Albright, Daniel. 2000. *Untwisting the Serpent: Modernism in Music, Literature, and the Other Arts*. Chicago/London: University of Chicago Press.

———, ed. 2004. *Modernism and Music: An Anthology of Sources*. Chicago/London: University of Chicago Press.

Auner, Joseph. 2003. *A Schoenberg Reader*. New Haven/London: Yale University Press.

Balbert, Peter. 1974. *D.H. Lawrence and the Psychology of Rhythm*. The Hague: Mouton.

Blissett, William. 1966. Lawrence, D'Annunzio, Wagner. *Wisconsin Studies in Contemporary Literature* 7 (1): 21–46.

Bonds, Mark Evan. 2014. *Absolute Music: The History of an Idea*. Oxford: Oxford University Press.

Brooker, Peter, Andrzej Gąsiorek, Deborah Longworth, and Andrew Thacker, eds. 2010. *The Oxford Handbook of Modernisms*. Oxford: Oxford University Press.

Bucknell, Brad. 2001. *Literary Modernism and Musical Aesthetics: Pater, Pound, Joyce and Stein*. Cambridge: Cambridge University Press.

Bynner, Witter. 1953. *Journey with Genius: Recollections and Reflections Concerning the D.H. Lawrences*. London: Peter Nevill.

Carpenter, Edward. 1908. Music-Drama in the Future. *New Age*, August 15, 311–312.

Dahlhaus, Carl. 1989. *Between Romanticism and Modernism*. Trans. Mary Whittall. Berkeley: University of California Press.

———. 1991. *The Idea of Absolute Music*. Trans. Roger Lustig. Chicago/London: University of Chicago Press.

Enns, Anthony, and Shelley Trower, eds. 2013. *Vibratory Modernism*. Basingstoke: Palgrave Macmillan.

Fillion, Michelle. 2010. *Difficult Rhythm: Music and the Word in E.M. Forster*. Urbana/Chicago/Springfield: University of Illinois Press.

Forster, E M. 1990. *Aspects of the Novel*. London: Penguin.

Gibbons, Thomas. 1988. "Allotropic States" and "Fiddle-Bow": D.H. Lawrence's Occult Sources. *Notes and Queries* 35 (3): 338–341.

Huxley, Aldous. 1932. Introduction. In *The Letters of D.H. Lawrence*, ix–xxxiv. London: William Heinemann.

Ingram, Allan. 1990. *The Language of D.H. Lawrence*. Basingstoke: Palgrave Macmillan.

Jones, Bethan. 2003. Music. In *Encyclopedia of Modernism*, ed. Paul Poplawski, 267–271. Westport: Greenwood Press.

Kinkead-Weekes, Mark. 1996. *D.H. Lawrence: Triumph to Exile, 1912–1922*. Cambridge: Cambridge University Press.

Kramer, Lawrence. 2002. *Musical Meaning: Toward a Critical History*. Berkeley/Los Angeles: University of California Press.

Krockel, Carl. 2007. *D.H. Lawrence and Germany: The Politics of Influence*. Amsterdam/New York: Rodopi.

Lawrence, Ada, and G. Stuart Gelder. 1966. *Young Lorenzo: Early Life of D.H. Lawrence*. New York: Russell & Russell.

Martin, Stoddard. 1982. *Wagner to "The Waste Land": Swinburne, Wilde, Symons, Shaw, Moore, Yeats, Joyce, Lawrence, Eliot*. London: Macmillan.

Michelucci, Stefania, and Paul Poplawski. 2015. D.H. Lawrence and the Arts: A Sketch of the Critical Heritage. *D.H. Lawrence Review* 40 (1): 1–20.

Murry, John Middleton. 1911. Art and Philosophy. *Rhythm* 1 (1): 9–12.

Nicolson, Nigel, ed. 1978. *Reflection of the Other Person: The Letters of Virginia Woolf, 1929–1931*. Vol. 4. London: The Hogarth Press.

Nietzsche, Friedrich. 1911. *The Case of Wagner*. Trans. Anthony M. Ludovici. Edinburgh/London: T.N. Foulis. Project Gutenberg. http://www.gutenberg.org/files/25012/25012-pdf.pdf

Northcott, Bayan. 2012. Introduction. In *Voicing Pierrot*, ed. Jane Manning, 9–10. Amaroo: Southern Voices.

Oates, Joyce Carol. 1978. Lawrence's *Götterdämmerung*: The Apocalyptic Vision of *Women in Love*. *Critical Inquiry* 4 (3): 559–578.

Pater, Walter. 1873. The School of Giorgione. In *The Renaissance: Studies in Art and Literature*. http://www.victorianweb.org/authors/pater/renaissance/7.html

Poplawski, Paul. 1996. *D.H. Lawrence: A Reference Companion*. Westport/London: Greenwood Press.

Ravilious, C.P. 1973. Lawrence's "Chladni Figures". *Notes and Queries* ccxviii: 331–332.

Salter, Leo. 2008. Lawrence, Newton and Einstein. *Etudes Lawrenciennes* 38: 25–39.

Sausman, Justin. 2013. From Vibratory Occultism to Vibratory Modernism: Blackwood, Lawrence, Woolf. In *Vibratory Modernism*, ed. Anthony Enns and Shelley Trower, 30–52. Basingstoke: Palgrave Macmillan.

Schopenhauer, Arthur. 1909. *The World as Will and Idea*. Trans. W.B. Haldane and J. Kemp. London: Kegan Paul. https://www.gutenberg.org/files/38427/38427-pdf.pdf

Sherry, Vincent. 2015. *Modernism and the Reinvention of Decadence*. Cambridge: Cambridge University Press.

———, ed. 2017. Introduction. In *The Cambridge History of Modernism*. Cambridge: Cambridge University Press.

Spencer, Herbert. 2013. On the Origin and Function of Music. *Essays on Education and Kindred Subjects*. Print on Demand by Amazon UK.

Stevens, Hugh. 2014. From *Genesis* to the *Ring*: Richard Wagner and D.H. Lawrence's *Rainbow*. *Textual Practice* 28 (4): 611–630.

Stewart, Jack. 1999. *The Vital Art of D.H. Lawrence: Vision and Expression*. Carbondale/Edwardsville: Southern Illinois University Press.

Sutton, Emma. 2002. *Aubrey Beardsley and British Wagnerism in the 1890s*. Oxford: Oxford University Press.

———. 2013. *Virginia Woolf and Classical Music*. Edinburgh: Edinburgh University Press.

Waddell, Nathan. 2017. Modernism and Music: A Review of Recent Scholarship. *Modernist Cultures* 12 (2): 316–330.

Wilson, Leigh. 2013. *Modernism and Magic: Experiments with Spiritualism, Theosophy and the Occult*. Edinburgh: Edinburgh University Press.

Wolf, Werner. 1999. *The Musicalization of Fiction: A Study in the Theory and History of Intermediality*. Amsterdam/Atlanta: Rodopi.

Woolf, Virginia. 2009. Character in Fiction. In *Selected Essays*, ed. David Bradshaw, 37–54. Oxford: Oxford University Press.

Worthen, John. 1992. *D.H. Lawrence: The Early Years, 1885–1912*. Cambridge: Cambridge University Press.

CHAPTER 2

"The Insidious Mastery of Song": Cadence and Decadence in the Early Poems

Introduction

Tales of sing-songs and musical evenings are a rich seam running through memoirs about Lawrence. Jessie Chambers attests that Lawrence's favourite subject at college was "music, which of course was singing. He liked the Folk songs, particularly the ballad of 'Henry Martin' and 'I sowed the seeds of love'. We bought the song book in use at College, *A Golden Treasury of Song*, and had great times singing 'I triumph, I triumph', 'The Lay of the Imprisoned Huntsman', 'Vulcan's Song' and practically everything in the book" (Chambers 1980: 80). She conflates her sources here in an interesting way, since Palgrave's *The Golden Treasury of English Songs and Lyrics* is not a song book but an anthology of poems (as she accurately recalls a few pages later): this "became a kind of bible to us. Lawrence carried the little red volume in his pocket and read to me on every opportunity, usually out in the fields" (Chambers 1980: 99). Chambers seems to have muddled one red volume with another that she also mentions, namely, *The National Song Book* (1906), but her confusion of songs and poems suggests two important themes for approaching Lawrence's interest in music.[1]

Firstly, lyric poetry had once been united with song; in the Greek mythology of Euterpe as one of the nine Muses (who also provide the root of the word music)[2] and in the European traditions of bards and troubadours. In many ways, Palgrave's anthology is a celebration of the proximity

© The Author(s) 2019
S. Reid, *D.H. Lawrence, Music and Modernism*,
Palgrave Studies in Music and Literature,
https://doi.org/10.1007/978-3-030-04999-7_2

of poetry and song, as emphasised by the word "Songs" in its title. Many of its poems deal with this shared artistic heritage, including Milton's "At a Solemn Music", which begins: "Blest pair of Sirens, pledges of Heaven's joy / Sphere-born harmonious Sisters, Voice and Verse!" (Palgrave 1990: 106). This poem—like many in the volume—had also been set to music; Hubert Parry's "Blest Pair of Sirens" (1887) was a commission by Charles Villiers Stanford, editor of *The National Song Book*. The relationship between poetry and song evidently interested Lawrence, since Chambers notes that "Against Shirley's 'Death the Leveller' he wrote in my copy [of Palgrave's *Treasury*]: 'This poem De Quincey says he heard sung in a chamber of a tiny Welsh inn where he was staying awhile during his rambles. The unseen singer was a young Methodist girl, and although used to operatic performances De Quincey was more pleased and delighted with her song than he had ever been before or since'" (Chambers 1980: 100). Lawrence, as I illustrate below, particularly enjoyed spontaneous and informal renditions of song. To what extent, then, did he approach poetry through the cadences of song and by treating the metre of poetry like the rhythms of music? This is a central question for this chapter, which also builds a foundation for an exploration throughout this book of how the musicality of Lawrence's poetic rhythms influenced his prose writing.

Secondly, Lawrence's practice of reciting poems aloud highlights the fundamental relationship between "Voice and Verse" (as Milton puts it), but what he recited is also significant. Chambers stresses the importance of the Romantic poets within Palgrave's *Treasury* and to Lawrence in particular:

> He must have read almost every poem to me at one time or another, but those that stand out most clearly in my memory are Shelley's "The Invitation", "The Recollection", "Rarely, rarely comest thou", "Ode to the west wind", and "Swiftly walk over the western wave". Of Wordsworth there was "The Solitary Reaper", "I wandered lonely as a cloud", and the "Ode on Intimations of Immortality", while Keats' "La Belle Dame Sans Merci" seemed to have the tang of our own dank meadows. These, with others, he would read to me over and over again, and he pointed out that Book IV [1800–1850] comprised nearly half the volume. (Chambers 1980: 99)

The "dank meadows" invoked here are redolent of the earthiness of folk songs and the decayed Romanticism of the *fin de siècle* through which the young writer mediated the legacy of Romantic transcendence; a trajectory this chapter traces through the development of Lawrence's early poetry.

I begin with an overview of the folk songs and hymns of Lawrence's Eastwood upbringing and an exploration of their influence on poems such as "Cherry Robbers". After the publication of his first collection *Love Poems and Others* (1913), a debate with Edward Marsh about rhythms demonstrates an overtly musical approach to metre in his "All of Roses" sequence that draws on the decadent musicality of Ernest Dowson. Finally, the evolution of his poem "Piano" (1918) shows how Lawrence also worked through the poetry of Baudelaire and Hardy to come to terms with the legacies of decadence and Romanticism in what he now understood as "the insidious mastery of song" (*Poems* 108). Vincent Sherry has argued persuasively that for modernists like Pound and Yeats, their negotiations with "the legacy of the Nineties" emerged in their writing as "a subtler music" (Sherry 2015: 3). This is demonstrably the case for Lawrence, who met Pound and Yeats soon after his arrival in London (*IL* 145), and, like them, he also brought his own distinctive musical background into his art.[3]

SING-SONGS IN EASTWOOD

Although England was regarded by some as the "Land without Music", Dave Russell argues that "in the Victorian and Edwardian periods [it] was an extraordinarily musical place", where "The home, the street, the public house and the public park were almost as much musical centres as the concert hall and the music hall" (Russell 1997: 1). Lawrence's hometown of Eastwood was no exception, as evidenced by numerous accounts. The first part of Edward Nehls's composite biography of Lawrence (Nehls 1957: 5–78), as well as individual memoirs published by those who witnessed his early life, cumulatively suggest that the social and musical experiences of the writer were formed within an environment of communal singing.

May Holbrook (née Chambers, the older sister of Jessie) emphasises Lawrence's attention to the words of the hymns he sang in church and his alacrity for continuing the singing at home on Sunday evenings (as was customary throughout England at this time)[4]:

> When he stood to sing, tall and slim, he was straight but easy and graceful, one hand holding the hymn book ... He sang with pleasure but always with that expression of intellectual detachment, as though his mind were analyzing the words and what they sought to convey ... He still insisted on taking those of us who would go to his home where they sang around the piano. I heard them as I passed their window to my home. (Holbrook n.d.: 58)

While Lawrence's primary identification was with language, his early experiences of music stimulated his "wonder" of how words sound, as explored in his first essay "Art and the Individual" (1908) and again in his late essay "Hymns in a Man's Life" (1928). The Congregational hymns he learned as a child remained ingrained; more deeply, he admitted, than the "lovely poems" of Wordsworth, Keats, Shakespeare, and Goethe, which although "woven deep into a man's consciousness, are still not woven so deep in me as the rather banal nonconformist hymns that penetrated through and through my childhood" (*LEA* 130). Lawrence records his delight in the "wonderful sound" of the "word Galilee" and how "Just the words 'Sun of my soul, thou saviour dear,' penetrated me with wonder, and the mystery of twilight" (*LEA* 130, 132–3).[5] As Roger Dataller asserts, it is not ridiculous to attribute a "debt" to Moody and Sankey's hymn-book that might compare with "Lawrence's 'debt' to Hardy or to Whitman, to Blake or to Baudelaire" (Dataller 1952: 673). I propose a similar debt to a broad spectrum of songs, explored here in terms of his poetry but which also infuses his prose, as discussed in subsequent chapters.

Lawrence's younger sister Ada provides further insight into his musical background. The piano in the parlour—which he made a brief and "exasperated" attempt to play (Lawrence and Gelder 1966: 53–54)—had much deeper significance than an unused status symbol and would later be commemorated in his much-anthologised poem "Piano".[6] Ada writes:

> Some of our happiest hours were spent at our old piano with its faded green silk front. It had to be touched gently to bring out the tinkling notes. Bert bought me Chopin waltzes, music by Tchaikowsky [sic] and Brahms, Boosey's song books, and opera selections. He could not play but sat by my side for hours at a time encouraging me to practice difficult pieces ... We sang duets—Mendelssohn's *Maybells and Flowers*, *The Passage Bird's Farewell*, and Rubenstein's *Song of the Birds*, but no one else heard them. There were sing-songs at Hagg's Farm but our duets were never given there. He only sang them for his and my amusement. (Nehls 1957: 53)

These pieces are mostly by Romantic composers and some reflect the metaphor of bird-song favoured by the Romantic poets, Wordsworth, Keats and Shelley, who were well represented in Palgrave's *Treasury* (Chambers 1980: 99).

By contrast, the sing-songs at Haggs Farm were more wide-ranging and boisterous, and these became an important feature of Lawrence's increasingly close relationship with the Chambers family. As no-one at the

Haggs could play the "ancient piano" bought especially for these "family concerts", David Chambers (Jessie's brother) recalls that "Lawrence persuaded his sister Ada, somewhat reluctantly, to come from time to time to play for us" (Chambers 2017: 34). More frequently:

> We sang *Friars of Orders Grey, Two Grenadiers, Caro Mio Ben, Larboard Watch* and a host of others which I can never hear even now without an echo of those family sing-songs with Bert conducting and singing all parts as required although he had by far the poorest singing voice of us all. And when he left us to start out on his two and a half mile walk through fields and woods, heavy with sticky mud or bathed in translucent moonlight, we gathered outside and sang in full-throated family chorus what would now be called our signature tune—*A Tavern in the Town*—or shattered the midnight stillness by a final crashing rendering of *Larboard Watch*. (Nehls 1957: 48)

This mixed repertoire includes songs by Lawrence's "beloved Schumann and Giordani" (*IL* 67). The latter's "Caro Mio Ben" also features in Lawrence's story "A Prelude", written in 1907 and based on the Chambers family (*LAH* 14); an early example of how he used specific songs to heighten the emotional content of his fiction. There are also "popular" English songs, such as the naval shanty "Larboard Watch" (featured in *Kangaroo* [*K* 44]) and the drinking song "A Tavern in the Town" (referenced in *Sons and Lovers* [*SL* 138]).[7] Holbrook recollects other "songs grave and gay" that Lawrence shared with the Chambers family around their piano: "so many that a list would look like an index of a song book".

> We began with 'Bill beans and jolly big lumps of fat' to the tune of the 'Soldier's Chorus' [from *Faust*, by Gounod], then the Soldier's Chorus proper and 'Who is Sylvia' [set by Schubert but also by W.G. Goodworth in *The Oxford Song Book*]. 'Ariel's Song' [possibly in the setting by Arthur Sullivan] followed, then 'Golden Slumbers' [a lullaby, 'Cradle Song' by Thomas Dekker]. (Nehls 1957: 48)[8]

Music also provided the rhythms at social gatherings where the younger Lawrences danced with friends to the violin played by Ada's future husband, although "as poor Eddie could only play from memory the waltz *Love's Golden Dream is O'er*, [they] had *Love's Golden Dream* for waltz, polka, and valeta" (Nehls 1957: 20). The abiding influence of hymns was a legacy of his mother Lydia's religious upbringing under her father John Newton (a composer of hymns as well as a lace-maker),[9] but Lawrence learned dancing from his father; Arthur Lawrence was a fine dancer who, as John Worthen states, "actually taught dancing, though it is not known where or for how long" (Worthen 1992: 12). Holbrook describes Lawrence teaching the Chambers siblings to dance—"First he taught us songs for dance tunes. 'The Lowther Arcade' was sung by the rest while he taught me the steps"—and how when questioned about the source of his expertise, "reddening, he admitted it was his father" (Holbrook n.d.: 21).

The troubled relationship between Lawrence's parents and his identification with his mother is reflected in his autobiographical novel *Sons and Lovers* (1913), in which the father figure, Walter Morel, "had a pleasant way of whistling, lively and musical. He nearly always whistled hymns. He had been a choir-boy with a beautiful voice, and had taken solos in Southwell cathedral. His morning whistling alone betrayed it" (*SL* 27). The rather bitter final sentence here suggests that the adult collier abandoned any interest in singing hymns, except when he was "maudlin" (*SL* 31). There is no evidence that Arthur Lawrence continued his choral activities (there were local male voice choirs for Eastwood and Greasley and for Pye Hill and district, but the Eastwood Collieries Male Voice Choir was only established in 1920).[10] However, he did help to organise at least two musical evenings in Eastwood that are not disclosed in his son's writings (Moran 2015: 29–31). In 1899, a "grand concert" at the Mechanics Hall raised £17 for a colleague injured in the mine: an 11-piece band began with a rousing march called "Honest Toil" (by Lancashire composer William Rimmer), followed by a variety of musical numbers and comic songs, concluding with the famous hymn "Lead Kindly Light" (a favourite of drunken miners, according to Gertrude Morel in *Sons and Lovers* [*SL* 31]). Another fund-raising concert followed the next year, in the General Havelock Inn, which combined comic songs such as "Some One to Mind the Children" with sentimental songs including "Break the News to Mother".

Lawrence also suppressed references to music hall in his early work, although some of the events he fictionalised in *The Lost Girl* (1920) were drawn from his life in Eastwood.[11] As Ada recalls, "Bert and I went often to the home of *The Lost Girl*. The cinema depicted in that novel actually existed, and when Alvina (her real name was Florence [Cullen]) was ill, I played the piano for her during a performance" (Nehls 1957: 54). In this novel, Lawrence describes the excitement of "the whooping, whistling, excited audience" on opening night: "Time came, and the colliers began to drum their feet" and "Alvina looked almost indecently excited"

(*LG* 109–110). Similarly, other accounts of church-going in Eastwood are less pious than *Sons and Lovers* might suggest. When Paul Morel watches Miriam sing a hymn, it strikes him that "Her comfort and her life seemed in the after-world" (*SL* 457), whereas in Part 1 of *Mr Noon* (posthumously published in 1934) as Emmie sits in the choir-loft of the chapel her mind is occupied entirely by her post-chapel liaisons with Gilbert: "Fallen angels indeed" (*MN* 47). In the short story "The Last Straw [Fanny and Annie]" (1922), it is a male chorister, Harry who "handled his aitches so hopelessly" (*EME* 159), who causes a scandal when the fruit of his extra-marital affair is announced in chapel. This juxtaposition of the sacred and profane, mirrored in the hymns and folk songs of Lawrence's youth, continued to percolate through his oeuvre.

In this respect, as in others, Thomas Hardy was an important forebear for Lawrence, since he drew on a similar musical background in his poetry and prose. In the archives of Dorset County Museum in Dorchester is "a vast store of music and songs which the Hardy family had written down over many years", including two of his grandfather's handwritten song-books: "At one end are written the old songs and music, and at the other end there are the hymns and carols played in church" (Griffin and Sartin 2013). The advent of *The National Song Book*, and, later, *The Oxford Song Book* (Buck 1916), alleviated the need for Lawrence to compile one of his own, although he did write out songs for his friends. The D.H. Lawrence collection at the Harry Ransom Center at the University of Texas at Austin includes the manuscript of three songs transcribed by Lawrence for Catherine Carswell—"Twankydillo", "The Lincolnshire Poacher", and "Widdicombe Fair"—together with a fourth, "The Cherry Tree", in the handwriting of Dollie Radford.[12] The manuscript of a further two songs—"Auprès de ma blonde" and "The Elephant Battery"—were included with Lawrence's letters to Anna Winchell Bóttern. His continuing interest in British and other European songs is further evidenced by requests to friends to send him music during his travels of the 1920s. Notably, in January 1923, he wrote from the Del Monte Ranch in New Mexico to request music for his sing-songs with Knud Merrild on flute and Kai Götzsche on fiddle: "Could you send us a book of English songs, and one of German: just the *simple* ordinary good songs, with simple music. I would like, if you can get it, *The Oxford Song Book*, in English—If there is a simple Italian book, too ... It doesn't matter if there is only mandoline accompaniment" (*4L* 373).[13] His repertoire thus remained firmly rooted in the European songs of his youth.

Folk Song and Poetry: The Case of "Cherry Robbers"

Lawrence's sing-songs in Eastwood reflect a repertoire in Britain that was viewed by some to be unduly reliant on composers from overseas (Russell 1997: 1). Such was the prestige of foreign music in Britain "that many composers adopted foreign-sounding pseudonyms" (Richards 2001: 445), including Theodore Bonheur (aka Charles Arthur Rawlings, from London) whose "Love's Golden Dream Is O'er" provided the music for Lawrence's dances. A perceived need to bolster a national tradition and inspire a musical renaissance prompted the collection of putatively national songs. Cecil J. Sharp's first collection, *Book of British Song for Home and School*, appeared in 1902, although others had begun similar work in the final decades of the nineteenth century.[14] The British folk song was thus a relatively recent development, with the term arriving in the English dictionary in 1889, according to Sharp, translated from the German term "Volkslied" since no equivalent existed in English (Sharp 1965: 3). Sharp's folk-song project was enthusiastically embraced by many associates of the Royal College of Music (established to enhance the nation's musical proficiency in 1882), including the young composer Ralph Vaughan Williams and Stanford, whose *National Song Book* bore the subtitle: "A Complete Collection of the Folk-songs, Carols, and Rounds, suggested by the Board of Education ... Edited and Arranged for the Use of Schools".

Lawrence was thus introduced to British folk songs by the *National Song Book* when he was training to be a teacher at University College Nottingham (1906–1908). His favourites, "Henry Martin" and "I Sowed the Seeds of Love" (Chambers 1980: 80), were both songs collected by Sharp, the latter being the very first folk song Sharp collected from the aptly named John England (Sharp 1902: vi). The sowing of seed was a recurrent image in well-known hymns—such as "I plough the fields and scatter the good seeds on the land" (of German origin)—but in folk songs was often associated with the seminal sense of "seed". Together with coded use of "plucked flowers" to denote lost virginity, folk songs like "I Sowed the Seeds of Love" were of dubious suitability for schoolchildren, as exemplified by these verses (Sharp 1965: 186):

> For in June there is a red rosebud
> And that's the flower for me.
> So I pulled and pluckèd at the red rosebud
> Till I gainèd the willow tree.

For the willow tree will twist
And the willow tree will twine.
I wish I was in a young man's arms
That once had this heart of mine.

Nonetheless, Sharp set about providing piano arrangements for songs which he claimed had been "handed down among our peasantry from generation to generation, and [which] are still to be heard in country places" (Sharp 1902: vi). However, as England drily remarked, "There had been no piano in his song" (qtd. Rylance 2007: 18).

There is some irony, too, in Lawrence teaching songs of the "peasantry" (Sharp 1902: vi) that he learned at College to the Chambers family as they tended their animals and fields in Nottinghamshire. The Chambers had recently moved out of Eastwood to take up farming and their tenancy of Haggs Farm only lasted from 1888 until 1910 (Chambers 2017: 23)—they were no more "peasants" than Lawrence himself.[15] Also the folk songs he taught them were not local to Nottinghamshire but drawn from around Britain: "Henry Martin" was a traditional Scottish ballad and "I Sowed the Seeds of Love" was from Somerset, which was disproportionately represented in Sharp's collection. Subsequently, Lawrence became sceptical about the nationalism inherent in the folk-song project: the 1922 version of his short story "England, My England" mocks Egbert's attachment to "the old customs", exemplified by "collecting folk-songs and folk-dances" (*EME* 7), and his final novel, *Lady Chatterley's Lover* (1928), excoriates the "mechanical yells" of "Standard Five girls ... finishing the la–me–doh–la exercises" (*LCL* 152). Nor did he express any interest in the burgeoning school of "English" composers (mainly associated with the Royal College of Music), such as Vaughan Williams and Gustav Holst, who drew on traditional tunes.

Nevertheless, the rhythms of folk songs stayed with Lawrence throughout his life and inflected his writing in several ways, particularly through a tendency towards triple repetitions that they shared with hymns. Dataller observes that the repeated refrain of hymns—such as "Shall we gather at the *river*, / The beautiful, the beautiful, the *river*, / Gather with the Saints at the *river*" (my emphasis)—wove its way into Lawrence's consciousness and into the biblical rhythms found in passages of *The Rainbow* and *The Plumed Serpent* (Dataller 1952: 674–677). As Monica Nash observes, the ballad of "Henry Martin" also "employs a series of triple repetitions throughout", beginning its narrative with "three brothers" and incorporating a triple refrain in the penultimate line of each stanza (qtd. Nash 1999: 150):

> There were three brothers in Merry Scotland
> In Merry Scotland there were three
> And they did cast lots which of them
> Should go, should go, should go
> For to turn robber all on the salt sea

This song is referenced in *The White Peacock* (*WP* 292) and Nash notices how Lawrence mirrors the motif of three by evoking three musical layers of sound: "the rumble of the rocking chair marking out the rhythm, then the heavily accented voice of George Saxton, and finally the shrill, spontaneous, inarticulate (and presumably, tuneless) crooning of the baby" (Nash 1999: 151). However, the techniques of folk song are more closely rehearsed in the poetry of his Eastwood years.

Lawrence's three-stanza poem "Cherry Robbers" was "probably composed c. summer 1908" (*Poems* 825) and revised for publication in *Love Poems and Others* (1913). "Three dead birds" lie at its centre and there are triple (sometimes modified) repetitions of key words, including "cherries" in each stanza, each of which begins with a preposition modulating a progression in mood from "Under" (twice) to "Against".[16]

"Cherry Robbers"

Under the long dark boughs, like jewels red
  In the hair of an Eastern girl
Hang strings of crimson cherries, as if had bled
  Blood-drops beneath each curl.

Under the glistening cherries, with folded wings
  Three dead birds lie:
Pale-breasted throstles and a blackbird, robberlings
  Stained with red dye.

Against the hay-stack a girl stands laughing at me,
  Cherries hung round her ears.
Offers me her scarlet fruit: I will see
  If she has any tears. (*Poems* 8)

In this deceptively simple poem, the "scarlet fruit" offered by the girl bears a sexual meaning as in popular songs, such as "Cherry Ripe", "Strawberry Fair", and "The Cherry Tree". The latter was a favourite of Lawrence's (as noted above) and the imagery of his poem amplifies Joseph's reproof to Mary in the carol—"Let him gather the cherries / That got thee with child"—in the multiple associations of "stain" (also meaning blemish and stigma).

The striking central image of "Three dead birds" underlines the proximity of sex and death, which is the usual emphasis of critical interpretations of this poem (e.g. Gilbert 2007: 79). However, three is an important metric in folk songs and hymns, while the designation of these birds as "throstles and a blackbird" is also significant; indeed the title of an early version was "Throstles in the Cherry Tree" (*Poems* 1905). In *The White Peacock*, these species are associated explicitly with song and courtship: "Now be still, and I'll tell you what sort of music you make ... Like the calling of throstles and blackies, in the evening ... Like the ringing of bluebells ... Marriage music, Sir" (*WP* 84).[17] The throstle or song thrush is widely celebrated in poetry, notably in Thomas Hardy's poem "The Darkling Thrush" (1900), while the blackbird features in Wordsworth's "The Fountain", included in Lawrence's beloved Palgrave's *Golden Treasury* (Palgrave 1990: 317):

> The blackbird amid leafy trees,
> The lark above the hill,
> Let loose their carols when they please,
> Are quiet when they will.

For Wordsworth, as for Keats and Shelley, song birds enjoy an enviable freedom compared with the earth-bound poet, so what are we to make of their unexplained death in Lawrence's poem? The monosyllabic words "Three dead birds lie" toll like a warning, and that toll is reiterated in the rhythm two lines later of "Stained with red dye". The transcendent song birds of Romantic poems are replaced in "Cherry Robbers" by an abrupt fall into sexuality and death, which for Sandra Gilbert "captures the Swinburnean entanglement of the erotic and the sadistic" (Gilbert 2007: 79). Wilde's "The Burden of Itys" offers a further parallel, in which the song of the nightingale stirs unbearable memories of sexual violence and the poet speaks in sexually coded terms of "Dying in music" (Wilde 1881: l. 339). The proximity of "Cherry Robbers" to decadent poetry is further encoded in its imagery of falling; a fall into sexuality which is enacted in language of "hang", "drops", "hung", and "tears" (implicitly falling). As Sherry has noted, "the root sense of *décadence* (de-*cad*-ere) [is] to *fall* away" (Sherry 2015: 34), and since the word incorporates the musical term "cadence" there is also the sense of a falling or fallen cadence. The musicality of *fin-de-siècle* poetry, as well as the cadences of folk song, was thus useful to Lawrence in formulating his musico-poetics.

DECADENT MUSICALITY: BAUDELAIRE AND DOWSON

Sherry argues that modernist writers, such as Pound, sought to distance themselves from the *maladie fin de siècle* even as they borrowed from their immediate predecessors (Sherry 2015: 4–6).[18] He perceives the roots of modernism reaching back through Baudelaire, whose *Les Fleurs du mal* (1857) provided "the older testament of poetic decadence" (Sherry 2015: 11). Lawrence was well versed in such discourses, as suggested by his poem titled "Malade" (composed c. February 1910), which resonates with the rainy day imagery of Baudelaire's poem "Spleen" (No. 161 in *Les Fleurs du mal*) and uses a parallel metaphor of spiders to suggest the disturbed interiority (or "cave") of the poet's mind.[19] By 1910, Lawrence had decided that "Baudelaire's Fleurs de Mal ... are better than Verlaine" (*1L* 179), whose poetic doctrine of "De la musique avant toute chose" (*1L* 63) he had pondered in 1908. In "La Musique" (No. 175 of *Les Fleurs du mal*), as David Michael Hertz explains, Baudelaire "renders a personal reaction to music, a description of the experience of music. This is more important than a specific meaning of music for Baudelaire" (Hertz 1987: 21). This poem resonates strongly with Lawrence's attitudes to music and literature discussed in his early letters and practised in his early poetry and later prose, so I quote it below in full (Baudelaire 1954) and will return to it in the final part of this chapter.

"La Musique"[20]

La musique souvent me prend comme une mer!
Vers ma pâle étoile,
Sous un plafond de brume ou dans un vaste éther.
Je mets á la voile:

La poitrine en avant et les poumons gonflés
Comme de la toile
J'escalade le dos des flots amoncelés
Que la nuit me voile:

Je sens vibrer en moi toutes les passions
D'un vaisseau qui souffre;
Le bon vent, la tempête et ses convulsions

Sur l'immense gouffre
Me bercent. D'autres fois, calme plat, grand miroir
De mon désespoir!

["Music"

Music often transports me like a sea!
Toward my pale star,
Under a ceiling of fog or a vast ether,
I get under sail;

My chest thrust out and my lungs filled
Like the canvas,
I scale the slopes of wave on wave
That the night obscures;

I feel vibrating within me all the passions
Of ships in distress;
The good wind and the tempest with its convulsions

Over the vast gulf
Cradle me. At other times, dead calm, great mirror
Of my despair!]

Baudelaire's imagery of waves and vibrations resembles Lawrence's metaphor of the Chladni patterns of sound waves, discussed in my introductory chapter and which informs the focus of my chapters on *The Rainbow* and *Women in Love*. The rhythmic prose of these novels approaches what Baudelaire describes as an ambitious dream "of the miracle of a poetic prose, musical, without rhythm and without rhyme, supple enough and rugged enough to adapt itself to the lyrical impulses of the soul, the undulations of reverie, the jibes of conscience" (Baudelaire 1970: ix–x). Baudelaire's poems thus provide a tentative image in *Women in Love* for what Colin Clarke recognises as its "downward rhythm" (Clarke 1969: 36–42), as reflected in Birkin's suggestion that "we are fleurs du mal ... not roses of happiness" (*WL* 173). This rhythmic turn in Lawrence's prose was anticipated by developments in his poetry, mediated through Ernest Dowson and Baudelaire, as well as Hardy, which are explored in the remainder of this chapter.

Following the publication of *Love Poems and Others* (1913), Lawrence's attention to his "rhythms" was provoked by Edward Marsh, editor of *Georgian Poetry*. Lawrence complained to their mutual friend, Cynthia Asquith, that "Eddie-dear ... thinks I'm too Rag-Time" (*2L* 62), referring to the syncopated music from America which was becoming popular in music halls as well as with modernist composers.[21] Marsh's tastes were more conservative (Lawrence called him "a bit of a policeman in poetry" [*2L* 104]) and he looked instead to a revival of "Englishness" in poetry; a Georgian Renaissance somewhat akin to the folk-song revival among British composers. Lawrence, however, was thinking about his metre in overtly musical terms: in another letter, he lapses from poetic to musical terms in explaining to Marsh that "I seem to find about the same number of long, lingering *notes* in each line" (*2L* 104, my emphasis). The idea of a poem as a sort of musical score, influenced by Stéphane Mallarmé and also by Sidney Lanier's *The Science of English Verse* (1880), was espoused by several poets with whom Lawrence would soon discuss his evolving poetics, including Lascelles Abercrombie, Amy Lowell, and Harriet Monroe.[22] An earlier precedent is set by Pound in the Introduction to his translations of *Cavalcanti Poems* (1910), in which he wrote that "rhythm implies about it a complete musical form ... perfect, complete" and which he applies to poetry: "the rhythm set in a line of poetry connotes its symphony, which, had we a little skill, we could score for orchestra" (qtd. Bucknell 2001: 70). The idea of poetry as a form of music was thus highly topical among Lawrence's growing circle.

Lawrence's response had been that "Shelley and Byron ... might be good for my rhythms" (*2L* 63), but soon he claimed that Shelley had caused him to become "a *real* cropper in my belief in metre" (*2L* 105) and turned instead to Dowson. As his debate with Marsh about rhythm intensified, Lawrence went so far as to mark out the metre in his own poem "Roses on the Breakfast Table" and Dowson's poem "Cynara" noting that "I think I read my poetry more by length than by stress—as a matter of movements in space than footsteps hitting the earth ... I think more of a bird with broad wings flying and lapsing through the air, than anything, when I think of metre" (*2L* 102–103). Displacing the Romantic figure of the poet as a disembodied and transcendent song bird, Lawrence's spatial metaphor of a bird in flight emphasises physical movement that lapses as well as rises, implying a falling cadence of decadence that counters the spiritual transcendence of

Romanticism. He thus expresses a desire to escape the temporality and progressiveness of poetry in a different way than the "bodyless" Shelley, anticipating his argument with "To a Sky-lark" in *Study of Thomas Hardy* (*STH* 71), to which I will return.

Lawrence's increasingly free interpretation of poetic rhythm and form led him to argue that "It all depends on the *pause* – the natural pause, the natural *lingering* of the voice according to the feeling – it is the hidden *emotional* pattern that makes poetry, not the obvious form" (*2L* 104). "Cynara" thus provides an important exemplar because, as Carol Rumens observes:

> [Dowson's] art is not all music and movement; there is a cleverly choreo-graphed stillness as well. An exclamation mark after each address to Cynara creates a perfectly natural-seeming caesura. But it is an unusually forceful one, visual as well as aural. The pause extends for an extra half-beat, and adds emphasis to the name. In the body of the poem it is always "Cynara!", never simply "Cynara". (Rumens 2011: n.p.)

Christopher Pollnitz recognises a similar importance in the punctuation of Lawrence's poems, writing that "Every time I recovered a mid-line comma in my editing of the *Poems*, I felt I was edging a jot closer to recapturing what Lawrence called 'the natural *lingering* of the voice according to the feeling', and so to 'the hidden *emotional* pattern that makes poetry'" (Pollnitz 2015: 15). Dowson's clever choreography also appealed to early twentieth-century composers: "Cynara" was set by Delius (in 1907, completed 1929), "I was not sorrowful" by John Ireland (in 1912) and "Seraphita" by Schoenberg (in translation by Stefan Georg), as one of his "Four Orchestral Songs" (Op. 22, 1913–1916).[23]

Lawrence's "Roses on the Breakfast Table" is part of a sequence of four rose poems titled "All of Roses", published in *Poetry* (January 1914) and later collected in *Look! We Have Come Through!* (1917). The simple song-like structure of some of these rose poems (four-line stanzas, with ABCB rhyme scheme) reflects Dowson's adoption of the ballad-like villanelle, as do the more well-known ballads in *Look!* (note also his "Cynara"-like use of the exclamation mark).[24] The refrain at the end of each stanza of the "Cynara" poem—"I was desolate and sick of an old passion, / ... I have been faithful to thee, Cynara! In my fashion"—breaks up the linearity of poetic form; a technique that Lawrence echoed in his poem "The Ballad of a Wayward Woman" which reiterates "the land, the land, / The land of her glad surmise" (in lines also criticised by Marsh [2L 104 n.6]). As discussed above, triple repetition is a feature of the folk songs that Lawrence had deployed in his earliest poems, and so Lawrence's sequence of rose poems continues to combine elements of decadent poetry with the fecundity of the folk song as in the earlier "Cherry Robbers".[25]

The rose poems of *Look!* also mark a shift in Lawrence's thinking about sexuality as a flowering rather than a bearing of fruit (or loss of virginity), which anticipates developments in language and thought in the *Study of Thomas Hardy*. For instance, in the poem "Rose of All the World" (written c. 1912–1914):

> To me it seems the seed is just left over
> From the red rose-flowers' fiery transience;
> Just orts and slarts; berries that smoulder in the bush
> Which burnt just now with marvellous immanence. (*Poems* 178)

The use of dialect ("orts and slarts" meaning "bits and pieces, leftovers" [*Poems* 952]) lends a folk element to the biblical references, such as the burning bush (Exodus 3: 1–21), juxtaposing the sacred and the putatively profane to suggest a sign that might instead lead humanity towards sexual freedom, unencumbered by reproductive consequences. In this respect, Lawrence's poems of 1912–1914 foreshadow the themes of *The Rainbow*, just as his early poems explore similar themes to *The White Peacock* and *Sons and Lovers*. Accordingly, Anna Brangwen remarks that "God burned no more in that bush", contrasting the "barren" altar in Lincoln Cathedral with her pregnant state (*R* 188).

The development of *The Rainbow* involved wrestling with the literary legacy of Hardy, as amply demonstrated by Mark Kinkead-Weekes (1968), but this was also a struggle with the Romantic poets as remarked by John Worthen (2014). In *Study of Thomas Hardy*, Lawrence returned to Shelley to argue with "To a Sky-Lark", but Hardy had already done this in "Shelley's Sky-Lark" (1901), composed following a visit to Livorno where Shelley had written his poem. As Daniel Karlin observes, Hardy responds to a poem about "heavenly soaring and singing" and "unbodied joy" by concentrating on "the fate of the bird's material remains" (Karlin 2013: 74). In Hardy's poem, Shelley's lark (qtd. Karlin 2013: 74):

> … only lived like another bird,
> And knew not its immortality:

Lived its meek life; then, one day, fell—
A little ball of feather and bone;
And how it perished, when piped farewell,
And where it wastes, are alike unknown.

Hardy's premise of a fallen lark chimes with the "Three dead birds" of Lawrence's "Cherry Robbers", which, in this context, might also signify the triumvirate of dead Romantic poets that dominated the Palgrave *Treasury*: Shelley, Wordsworth, and Keats.

In wider terms, the musicality of Hardy's poetry and prose may also have been instructive to Lawrence in developing his own mature style. Before embarking on his own *Study of Thomas Hardy*, he read *Thomas Hardy: A Critical Study* (1912) by Lascelles Abercrombie (*1L* 544), which attends to how "Hardy's fiction, at its best, is like music ... for what a piece of music really means is simply the music, and just so the whole meaning of the story is—the story" (Abercrombie 1912: 114–115). But Hardy's poetry (to which Abercrombie devoted a chapter) may also have contributed to Lawrence's negotiation of the legacies of decadent musicality, as demonstrated by his working through to the final version of "Piano".[26]

MUSICAL DEVELOPMENT IN "PIANO"

The evolution of Lawrence's "Piano" traces his negotiation with a legacy of nineteenth-century thinking about music through to fruition. Baudelaire's opening image in "La Musique" of music sweeping up the poet like the sea ("La musique souvent me prend comme une mer!", quoted above) parallels Lawrence's image of being "cast / Down in the flood of remembrance" (*Poems* 108). This concluding line of "Piano" marks a seismic shift from the first draft titled "The Piano" (1906–1908), as the final version grows closer to Baudelaire's conception of music. Baudelaire's extended imagery of a ship amidst a sea of passions evokes, albeit obliquely, the mythical plight of Odysseus and his crew at the mercy of the song of the sirens. The rendition of siren song is an aspect of Lawrence's poem that is also transformed by his revisions, as I discuss below.[27] The ability of the poet to recognise the overwhelming effects of music, while retaining poetic control of his material, is an achievement that I.A. Richards recognised in "Piano" (Richards 1929: 105–117), even if his students and many early critics did not. Subsequent studies of manuscript sources have revealed that there were several versions of "Piano", which show, in Holly Laird's careful analysis, the extent to which Lawrence wrestled to control his material.[28] This control, I argue, is also achieved through an evolution in his conceptions of music.

"The Piano", one of Lawrence's earliest poems, was first drafted around the same time as his essay "Art and the Individual" (1908), which, as discussed in Chap. 1, extols the musicality of artistic language and declares that "Sentimentality is by far the most grievous disease that an artist can contract" (*STH* 142). Yet, that is precisely the "disease" that one of the earliest reviewers perceived in the final version of "Piano", when it was published in *New Poems* (1918), writing that although he was "swept along in the music of the poem", ultimately:

> Here, as elsewhere, [Lawrence] is at the mercy of his emotions ... There is this difference between him and older sentimentalists, that they were at the mercy of pleasant feelings, while he is often at the mercy of unpleasant; but it is still the same poet's disease, and in both cases the feelings seem too intense for their cause. (Qtd. Laird 1985–1986: 183–184)

Subsequently, many of Richards's students were similarly annoyed or even "nauseated" by the poem; responses which Richards interpreted as "the prejudice of a post-Victorian age" (Laird 1985–1986: 184), a discourse of "nausea", "disease", and the "unpleasant" that was closely associated with the decadent arts. In the wake of the Wilde trials, as Emma Sutton observes, literary decadence became "closely associated with pathology" (Sutton 2002: 71). Lawrence's participation in these discourses is evident in poems such as "Malade", but we can also see how he worked through some of these pathological attitudes to decadence as he reworked "The Piano", particularly in addressing the role of music in literature.

"Piano" became more rather than less expressive of emotion in its final version, since, as Laird observes, "what had been a novelistic anecdote of his family became a compressed epiphany of feeling" (Laird 1985–1986: 190). The first, five-stanza version, "The Piano", is similar in some respects to a passage in *The White Peacock*, in which the male narrator, his mother and his sister eschew any displays of musical sentiment: "'Nay,' said my mother 'the touch of the old keys on my fingers is making me sentimental—you wouldn't like to see me reduced to the tears of old age?'" (*WP* 7). In "The Piano", however, emotion is associated with three women engaged in making music, including the poet's mother, but particularly (in the final two of its original five stanzas) with the poet's love-struck sister and a female singer who is baring "the whole of her soul":

Or this is my sister at home in the old front room
Singing love's first surprised gladness, alone in the gloom.
She will start when she sees me, and blushing, spread out her hands
To cover my mouth's raillery, till I'm bound in her shame's heart-spun bands.

A woman is singing me a wild Hungarian air
And her arms, and her bosom, and the whole of her soul is bare
And the great black piano is clamouring as my mother's never could clamour
And my mother's tunes are devoured of this music's ravaging glamour.
(*Poems* 1400)

The alignment here of music with a domain of "feminine" accomplishment and emotionality is a residue of Victorian attitudes towards music, exemplified by passages such as the following from the Reverend H.R. Haweis's popular *Music and Morals* (1871), which had run to 16 editions by the turn of the century:

> The emotional force in women is usually stronger, and always more delicate, than in men. Their constitutions are like those fine violins which vibrate to the lightest touch. Women are the great listeners, not only to eloquence, but also to music. The wind has swept many an Aeolian lyre, but never such a sensitive harp as a woman's soul. ... Her attitude changes unconsciously with the truest, because the most natural, dramatic feeling. At times she is shaken and melts into tears, as the flowers stand and shake when the wind blows upon them and the drops of rain fall off. (Haweis 1875: 100–101)

Lawrence wrote apologetically to Blanche Jennings in December 1908 about Haweis (*1L* 100), having previously written to her in similar terms about the relative emotional proclivities of women compared with men:

> Set a woman's soul vibrating in response to your own, and it is her whole soul which trembles with a strong, soft note of uncertain quality. But a man will respond, if he be a friend, to the very chord you strike, with clear and satisfying timbre, responding with a part, not the whole, of his soul. It makes a man much more satisfactory. (*1L* 66)

He then persisted in gendering musical propensities in a similar way in *The White Peacock*, when the piano-playing Lettie reprimands the farmer George Saxton for his limited range: "You are a piano which will only play a dozen common notes" (*WP* 28).

Lettie uses music to flirt with her suitors—as the narrator observes, "she flattered herself scandalously through the piano" (*WP* 25)—thus reflecting a Victorian discourse of musical sirens who seduced men against their better judgement (exemplified by Becky Sharp in Thackeray's *Vanity Fair*, 1847–1848).[29] This is evident in "The Piano" in the description of the "devouring" and "ravaging glamour" of "a wild Hungarian air" sung by a woman, while baring her arms, her bosom, and her soul.[30] The wildness—and perhaps the foreignness—suggests a loss of control and the threat of a "glamour" which may also devour the poet. Even the sister's outpourings of love are associated with "shame" as the poet feels "bound in her shame's heart-spun bands". The poet, like Odysseus bound to the mast, struggles to resist the overpowering effects of siren song.

Many of these elements are excised in the final version of "Piano". The stanza featuring the sister is cut entirely—as is the sister—and the final stanza is transformed:

> So now it is vain for the singer to burst into clamour
> With the great black piano appassionato. The glamour
> Of childish days is upon me, my manhood is cast
> Down in the flood of remembrance, I weep like a child for the past. (*Poems* 108)

The gender of "the singer" is not specified and the emphasis no longer rests on a particular song. The newly introduced musical term "appassionato" is aligned with "the great black piano" rather than with sexual passions, while "glamour" is also detached from the singer and associated with a younger version of self. Indeed, what remains in "Piano", as in Baudelaire's "La Musique", is the overwhelming effects of music itself—figured by Lawrence as "the flood of remembrance"—for which the reader has been prepared by changes to the middle stanza:

> In spite of myself, the insidious mastery of song
> Betrays me back, till the heart of me weeps to belong
> To the old Sunday evenings at home, with winter outside
> And hymns in the cosy parlour, the tinkling piano our guide. (*Poems* 108)

The references to women, again, have been removed here—"The full throated woman" and her song, and also the gliding fingers of the poet's mother—so that it is song itself that asserts its "insidious mastery". At this mid-point in the poem, the poet feels this as a form of "betray[al]", but by its close he succumbs, finally, "to weep like a child for the past". As Laird observes, this is a breakthrough in the final version of the poem which "should be viewed as a personal anecdote of Dionysian breakdown, not something finally to be resisted, but a transformative moment" (Laird 1985–1986: 194). In this context, then, I will explore more closely what facilitates the transformation of Lawrence's poem, in terms of a development of his sympathy for decadent musicality and in relation to contemporary anxieties about the gendering of the singer-poet whose "manhood" here has been "cast / Down".

Laird astutely identifies a series of slippages backwards in time in the final version of "Piano", which have the following effect:

> Curiously like a failed Romantic lyric, the speaker falls from the present into the past without emerging renewed. He repeats this slippage backward three times, with each stanza mimicking the movement of the whole like a series of falling steps ... this version of his insistent demand stands strong in the lineage of the Romantics, as the earliest draft did not. (Laird 1985–1986: 192)

I posit a specific link with Wordsworth's concept of the "spot of time", in his autobiographical *Prelude* (1850), which, as Sherry explains, "redeems the experience of an adult poet with a remembered incident of childhood" (Sherry 2015: 38–40). But in Sherry's account, by the start of the twentieth century, the optimism of Wordsworth's notion of "renewal"—"my hope, the spirit of the Past, / For future restoration"—had decayed into a sense of loss in which "The temporal imaginary of decadence acknowledges the motive interest in this fusion [between past and present] but accepts and even embraces its necessary failure" (Sherry 2015: 37–38). Baudelaire's experience of time as "fugitive" and Swinburne's sense of "temporal dispossession" provide important precedents for modernist poets (Sherry 2015: 57, 67), and Lawrence was an admirer of both poets.[31] The falling back through time in "Piano" thus exemplifies a decayed Romanticism, in which falling cadences signify only loss. The final version of the poem assimilates Lawrence's loss of his mother since its first draft, but also what Sherry describes as a "sense of historical loss" (Sherry 2015: 38–40), catalysed here by the catastrophe of the First World War that broke out between the first and final versions of Lawrence's poem. Crucially, too, for Wordsworth the "spot of time" occurs when "The mind is lord and master" (Wordsworth 1888: 12.222)—a situation that Lawrence complicates by simultaneously displaying mastery of the poet's craft and depicting the experience of being overmastered by song.

The burden of Lawrence's term "mastery" relates to a nineteenth-century discourse that gendered the lyric poet as a female singer, in the tradition of Sappho, with Sapphic song also representing a model for transgressive male poets like Swinburne.[32] Accordingly, Yopie Prins perceives that "Swinburne's Sappho emerges ... as a decadent figure, a descending cadence, a song fallen into decline. Without repeating Sappho verbatim, Swinburne recalls her in his poetry by means of a rhythmic reiteration that takes the place of Sapphic song" (Prins 1999: 119). In the early twentieth century, many male poets who were demonstrably influenced by Swinburne nonetheless sought to distance themselves from him. While Yeats regarded himself as a singer-poet, he aligned himself with the male tradition of the bard rather than with putatively "female" lyricism; for instance, his well-known poem "Sailing to Byzantium" (1928) insists on falling back to the "old sages" (implicitly male) to be "the singing-masters of my own soul" (Yeats 1933: l. 20). Thomas Hardy, on the other hand, ostensibly paid tribute in his elegy for Swinburne, "A Singer Asleep" (1910), while also consigning his predecessor to a past from which Hardy carefully distances himself (Karlin 2013: 179). Accordingly, the closing lines of Hardy's poem read: "I leave him, while the daylight gleam declines / Upon the capes and chines" (qtd. Karlin 2013: 178). Crucial to Hardy's turning away, as Karlin observes, is Swinburne's relationship with Sappho, figured here as both "singing-mistress" and "music-mother" (qtd. Karlin 2013: 178):

> —His singing-mistress verily was no other
> Than she the Lesbian, she the music-mother
> Of all the tribe that feel in melodies;
> Who leapt, love-anguished, from the Leucadian steep
> Into the rambling world-encircling deep
> Which hides her where none sees.[33]

By the time Lawrence completed "Piano", he was writing an elegy to his own mother, but he had also embraced the "music-mother" Sappho in his *Study of Thomas Hardy* (written in 1914), in which he states: "It is so arranged that the very act which carries us into the unknown, shall probably deposit seed for security to be left behind. But the act, called the sexual act, is not for the depositing of seed. It is for leaping off into the unknown, as from a cliff's edge, like Sappho into the sea" (*STH* 53). Here, Lawrence engages an imagery of falling into sexuality as a creative act that is not procreative; the repeated word "seed" has biblical overtones, but also the sense of sexual freedom implied by folk songs such as "I Sowed the Seeds of Love". For Lawrence, like Swinburne, leaping into the sea is a source of poetic renewal (rather than Wordsworth's return to childhood innocence), and this development lends a different interpretation to "the flood of remembrance" in "Piano", which overwrites any allusion to the biblical flood that was God's judgement on "the wickedness of the human race" (Genesis 6.5). Thus, while there are references to the biblical fall into sexuality—in the poet being "cast / Down" by the "betray[al]" of song figured as an "insidious" serpent[34]—there are also suggestions of a fall into renewed poetic creativity.

In "Piano", Lawrence, in his own way, reinvented decadence (to borrow Sherry's phrase) for a modern age, then complicated decadent tropes further in *Women in Love*, when Ursula contemplates a Sapphic leap into the unknown to escape a decadent world in which "she had experienced all she had to experience, she was fulfilled in a kind of bitter ripeness, there remained only to fall from the tree into death" (*WL* 191). The implied proximity of death and manhood in "Piano" is evoked by "the flood of remembrance"—thus paving the way for later acts of silent remembrance of the millions of young men who lost their lives in the war—while at the same time drawing on the Swinburnian sea, which for Prins is "a recurring figure for pure rhythm" (Prins 1999: 119). For Lawrence, the concept of rhythm in lived experience as well as in music became an increasingly important aspect of his prose, as he worked out his theory of "rhythmic form" in *The Rainbow*. But first, he needed to work through the legacy of literary Wagnerism, implicit in the musicality of decadent poetry, but also important to questions of form and style in the early twentieth-century novel.

RECOMMENDED LISTENING

Folk songs:	"The Cherry Tree", "Henry Martin", "The Lincolnshire Poacher", "I Sowed the Seeds of Love", "Twankydillo".
Hymns:	"Evening", "Lead Kindly Light", "Sun of My Soul, Thou Saviour Dear".
Piano music:	Chopin (waltzes and nocturnes), Tchaikovsky *The Seasons*.
Popular songs:	"Larboard Watch", "Love's Golden Dream is O'er", "Tavern in the Town".
Song settings:	Giordani "Caro mio ben", Hubert Parry "Blest Pair of Sirens".

NOTES

1. In fact, there is further confusion because the three songs that Chambers attributes to *The Golden Treasury* do not appear in *The National Song Book* either; the more likely source is the *Oxford Song Book* series published by J. Curwen & Sons, which also included sol-fa notation. In their contributions to Nehls's composite biography, both Willie Hopkin (Nehls 1957: 24) and Emily Lawrence (Nehls 1957: 21) refer to *The Oxford Song Book*. To further confuse matters, many of Lawrence's favourite songs were later collected in Sir Percy C. Buck's *The Oxford Song Book* (London, New York & Toronto: Oxford University Press, 1916) and this is probably the volume that he frequently requested when travelling overseas in the 1920s (see note 12).

2. The Muses were Greek goddesses governing the arts and the science of Astronomy. Euterpe was the goddess of music, song, and lyric poetry.

3. In November 1909, Lawrence met Pound through Ford Madox Hueffer and Violet Hunt, and Yeats soon after (*1L* 145). In March 1910, Yeats and Pound were the "celebrities" at one of Ernest Rhys's gatherings (*1L* 156). For Rhys's account of this evening, at which Pound ate some tulips and Lawrence recited some of his love poems with his back to the company, see Nehls 1957: 129–131. Rhys also recalls that the most novel contribution was Winifred Emory's performance of a Yeats poem to the accompaniment of the psaltery: Yeats, he writes, "was bent on using the psaltery as a means of giving poetry a new musical vogue" (Nehls 1957: 131).

4. "Sunday evenings were a favourite time for neighbours to gather and perform" (Russell 1997: 1).

5. "Galilee" is a reference to the hymn "Evening", by Robert Morris, in Ira David Sankey's *Sacred Songs and Solos* (1881): see *LEA* 130 and 350 n. 130:29. Many hymns refer to "Galilee", including "Each Gentle Dove" identified by Peter Preston (2011: 198), in the context of a wider discussion of Lawrence's "Bibline" language.

6. For a discussion of the piano, and music, as a social marker in Lawrence's work, see Deutsch 2015: 117–120.

7. This was later recorded as "The Drunkard Song" by American singer Rudy Vallee in 1934. A recording is available on YouTube: https://www.youtube.com/watch?v=7S0H-veLKWY, an exaggeratedly sentimental version in which Vallee breaks into laughter.

8. "Golden Slumbers" has been immortalised by its inclusion in a "Medley" by the Beatles, a track on their iconic album *Abbey Road* (1969). Acoustic versions of the folk song are available on YouTube, for instance: https://www.youtube.com/watch?v=DShZcqG6s7M

9. According to the entry for John Newton (1802–1886) in the *Dictionary of Composers for the Church in Great Britain and Ireland*: "Around 1824, he joined the Nottingham Zion Chapel and reorganised the choir ... he moved

to the nearby town of Beeston in 1830. There he became choirmaster of the Wesleyan Chapel. Eventually returned to Nottingham, where he was choirmaster for the Parliament Street Chapel (1834–1842). Also worked with the Nottingham Choral Society. Composed hymn tunes. 'Sovereignty' was one of 28 by him in a collection The Pilgrim published at some time before 1839" (Humphries and Evans 1997: 245). The earlier, more famous John Newton (1725–1807), who was no relation, collaborated with the poet William Cowper to produce well-known hymns including "Amazing Grace".

10. For details of this successful choir, which immediately began winning prizes and still exists today, visit their website at http://www.ecmvc.org/about-us/history-of-the-choir/. Although miners often sang while working in the pit, colliery songs are not a feature of Lawrence's work.

11. Published in 1920, but probably begun in 1912–1913 (*LG* xix–xxii).

12. I am grateful to Terry Gifford for sharing his findings with me. His correspondence with the Harry Ransom Center is dated 7 May 1996; there are no references to help locate these manuscripts within the archive and unfortunately this remains the case, as my recent inquiries confirmed. The archives of the University of Nottingham hold a recorder owned by Catherine Carswell, who was described by her son as "musical" (Carswell 1981: vi).

13. In October 1926, Lawrence wrote to Vere Collins requesting another copy of "*The Oxford Book of Songs* (with music)" (*5L* 588). According to Carswell, Lawrence also had "a little manual of French songs which he carried about everywhere like a bible" (Carswell 1981: 105). In September 1926, he sent "a book of French songs" to his niece Margaret "Peggy" Needham (*5L* 564).

14. For an interesting account of the fractious relationship between Sharp and the forerunners of the folk-song movement, who have subsequently been sidelined in the record, see Francmanis 2002.

15. Before Edmund Chambers took over the tenancy of Haggs Farm in 1898, he had been a "provisions merchant" (according to his marriage certificate) in Nottingham and on moving to Eastwood a general labourer (Chambers 2017: 23).

16. Other early poems which would bear further investigation for various parallels with folk songs include "Gipsy", "The Collier's Wife", "Flapper", "In a Boat", "Wedding Morn", "Sigh No More", and the long poem "Whether or Not".

17. Probably, the best-known blackbird poem is Wallace Stevens's "Thirteen Ways of Looking at a Blackbird", which features "three blackbirds" and a poet "of three minds".

18. As Sherry relates here, Symons's *The Symbolist Movement in Literature* (1899) is in large part a recasting of his earlier "The Decadent Movement in Literature" (1893), which enabled Yeats and others to reinvent decadence (Sherry 2015: 4–6).

19. In "Spleen", "the dumb throngs of infamous spiders spin/Their meshes in the caverns of the brain" (Baudelaire 1909), while Lawrence's "Malade" depicts "The spiders with white faces, that scuttle on the floor of the cave!" (*Poems* 76).

20. Charles Baudelaire, "La Musique", with English translations by the composer Cyril Scott and others, see https://fleursdumal.org/poem/175

21. A hit review called *Hullo, Rag-time* (1912) popularised the genre, which went on to inform popular songs sung by British soldiers during the First World War, such as "We Are the Ragtime Infantry". The lyrics to the song humorously (if poignantly) send up the inefficient humanity of those caught up in what Lawrence called the war "machine". Here is one variation of the first verse:

We are Fred Karno's army,
We are the ragtime infantry.
We cannot fight, we cannot shoot,
What bloody use are we?
And when we get to Berlin
We'll hear the Kaiser say,
"Hoch, hoch! Mein Gott, what a bloody rotten lot,
Are the ragtime infantry.

https://movehimintothesun.wordpress.com/2011/02/13/we-are-the-ragtime-infantry/

22. For example, Amy Lowell in her *Dial* article "The Rhythms of Free Verse" (1918), Harriet Monroe *Poets and Their Art* (1926), and, to a more limited extent, Lascelles Abercrombie in *Principles of English Prosody* (1923).

23. Schoenberg's interest in Balzac's novel *Séraphita* continued in his unfinished oratorio *Die Jakobsleiter*, discussed in Chap. 4.

24. Of the four poems, the final pair have a simple song-like structure, "Roses on the Breakfast Table" and "I Am Like a Rose". The longer poem, "Rose of All the World", which immediately follows this sequence in *Look!*, has a similar structure.

25. Dowson's symbolism was inherited from Baudelaire—the passion in "Cynara" is "sick" and his roses reminiscent of *Les Fleurs du mal*—and provided an important precursor to the modernist poetics of Yeats and Pound, as Vincent Sherry observes (2015: 70–72).

26. As this book went to press, Volume III of *The Poems* was published: this usefully collects for the first time three variants of "The Piano" that preceded "Piano". These variants have been closely examined by Holly Laird (1985–1986), whose insightful essay informs my discussion: for reasons of space, I focus on changes between the earliest version, "The Piano [1]", and the final version, "Piano".

27. While "Piano" is the most-quoted example of musicality in Lawrence's oeuvre, James Joyce also experimented with siren song in what Werner Wolf characterises as his "best-known experiment with musicalized fiction: the famous 'Sirens' episode in Ulysses (1918/22)" (Wolf 1999: 127).

28. As noted above, three variants of "The Piano" are newly published in *Poems III*. See also Cushman (2001) on versions of "Piano" as a pedagogical tool, and my previous discussion of versions of "Piano" in Reid 2011.

29. For a detailed account, see Chapter 1 of da Sousa Correa 2003.

30. It is difficult to know what this "wild Hungarian air" might be. Brahms and Liszt wrote instrumental Hungarian dances, but Lawrence may be conflating these with Brahms's folk songs. George Neville recalls, for instance, an evening in Blackpool when "At Lawrence's request [a violinist] gave us some Brahms Folk Songs of the Baltic, and we sang them quietly in German" (Neville 1981: 146).

31. Several of Swinburne's poems are mentioned in Lawrence's letters, and in September 1916 he wrote that "I put [Swinburne] with Shelley as our greatest poet. He is the last fiery spirit among us" (*2L* 654).

32. An interesting discussion of the gender positioning of poets is threaded through the excellent study by Daniel Karlin (2013).

33. The full poem is available at http://www.poetryatlas.com/poetry/poem/574/a-singer-asleep.html

34. See also Laird who perceives the speaker's complaints of "betrayal and treachery" as "much like 'the voice of my education' in 'Snake'" (Laird 1985–1986: 197).

References

Abercrombie, Lascelles. 1912. *Thomas Hardy: A Critical Study*. New York: Mitchell Kennerley.

Baudelaire, Charles. 1909. Spleen. In *Poems and Baudelaire Flowers*. Trans. Jack Collings Squire. London: The New Age Press. https://fleursdumal.org/poem/161

———. 1954. Music. In *The Flowers of Evil*. Trans. William Aggeler. Fresno: Academy Library Guild. https://fleursdumal.org/poem/175

———. 1970. *Paris Spleen, 1869*. New York: New Directions.

Buck, Percy. 1916. *The Oxford Song Book*. Vol. I. London: Lowe and Brydone.

Bucknell, Brad. 2001. *Literary Modernism and Musical Aesthetics: Pater, Pound, Joyce and Stein*. Cambridge: Cambridge University Press.

Carswell, Catherine. 1981. *The Savage Pilgrimage*. Cambridge: Cambridge University Press.

Chambers, Jessie [E.T.]. 1980. *D.H. Lawrence: A Personal Record by E.T.* Cambridge: Cambridge University Press.

Chambers, Jonathan David. 2017. Memories of D.H. Lawrence. In *Miriam's Farm: The Story of Haggs Farm, D.H. Lawrence and the Chambers Family*, ed. Clive Leivers, 29–39. Nottingham: Russell Press.

Clarke, Colin. 1969. *River of Dissolution: D.H. Lawrence and English Romanticism*. London: Routledge & Kegan Paul.

Correa, Delia da Sousa. 2003. *George Eliot, Music and Victorian Culture*. Basingstoke: Palgrave Macmillan.

Cushman, Keith. 2001. The Tuning of "Piano". In *Approaches to Teaching the Works of D.H. Lawrence*, ed. M. Elizabeth Sargent and Garry Watson, 190–192. New York: MLA.

Dataller, Roger. 1952. Taos in Eastwood. *The Adelphi*, 673–681.

Deutsch, David. 2015. *British Literature and Classical Music: Cultural Contexts 1870–1945*. London: Bloomsbury.

Francmanis, John. 2002. National Music to National Redeemer: The Consolidation of a "Folk-Song" Construct in Edwardian England. *Popular Music* 21 (1): 1–25.

Gilbert, Sandra M. 2007. D.H. Lawrence's Place in Modern Poetry. In *The Cambridge Companion to Twentieth-Century English Poetry*, ed. Neil Corcoran, 74–86. Cambridge: Cambridge University Press.

Griffin, Edward, and Bonny Sartin. 2013. Thomas Hardy's Musical Heritage. *Dorset Magazine*. http://www.dorsetmagazine.co.uk/people/thomas-hardys-musical-heritage-1-1638349

Haweis, Rev. H.R. 1875. *Music and Morals*. London: Daldy, Isbister, & Co.

Hertz, David Michael. 1987. *The Tuning of the World: The Musico-Literary Poetics of the Symbolist Movement*. Carbondale/Edwardsville: Southern Illinois University Press.

Holbrook, May. n.d. D.H. Lawrence: Childhood and Boyhood. University of Nottingham, Manuscripts and Special Collections, La Ch 103.

Humphries, Maggie, and Robert Evans, eds. 1997. *Dictionary of Composers for the Church in Great Britain and Ireland*. London: Mansell.

Karlin, Daniel. 2013. *The Figure of the Singer*. Oxford: Oxford University Press.

Kinkead-Weekes, Mark. 1968. The Marble and the Statue: The Exploratory Imagination of D.H. Lawrence. In *Imagined Worlds: Essays in Some English Novels and Novelists in Honour of John Butt*, ed. Maynard Mack and Ian Gregor, 371–418. London: Methuen.

Laird, Holly A. 1985–1986. The Poems of "Piano". *D.H. Lawrence Review* 18 (2–3): 183–199.

———. 1988. *Self and Sequence: The Poetry of D.H. Lawrence*. Charlottesville: University Press of Virginia.

Lawrence, Ada, and G. Stuart Gelder. 1966. *Young Lorenzo: Early Life of D.H. Lawrence*. New York: Russell & Russell.

Moran, James. 2015. *The Theatre of D.H. Lawrence*. London: Bloomsbury.

Nash, Monica. 1999. D.H. Lawrence and Folk Music. *Journal of the D.H. Lawrence* Society: 150–170.

Nehls, Edward. 1957. *D.H. Lawrence: A Composite Biography, Vol. I 1885–1919.* Madison: University of Wisconsin Press.

Neville, G.H. 1981. *A Memoir of D.H. Lawrence: The Betrayal.* Ed. Carl Baron. Cambridge: Cambridge University Press.

Palgrave, Francis Turner. 1990. *The Golden Treasury of English Songs and Lyrics.* London: J.M. Dent & Sons.

Pollnitz, Christopher. 2015. Using the Cambridge Poems and Auditing Lawrence's Sacred Dramas. *D.H. Lawrence Review* 40 (2): 11–33.

Preston, Peter. 2011. Bathed in the Word of the Lord? Lawrence, Bunyan and the Bibline. In *Working with Lawrence: Texts, Places, Contexts,* 191–205. Nottingham: CCCP.

Prins, Yopie. 1999. *Victorian Sappho.* Princeton: Princeton University Press.

Reid, Susan. 2011. "The Insidious Mastery of Song": D.H. Lawrence, Music and Modernism. *Journal of D.H. Lawrence Studies* 2 (3): 109–130.

Richards, I.A. 1929. *Practical Criticism.* New York: Harcourt, Brace & World.

Richards, Jeffrey. 2001. *Imperialism and Music: Britain, 1876–1953.* Manchester: Manchester University Press.

Rumens, Carol. 2011. Poem of the Week: Non sum qualis eram bonae sub regno Cynarae by Ernest Dowson. *The Guardian,* March 14.

Russell, Dave. 1997. *Popular Music in England, 1840–1914: A Social History.* Manchester/New York: Manchester University Press.

Rylance, Rick. 2007. The Reception of Lawrence's Englishness in an International Perspective. In *The Reception of D.H. Lawrence in Europe,* ed. Christa Jansohn and Dieter Mehl, 14–22. London: Continuum.

Sharp, Cecil J. 1902. *A Book of British Song for Home and School.* London: John Murray.

———. 1965 [1907]. *English Folk Songs: Some Conclusions.* Ed. Maud Karples. London: Mercury Books.

Sherry, Vincent. 2015. *Modernism and the Reinvention of Decadence.* Cambridge: Cambridge University Press.

Sutton, Emma. 2002. *Aubrey Beardsley and British Wagnerism in the 1890s.* Oxford: Oxford University Press.

Wilde, Oscar. 1881. *The Burden of Itys. Poems.* Boston: Robert Brothers. http://www.bartleby.com/143/25.html

Wolf, Werner. 1999. *The Musicalization of Fiction: A Study in the Theory and History of Intermediality.* Amsterdam/Atlanta: Rodopi.

Wordsworth, William. 1888. *The Prelude, Book Twelfth. Complete Poetical Works.* London: Macmillan. https://www.bartleby.com/145/ww298.html

Worthen, John. 1992. *D.H. Lawrence: The Early Years, 1885–1912*. Cambridge: Cambridge University Press.

———. 2014. Lawrence and Some Romantic Poets. *Journal of D.H. Lawrence Studies* 3 (3): 11–32.

Yeats, W.B. 1933. Sailing to Byzantium. In *The Poems of W.B. Yeats: A New Edition*, ed. Richard J. Finneran. London: Macmillan. https://www.poetryfoundation.org/poems/43291/sailing-to-byzantium

CHAPTER 3

Lawrence's Case of Wagner: *The White Peacock* and *The Trespasser*

INTRODUCTION

Lawrence's first novel, *The White Peacock* (1911), draws widely on the music he enjoyed in his formative years. The farmer George Saxton (based on Alan Chambers) is associated with Lawrence's favourite folk songs, including "Henry Martin" and "I Sowed the Seeds of Love", and the piano repertoire of Lettie Beardsall has significant overlaps with his sister Ada's; a long list of composers in this novel includes Debussy, Gounod, Handel, Lehmann, Mozart, Schubert, Strauss, Tchaikovsky, Wagner, and Wolf. *The White Peacock* brings together Lawrence's interests in folk song and parlour music and juxtaposes these with references to Bizet's opera *Carmen* (1875), about a Spanish gypsy (whose name shares the root of the Latin word for song or poem).[1] The exoticism of *Carmen* offers a glimpse of a wilder life, which shocked the audience at its Paris premiere for its "realist" depiction of "lifelike, working-class characters ruled by their passions" (Curtiss 1958: 397), and thus provides a counterpoint to the themes of *The White Peacock*. In Lawrence's early novels, operatic references also helped to structure the narrative; a device deployed by several of his contemporaries, including E.M. Forster, Ford Madox Hueffer, George Moore, and H.G. Wells. The intermediality of words and music in opera would become particularly useful in canonical works of modernism, including James Joyce's *Ulysses* (1922), in which "the operatic material … is integral to its plot and technique" (Begam and Wilson Smith 2016: 2).

© The Author(s) 2019
S. Reid, *D.H. Lawrence, Music and Modernism*,
Palgrave Studies in Music and Literature,
https://doi.org/10.1007/978-3-030-04999-7_3

Lawrence's first attempts to use opera in his fiction, particularly in his second novel *The Trespasser* (1912), were thus bold and progressive in their experimentation and contributed in several ways to the development of his later, more accomplished, fictions.[2]

This chapter begins by exploring how Lawrence's allusions to Bizet's *Carmen* give shape to *The White Peacock*, as a prelude to considering his engagement with literary Wagnerism in *The Trespasser*. Intriguingly, Lawrence reverses the trajectory of Nietzsche, whose initial enthusiasm for Wagner gave way to denunciation in *The Case of Wagner* (1888) and praise instead for *Carmen*'s "Free[dom] from the *lie* of the grand style!" (Nietzsche 1911: 2). Nietzsche's attack on Wagner as a "disease" (Nietzsche 1911: xxx) informed the pathological discourse of decadence, which Lawrence actively courted in *The Trespasser* and explored further in his discussion of leitmotif in his review of "German Books" (1913). Leitmotif— defined at its simplest as a "short, constantly recurring musical phrase" (Kennedy 1987)—is an element of music comparable to the use of themes in literature that decadent writers, particularly, sought to emulate in the highly concentrated style of Wagner. By the *fin de siècle*, as Emma Sutton describes, Wagnerism was a cultural phenomenon that provided artists with "a spectrum of models against which to align or against which to define themselves" (Sutton 2002: 3), and which continued to cast a long shadow into the early modernist period (Martin 1982: vii). The extent to which Lawrence embraced or resisted the influence of literary Wagnerism is the focus of most of this chapter and continues as a theme running through the rest of this study.

Several critics have noted the prevalence of Wagnerian references in Lawrence's work. For Elizabeth Mansfield "the early pages of *The Rainbow* … are … the most Wagnerian in Lawrence" (*T* 327), and Stoddard Martin boldly claims that Lawrence wrote "a complete *Ring*, albeit in jumbled order and with only two of the four pieces consciously linked: *The Trespasser* as *Die Walküre*, *Sons and Lovers* as *Siegfried*, *The Rainbow* as *Rheingold*, and *Women in Love* as *Götterdämmerung*. He had also written his *Parsifal* in *The Plumed Serpent*" (Martin 1982: 178). Lawrence's friend Witter Bynner had already described *The Plumed Serpent* as "Wagner without music" (Bynner 1953: 212). In March 1930, Paul Rosenfeld summarised the body of Lawrence's work, following his recent death, remarking that "it can be said of D.H. Lawrence, more justly than of Wagner even, that his work was the picture of the relationship of a pair of people, serially continued" (qtd. Draper 1986: 336). An exploration of Lawrence's trespassing into the domain of Wagnerism may therefore add another strand to our understanding of his development as a writer, who saw the appeal of a decadent musicality even as he sensed its dangers. Already, in these early fictions, Lawrence was learning to balance other musical influences against the dominance of Wagner. This chapter ends with a consideration of Debussy's use of leitmotif in *Pelléas et Mélisande* (1902), and how his opera, mentioned near the beginning of *The Trespasser* (*T* 52), offers an alternative to the loss of boundaries inherent in Wagnerian music drama.

CARMEN AND *THE WHITE PEACOCK*

In December 1908, Lawrence wrote to Blanche Jennings: "I prefer a little devil—a Carmen—I like not things passive" (*1L* 103). He was drawing a comparison between the passivity of the girl depicted in Greiffenhagen's erotic painting *An Idyll* (1891) and the more active representation of sexuality embodied by Bizet's Carmen.[3] These contrasting depictions of passion are deployed in *The White Peacock*, through their associations with Lettie and her brother Cyril (the novel's narrator) and their triangular relationship with George. Lettie, we are told, "danced elegantly, but with a little of Carmen's ostentation—her dash and devilry" (*WP* 96). Her dance is a performance, designed to attract George, much as the "vamp[ish]" rhythms of Carmen's music are designed to "make José [the leading man]—and the listener—aware both of her body and also (worse yet) of their own bodies" (McClary 1991: 57). *An Idyll* has a comparable effect on George: "He was breathlessly quivering under the new sensation of heavy, unappeased fire in his breast, and in the muscles of his arms. He glanced at her bosom and shivered" (*WP* 29). However, despite Lettie's initial pretensions to "devilry", neither she nor George pursue their mutual attraction.

Lettie declares that she "won't be kept in bounds" (*WP* 84) and she envies the freedom of birds, appealing to George: "'Don't you wish we were wild—hark, like wood-pigeons—or larks—or, look, like peewits! Shouldn't you love flying and wheeling and sparkling and—courting in the wind!'" (*WP* 208). Here she echoes Carmen's opening aria, "La Habañera" (Fig. 3.1):

> L'amour est un oiseau rebelle
> Que nul ne peut apprivoiser
> Et c'est bien en vain qu'on l'appelle
> S'il lui convient de refuser.

Fig. 3.1   Opening of "La Habañera" from Bizet's *Carmen*

[Love will like a wild bird fly
Careering whither it may choose
Vainly for help we cry
If its fancy is to refuse.][4]

Lettie's allusion to wild birds is deeply ironic because, by the end of the novel, she allows herself to be tamed into "a small indoor existence" (*WP* 291). Likewise, although George replies to Lettie that he does not see why they cannot be free "as the larks", he too is "afraid to make the struggle, to rouse himself to decide the question for her" (*WP* 208). In *The White Peacock*, tragedy arises from the inhibition of sexual freedom, with both Lettie and George choosing loveless marriages over their passion for each other. The novel closes with a description of George as "a condemned man" (*WP* 325). Lettie has induced the same sort of hopelessness and self-destructiveness in George as Carmen does in José; she has toyed with his animal attractions, referring to him as her "Taureau" (*WP* 21) in an allusion to the final bullfight scene in *Carmen*. In the opera, tragedy ensues from Carmen's refusal to give up her sexual freedom and she dies at the hands of her thwarted lover. And so, while *Carmen* demonstrates the destructiveness of José's sexual insecurities and possessiveness, *The White Peacock* demonstrates a parallel destructiveness arising from a failure to fall into sexuality.

In the context of nineteenth-century sexual politics, José proves himself to be "a dangerously weak link in the patriarchal chain of command" in succumbing to a femme fatale figure, as Susan McClary argues (McClary 1991: 60). George's passivity represents a similarly equivocal and subversive version of normative masculinity. Moreover, when he does take a role in playing out a re-enactment of Greiffenhagen's *An Idyll* this is not with Lettie but with Cyril. In the bathing scene in the chapter titled "A Poem of Friendship", Cyril describes how "I left myself quite limply in his hands, and, to get a better grip of me, [George] put his arm round me and pressed me against him, and the sweetness of the touch of our naked bodies one against the other was superb" (*WP* 222).[5] This isolated episode is never repeated as Cyril also fails to assert his unspoken attraction for George and withdraws increasingly into the role of rootless flâneur; thus fulfilling a comparable role to the narrator in Prosper Mérimée's novella *Carmen* (1845), on which the libretto for Bizet's opera was based.[6]

During his descent into passivity, Cyril accompanies George and his newly wedded wife Meg to the theatre and observes them watching *Carmen*:

> "Carmen" fascinated them both. The gaudy, careless Southern life amazed them. The bold free way in which Carmen played with life startled them … On the stage the strange storm of life clashed in music towards tragedy and futile death. The two were shaken with a tumult of wild feeling. When it was all over they rose bewildered, stunned, she with tears in her eyes, he with a strange wild beating of his heart. (*WP* 248)

The "strange wild beating" of George's heart echoes the exotic rhythms of Carmen's arias, such as "La Habañera" (see Fig. 3.1), which mimics the beatings of a bird's wings (Nowinski 1970: 899). But the subtext here is the absent presence of Lettie—the novel's Carmen figure who George really wanted to marry—and the present absence of Cyril, who also failed to act upon his desires.

The scene at the opera thus plays a key part in the structure of Lawrence's novel, revealing underlying passions and their consequences in a similar way to the opera scene in Forster's first novel, *Where Angels Fear to Tread* (1905). Here a melodramatic performance of *Lucia di Lammermoor* in a provincial Italian town breaks the deadlock between the English visitors and the Italian man they have come to persuade to part with his half-English daughter. The passion of Donizetti's opera—and the excited response of the Italian audience—breaks down English reserve and prompts the visitors to follow their instincts (see also Fillion 2010: 27). Conversely, Lawrence's characters fail to assert themselves,[7] but his parallel use of an opera scene suggests a structuring device to which he returned in *Sons and Lovers* (1913)—in which Paul Morel consummates his passion for Clara Dawes after an evening at the theatre (*La Dame aux Camélias* being the base text for Verdi's *La Traviata*)—and in a chapter of *Aaron's Rod* (1922) featuring a performance of Verdi's *Aïda*. But in Lawrence's second novel, *The Trespasser* (1912), as for Forster in his second novel *The Longest Journey* (1907), Wagner presents an irresistible framework. Indeed, Lawrence's move in that direction is anticipated by Lettie's rendition of "O Star of Eve" from *Tannhäuser* in her final scene with George (*WP* 301).

By turning from Bizet to Wagner, Lawrence reverses the trajectory of Nietzsche's *The Case of Wagner*, which states:

Bizet's music seems to me perfect. It comes forward lightly, gracefully, stylishly. It is lovable, it does not sweat. "All that is good is easy, everything divine runs with light feet": this is the first principle of my aesthetics. This music is wicked, refined, fatalistic, and withal remains popular,—it possesses the refinement of a race, not of an individual. It is rich. It is definite. It builds, organises, completes, and in this sense it stands as a contrast to the polypus in music, to "endless melody". Have more painful, more tragic accents ever been heard on the stage before? And how are they obtained? Without grimaces! Without counterfeiting of any kind! Free from the *lie* of the grand style!—In short: this music assumes that the listener is intelligent even as a musician,—thereby it is the opposite of Wagner, who, apart from everything else, was in any case the most *ill-mannered* genius on earth (Wagner takes us as if … , he repeats a thing so often that we become desperate,—that we ultimately believe it). (Nietzsche 1911: 2)[8]

Lawrence appreciated the possibilities of *Carmen* to be "wicked, refined, fatalistic, and ... popular", but for building form and style he also saw the potential of literary Wagnerism in a range of novels that he had read, including those by George Moore, H.G. Wells, and his mentor Ford Madox Hueffer (later Ford). Such was "the scale of Wagnerism" by the beginning of the twentieth century that for some it was "*the* representative characteristic of contemporary European culture" (Sutton 2002: 3), but for Lawrence this culture was also a subject for critique.

THE TRESPASSER IN THE LAWRENCE CANON

When Lawrence's second novel appeared in 1912, it was condemned by some reviewers, who warned—in similar terms to those used by critics of Wagnerian decadence and degeneration, notably Nietzsche and Max Nordau—that "these things must not be written ... if readers are not to be sickened and—bored" (qtd. *T* 25). Subsequently, critics have tended to concur with F.R. Leavis's assessment that *The Trespasser* "is hard to read through, and cannot be said to contain any clear promise of a great novelist" (Leavis 1962: 19). Most have tended to view the novel, with a mixture of embarrassment and perplexity, as something of a "trespasser in the Lawrence canon", as William Blissett has quipped (Blissett 1966: 23).[9] What happens, though, if we take Lawrence's Wagnerism seriously enough to consider how his experiments in *The Trespasser* contributed to his thinking about form, during the writing of this novel and as he worked towards the next?

To some degree Lawrence's own misgivings about his novel foreshadowed its reception. As he completed the final draft for publication, he wrote to Edward Garnett in January 1912 that "At the bottom of my heart I don't like the work ... I hate it for its fluid, luscious quality" (*1L* 351), and yet he also regarded it as an achievement: "It really isn't bad ... At any rate, not many folk could have done it, however they may find fault" (*1L* 358). Even after a four-year interval and two further novels, in November 1916, when he was drafting his fifth (*Women in Love*), he drew a favourable comparison with the work of an internationally renowned writer: "Take even D'Annunzio and my *Trespasser*—how much cruder and stupider DAnnunzio [sic] is, really" (*3L* 41). This reference is interesting, too, because Gabriele D'Annunzio's novels are saturated by Wagner, including two which Lawrence mentioned around this time (*3L* 43): *Il Fuoco* (1900, trans. as *The Flame of Life* [1900]) and *Il Trionfo della Morte*

(1894, trans. as *The Triumph of Death* [1898]). The latter has been described as "an experimental text striving to be a *Gesemtkunstwerk* [sic]" (Galbo 2017: 49), and although it remains unknown whether Lawrence had read D'Annunzio before writing *The Trespasser*, he may yet have arrived at a recognition of the possibilities of the Wagnerian "total artwork" from other primary and secondary sources; that is, from his own experiences of Wagner's music and the literary Wagnerism of novels he had read, including Moore's *Evelyn Innes* (*1L* 142, 154) and Wells's *Ann Veronica* (*1L* 154).[10]

Lawrence insisted to Garnett that his novel had "true form" (*1L* 330), so what then might this form owe to Wagner and his concept of the artwork, as well as to the cultural discourse of Wagnerism? To what extent does Lawrence also begin to critique the legacy of Wagnerian leitmotif and its perceived decadence? By the time that he was writing *The Trespasser*, the primacy of music within Wagner's unification of the arts had already been questioned by writers including Nietzsche and Mallarmé, both of whom are led, as David Roberts demonstrates, "to confront the question of *aesthetic illusion* and to ponder the staging of the absolute in the age of aesthetics that is also the age of nihilism" (Roberts 2011: 79). Some composers were also exploring alternatives to what Debussy described as "the slavery of the 'leit-motif'" (qtd. Nichols and Langham Smith 1994: 185).

In this context, Lawrence's ambivalence about his achievement in *The Trespasser* may be closely related to his equivocal relationship with Wagner's operas: these have always divided opinion and Lawrence's responses mirror their wider reception. In December 1908, he wrote: "Surely you know Wagner's operas—*Tannhäuser* and *Lohengrin*. They will run a knowledge of music into your blood better than any criticisms" (*1L* 99).[11] Wagner thus inspired an early hint of Lawrence's later notion of "blood consciousness", which he began to formulate in a well-known letter to Ernest Collings of 17 January 1913: "My great religion is a belief in the blood, the flesh, as being wiser than the intellect" (*1L* 503). In *The Trespasser*, however, the pulsing of blood and heartbeats is a more ominous refrain, associated with Siegmund, the doomed violinist: from finishing his last performance at the theatre, when he feels as if "Phrases from the opera tyrannised over him, he played the rhythm with all his blood" (*T* 52), until he returns from his tryst with Helena on the Isle of Wight, "his whole self beating to the rhythm" of the "Ride of the Valkyries": "it hurt him with its heavy insistence of catastrophe" (*T* 165).

Siegmund is named for the hero of *Die Walküre* (the second opera in Wagner's tetralogy of the *Ring*), who falls in love with his sister Sieglinde and begets the eponymous hero of the third instalment, *Siegfried*, before he is sacrificed in the war between gods and mortals. These associations haunt Siegmund and Helena in *The Trespasser*, as they haunted the relationship of the real-life lovers on whom they are based: Helen Corke and her lover H.B. Macartney called themselves Siegmund and Sieglinde.[12] Corke (writing about herself as the fictional Helena) later wrote:

> Lawrence discovered that Wagner's *Ring* had a special fascination for Helena. She had seen the whole of the music-drama at Covent Garden, and possessed a pianoforte and vocal score of Walkure [sic]. Sometimes she would tap out motifs absently on the piano; more than once she had played the interlude with which the orchestra indicates Siegmund's watch over the sleeping Sieglinde. (Corke 1974: 231)

In October 1909, Lawrence and Corke attended *Tristan und Isolde* at Covent Garden, and henceforth Corke feels that she is "Isolt [sic] as well as Sieglinde—but a more unfortunate Isolt. I came from Cornwall to find my Tristan—but I found only his grave" (*T* 287). Despite Lawrence's report of feeling "very disappointed ... *Tristan* is long, feeble, a bit hysterical, without grip or force. I was frankly sick of it" (*1L* 140), themes from *Tristan und Isolde* permeate the version of the saga that he started to write in April 1910.

The enervating effects of Wagner's music were well documented by this time: asserted by intellectuals like Nietzsche and Nordau, but also by psychologists and physicians, and disputed by "Wagnerites" like George Bernard Shaw. Lawrence thus engaged with a discourse of sickness, neurasthenia, and "effeminacy" that had been marshalled against Wagner as "*The artist of decadence*" (Nietzsche 1911: 11, original emphasis).[13] By April 1911, he seems to have dismissed Wagner, who was too concerned with "immortal soul" and "the ultimate", as compared with Italian opera that "run[s] all on impulse": "Damn Wagner, and his bellowings at Fate and death" (*1L* 247). Later that year, he saw *Siegfried*: "It was good, but it did not make any terrific impression on me" (*1L* 327). Yet, as he proceeded to redraft his novel in early 1912, he continued along Wagnerian lines, with reference to the incestuous love of Siegmund and Sieglinde in *Die Walküre* and the potentially adulterous if unconsummated love of Tristan and Isolde. Although these themes were suggested in the source material written by Corke, Lawrence was knowingly trespassing against several social and cultural taboos when he deployed Wagner as his vehicle for the tragic affair of Siegmund and Helena.

IM/PERFECT WAGNERITES: LAWRENCE AND FORD MADOX HUEFFER

Samuel R. Delany asserts that "in the post-Edwardian pantheon, any writer who took herself or himself seriously had to appeal to Wagner in some way, whether by direct reference or by implication" (Delany 1996: 73). Helen Corke's tragic experience provided an opportunity for Lawrence's closer engagement with Wagnerism; indeed, her self-identification with Sieglinde made this inevitable. But it was difficult to escape Wagner in early twentieth-century England: his music was espoused by a cultural elite but also had popular appeal, thanks to initiatives such as Wagner Mondays at the affordable London Promenade Concerts.[14] Wagner had penetrated as far as Lawrence's hometown of Eastwood, where according to Hueffer:

> I have never anywhere found so educated a society ... Lawrence, the father, came in from down the mine of a Saturday evening. He threw down a great number of coins on the kitchen table and counted them out to his waiting mates. All the while the young people were talking about Nietzsche and Wagner and Leopardi and Flaubert and Karl Marx and Darwin and occasionally the father would interrupt his counting to contradict them. (Saunders 2012: 283)

Hueffer's fanciful description is largely borne out by (perhaps even inspired by) the range of cultural references in *The White Peacock*. Certainly, Wagner was performed within reach of Eastwood, as Lawrence and Jessie Chambers heard *Tannhäuser* at Nottingham Theatre (Chambers 1980: 109), and, in any case, piano reductions would have been as much a part of the domestic repertoire as they were elsewhere (see, for example, *WP* 301).

For George Bernard Shaw, who addressed *The Perfect Wagnerite: A Commentary on the Niblung's Ring* (1898) "to the ordinary citizen", the hope was that Wagner's operas would raise "the miners of England ... from pious respectability to a happy consciousness of and interest in fine art, without which all their piety and respectability will not save their children from resorting to cruel sports and squalid sensualities in their natural need for enjoyment" (Shaw 1986: 92, 307). Hueffer was ambivalent about such programmes of social improvement, noting somewhat disparagingly in his memoirs of 1911 that "today I never go to a place of entertainment where miscellaneous music is performed for the benefit of the poorest classes without hearing at least the overture to *Tannhäuser*" (qtd. Deutsch 2015: 1). Nonetheless, Hueffer, the founding editor of the *English Review* (from 1908 to 1910), was delighted to discover a miner's son with literary aspirations who could enlighten his readers about the life of those "poorest classes". John Worthen observes of their meeting in 1909 that "it is unlikely to have been a coincidence that this was the moment when Lawrence wrote "Odour of Chrysanthemums" and *A Collier's Friday Night*—work unlike anything he had previously written" (Worthen 2005: 67). But Hueffer also played a crucial role in Lawrence's deliberations about the novel form during the drafting of *The Trespasser* and its aftermath, which merits closer investigation.

Hueffer was a Wagnerite, who belonged to what Shaw described in *The Perfect Wagnerite* as an "inner circle of adepts" (Shaw 1986: 193): his father Francis Hueffer, a musicologist and music critic, had written the first book on Wagner in English, *Richard Wagner and the Music of the Future: History and Aesthetics* (1874), followed by the more popular *Richard Wagner* (1881). Following this paternal example, an early, unpublished essay titled "Wagner Educationally Considered" had been intended as the basis of Hueffer's own book about Wagner's "greatness", while his early musical compositions (including some 80 unpublished pages written between 1894 and 1905) have been said to show a particular "harmonic allegiance to Wagner" (Stang and Smith 1989: 187, 213). His Wagnerism transferred to his literary endeavours and, as Sondra J. Stang and Carl Smith observe, "*The Shifting of the Fire* [1892], his first published novel, is saturated in Wagner (and Berlioz), leaning hard on the *leitmotiv* in its structural organization" (Stang and Smith 1989: 218). Arguably, all Hueffer's early novels followed a similar formula, including his eleventh, *A Call* (1909), described by his biographer Arthur Mizener as "the slowly accelerated revelation of motive and meaning in a series of carefully dramatic scenes" (Mizener 1971: 199).[15] Lawrence, who read this book soon after meeting Hueffer, considered it to have "more art than life" (*1L* 141). This foreshadowed a clash of styles between the two writers. Although Hueffer tried to nurture what he recognised as Lawrence's "genius" through the drafting of *The White Peacock* (1911), their ways parted over *The Trespasser* when, as Max Saunders surmises, "both men realized the irreconcilability of their views on art" (Saunders 2012: 312).

In September 1910, Hueffer's comments on a draft of *The Trespasser* prompted Lawrence to protest that "He belongs to an opposite school of novelists to me: he says prose *must* be impersonal, like Turgenev or Flaubert. I say no" (*1L* 178). Yet, Lawrence took Hueffer's advice to heart: in *The Trespasser* both Flaubert (*T* 111) and Turgenev (*T* 209) are referred to rather self-consciously, while the novel's "triple time scheme" is perceived by Michael Bell as a strategy by which "Lawrence impersonalises his study of the central relationship" of Siegmund and Helena (Bell 1992: 26). Lawrence also declared, as he embarked on his third novel provisionally titled "Paul Morel", that it would be the antithesis of his earlier work: "not a florid prose poem, or a decorated idyll running to seed in realism: but a restrained, *somewhat* impersonal novel" (*8L* 4). A year later, in December 1911, when corresponding with Edward Garnett about the publication of his "Siegmund book", Lawrence further disclosed that Hueffer had called it "a rotten work of genius. It has no construction or form—it is execrably bad art, being all variations on a theme. Also it is erotic—not that I, personally, mind that, but an erotic work *must* be good art, which this is not" (*1L* 339).[16]

Hueffer's musical allusion to "variations on a theme" links the alleged eroticism of Lawrence's novel with its Wagnerism. In Wells's scandalous novel *Ann Veronica* (which Lawrence read in January 1910 [*1L* 154]), the eponymous heroine is taken to a performance of *Tristan und Isolde* as part of a planned seduction, prompting Lawrence to ask Garnett: "Is Hueffer's opinion worth anything, do you think? Is the book *so* erotic? I don't want to be talked about in an *Anne* [sic] *Veronica* fashion" (*1L* 339). Moore's *Evelyn Innes* (1898) was also "full of music and passion" (*T* 289), as Corke observed when Lawrence lent it to her soon after they attended *Tristan und Isolde*. In an interview published in *The Musician*, Moore explained that he had adopted the technique of leitmotif—which he felt was "unconsciously" deployed by Flaubert and which D'Annunzio "had done something to systematize"—to develop his art as a "psychological novelist" (Martin 1982: 103). There were therefore numerous examples of literary Wagnerism available to Lawrence when he worked on *The Trespasser*, although these differed in their emphasis on Wagner as a story-teller or as a musician. Often novelists borrowed more from the subject matter of Wagnerian opera than from its musical style, but, as Stoddard Martin observes, Moore's later novel *The Brook Kerith* (1916) moved closer to "achiev[ing] a narrative equivalent to Wagner's 'unending melody'". Here the fluidity of style was such that even the Wagnerite Shaw complained that after reading "about thirty pages ... It began to dawn on me that there was no mortal reason why Moore should not keep going on like that for fifty thousand pages, or fifty million for that matter" (qtd. Martin 1982: 114).

This Wagnerian sense of "endless melody" is perhaps another factor informing Hueffer's criticism of *The Trespasser* as being "*all* variations on a theme" (my emphasis), which implies a lack of the structure and resolution (in musical terms) that Hueffer valued. In sonata form—later defined by Hueffer as his ideal of literary form—variations are only part of a tripartite structure consisting of exposition, development, and recapitulation. Although it is possible to read *The Trespasser*, as Michael Black does, as a novel with "a very tight structure ... which has three movements" (Black 1986: 80), it yet falls far short of sonata form as Hueffer describes it. In *Thus to Revisit: Some Reminiscences* (1921), in an imaginary dialogue with an "Eminent Novelist" (namely Wells), Hueffer argues for limiting the notion of "Freedom" in development and advocates "emphatic" restatement of the themes in recapitulation. Later in life, "he repeatedly expressed his longing to write ... a novel like a fugue, in which the treatment counted for everything and the subject in itself was of far less consequence (as in Bach, 'abstract variations on an aesthetic, given theme' ...)" (Stang and Smith 1989: 219). Such descriptions bear out Corke's report of Lawrence's complaint that for Hueffer "What mattered in a novel was style, not content" (Corke 1971: 120). In his continuing quest for a Paterian synthesis of content and form, discussed in Chap. 1, Lawrence was after both.

Lawrence's active interest in music was no match for Hueffer's technical knowledge, regarding sonata form, fugue, or Wagner. Some critics have therefore been sceptical of Lawrence's musical achievements,[17] but as Black observes, even if "Lawrence's knowledge of [Wagner's] operas could not be more superficial ... his grasp of the musical method is that of an artist seizing on something he was already intuitively working towards" (Black 1986: 80). Accordingly, Black perceives *The Trespasser* as "a carefully worked-out motivic web which is the literary equivalent of Wagner's use of themes in the orchestral music of his operas" (Black 1986: 80). He contends that in Lawrence's novel, as in Wagnerian opera, "the wider implications are provided by the whole texture of the writing, and not just by the thoughts and conversations of the characters or direct address by the author" (Black 1986: 79). This perceived focus on texture rather than structure—or even on texture *as* structure—is particularly Wagnerian, since as Burton D. Fisher explains, "Wagner would elevate the emotional temperature of his drama through symphonic development of those musical 'motifs of memory', thematic ideas or leitmotifs, that would be altered and varied for psychological and dramatic impact, and reach their full expression through a woven symphonic texture" (Fisher 2017: 25).

However, Lawrence is by no means uncritical of the "emotional" consequences of "symphonic texture". Siegmund provides a working definition of the novel's symphonic method in his ominous declaration to Helena: "You seem to have knit all things in a piece for me. Things are not separate: they are all in a symphony. They go moving on and on. You are the motive, in everything" (*T* 98–99). As Bell observes, "Siegmund's reference to a 'symphony' here becomes an image of cosmic merging by which all separateness is lost", noting further that "The allusion to such a specifically Wagnerian conception of the orchestra here picks up the earlier desire for a fulfilling, but destructive, merging with the waves on the beach" (Bell 1992: 34). Black comments that Lawrence's experiment may have suggested a model for Virginia Woolf's *The Waves* (Black 1986: 81), her 1931 novel narrated by six consciousnesses which merge like waves in the sea. However, *The Trespasser* warns against the self-destructiveness of merger with the other. If, as Bell suggests, Lawrence's novel exemplifies a "concentration on the medium of music itself as a possible 'language' of feeling" (Bell 1992: 32), then it is an ambivalent study, which points to the dangers of dissolving the boundaries of the self.

Earlier in the novel, Siegmund and Helena disagree about the music that best evokes a sunset, which provides further musical context for the novel's impulse towards a unity that subsumes separate identity. Siegmund chooses a Beethoven symphony (unspecified)[18] and Helena chooses the Grail music from *Lohengrin* (*T* 61–62), shown in (Fig. 3.2). Lawrence borrowed this conversation almost verbatim from Corke's "Freshwater Diary" (*T* 295), but its context within the novel suggests that he may have discerned the significance of leitmotif in the opera. According to the composer Liszt, a contemporary and friend of Wagner:

> The distinguishing feature of the music of "Lohengrin" is unity of conception and style; there is not a single melodic phrase, still less an ensemble, nor indeed a passage of any kind, the peculiar nature and true meaning of which would be understood if it were separated from its connection with the whole work. Every part connects, binds together and enhances the rest. All is of a piece, and so united that the parts cannot be torn asunder.[19]

Gralmotiv

Fig. 3.2   The motif of the Grail from Wagner's *Lohengrin*

In musical terms, Helena's identification with leitmotif mirrors her desire for fusion with her lover, in which they will cease to have individual being and become "one being, Two-in-one, the only Hermaphrodite" (*T* 64). This model of androgyny is also strongly suggested in Aubrey Beardsley's illustrations of *Tristan und Isolde*, which for Sutton identifies Wagner's protagonists as "contemporary decadent figures, [while] it also suggests their 'morbid' solipsism: the nihilistic, self-destructive quality of their desire" (Sutton 2002: 43).[20]

The paradigm for the destructive merger of self with the lover is *Tristan und Isolde*, the opera which Lawrence introduced into Corke's narrative. As Bell notes, *Tristan und Isolde* is "the numinously tragic culmination of a particular tradition of romantic love in which passion is seen as intrinsically incompatible with the everyday social realm" (Bell 1992: 28). Wagner encapsulates the unfulfilled longing of his tragic hero in his so-called Tristan chord (Fig. 3.3), which is "strongly dissonant and has extremely complex harmonic properties" (see Maehder 2011: 99). The effect is heightened by delaying the resolution of tension: only at the culmination of four hours of music does the chord resolve, when the lovers are both dead. In *The Trespasser*, Helena survives the suicide of her lover and so there is no resolution in the Wagnerian sense. Indeed, as Bell asserts, Lawrence's "book is ambivalently poised between romantic tragedy and a critique of romance" and further "that its penetrating critique of romantic feeling is simultaneously an advance towards the conception which will challenge it" (Bell 1992: 29). Lawrence's ambivalence

Fig. 3.3   The "Tristan chord" from Wagner's *Tristan und Isolde*

towards leitmotif, I would argue, is a specific means of working out his "mature" style.

Leitmotif offers a useful way of manipulating the temporal aspects of music or plot, both of which usually unfold over time. In one sense, the "motivic web" that Black perceives in *The Trespasser* suspends narrative progression to create a spatial dimension of "no time, it was Romance, going back to Tristan" (*T* 55). But, as Fisher explains, "The great virtue of leitmotifs is that they work on multiple levels: they not only foreshadow the future, but by evoking the past they can provide the present with an infinitely greater immediacy" (Fisher 2017: 25). In this respect, as Bell points out, Lawrence produces a "fiction of the present" which resembles the rationale for his later poetry, which he outlines in the Preface to *New Poems* (1920): "In the immediate present there is no perfection, no consummation, nothing finished. The strands are all flying, quivering, intermingling into the web, the waters are shaking the moon" (*Poems* 646). Here Lawrence looks to Whitman—whose "heart beats with the urgent, insurgent Now" (*Poems* 647)—rather than to Wagner, a balance which shifts in tandem with his evolving critique of the temporal implications of leitmotif. Nonetheless, *The Trespasser* works towards the more successful experiments with poetic prose and the mythic method in *The Rainbow*, as Black has briefly suggested (Black 1986: 81). Lawrence's negotiations of leitmotif, through the work of Gustave Flaubert, Thomas Mann, and Debussy, are crucial to this development, as explored in the remainder of this chapter.

TRISTANISING: LEITMOTIF IN THOMAS MANN
AND FRIEDRICH NIETZSCHE

Lawrence's review titled "German Books" (1913), published a year after *The Trespasser*, offers useful insight into his evolving ambivalence about the literary application of leitmotif. Here he writes specifically of the use of leitmotif as an aspect of form and his critique of Mann's aestheticism opens into questions of the stylistic excesses that critics have attributed to his own early vision. Lawrence's review, therefore, resonates with Vincent Sherry's thesis that modernist aesthetics is rooted in the decadence that it attempted to disavow. As Sherry argues, while modernist writers constantly aspired to capture "Now-ness", this must always become lost in the past, and so "This sense of the present moment being written as the memory of its possibilities of presence takes the radical meaning of modernism, or Just-Now-ism, and ties it to the root sense of *décadence* (de-*cad*-ere), to *fall* away" (Sherry 2015: 34, original emphases). In the case of Wagner, the repetition throughout a work of motifs, such as the Tristan chord, represents an intrusion of past memories into the listening present in a way that unsettles our sense of time. Fredric Jameson thus observes that in Wagnerian opera "leitmotif is the scar left by destiny on the musical present" and repetitions represent "substantive moments in their own right, where characters confront the weight of destiny as it drags on their life in the present of time" (Jameson 2013: 19). But, at the same time, as he continues:

> the leitmotif also occupies and consummates a different kind of temporality, which, adapting Hegel, we may call "the immense privilege of the musical present" … And if it should be objected that it is scarcely possible to conceive of some pure present in a temporal art like music, … attention to the timbre and colour of the musical event … is bound to shift the experience of sound away from its movement in time, and far more decisively to the approach of some paradoxical new musical atemporality. (Jameson 2013: 22)

In the former sense of "scar[s] left by destiny", then, we have the "bellowings at Fate and death" that Lawrence soon objected to in Wagner (*1L* 247), but on the other hand leitmotif brings a sense of atemporality that was effective in setting the static atmosphere of "no time" in *The Trespasser* (*T* 55). And yet, Lawrence was aware, as he revised the novel for publication during January 1912, of a conflict between "the fluid, luscious quality"

that he "hate[d]" and "its steady progressiveness" that "surprise[d]" him
(*IL* 351). If the former quality derives from the excesses of a Wagnerian
style, the surprising "progressiveness" that emerges in spite of Wagnerism
is regarded by Lawrence as a strength in his method that merits closer
attention in terms of his developing aesthetics (Black 1986: 80).

Lawrence talks again of the virtues of progressiveness in his review of
Georgian Poetry (published in *Rhythm* in March 1912, shortly before *The
Trespasser*), which he praises as an awakening to "morning" from "the terror of night", thus reversing the imagery of *Tristan und Isolde* that extols
the night as a relief from the madness of day and which Lawrence had
borrowed in *The Trespasser*. Indeed, Lawrence takes a turn against opera
to explain how an all-consuming notion of passion is fundamentally at
odds with a philosophy of life as "progressive":

> Love is the greatest of all things … It is sex-passion, so separated, in which
> we do not believe. The "Carmen" and "Tosca" sort of passion is not inter-
> esting any longer, because it can't progress. Its goal and aim is possession,
> whereas possession in love is only a means to love. And because passion can-
> not go beyond possession, the passionate heroes and heroines—Tristans and
> what-not—must die. We believe in the love that is happy ever after, progres-
> sive as life itself. (*IR* 204)

The fatal limitations of opera therefore cannot supply the model for art
that is as "progressive as life"—as Lawrence's subsequent review of Mann's
Death in Venice (1912) demonstrates.

Lawrence, like Mann in his novella, does not mention Wagner directly
but he blames Mann's rigid adherence to the technique of leitmotif for the
resulting decadence of his novella, which "is absolutely, almost unintentionally, unwholesome. The man is sick, body and soul. He portrays himself
as he is, with wonderful skill and art portrays his sickness … It portrays one
man, one atmosphere, one sick vision" (*IR* 211). Mann's work is therefore
the antithesis of what Lawrence would formulate at greater length in *Study
of Thomas Hardy* (1914) because it "has none of the rhythm of a living
thing, the rise of a poppy, then the after uplift of the bud, the shedding of
the calyx and the spreading wide of the petals, the falling of the flower and
the pride of the seed-head" (*IR* 212). Although Lawrence is reaching
towards another vision of "excess" (*STH* 9), associated with an organic and
life-affirming flowering of life in tension with Baudelaire's *Les Fleurs du
mal* and the *maladie* of decadence, he must yet acknowledge "the falling

of the flower" and so remain implicated in decadence and degeneration. Moreover, he also replicates the juxtaposition of old and young represented in Mann's *Death in Venice* by the ageing protagonist's pursuit of youthful male beauty. Indeed, although the decadent Aschenbach feels satisfied that the young man seems "very delicate, he's sickly ... he'll probably not live to grow old" (Mann 2003: 124), youth is spared in Mann's tale and it is the older man who dies, while Lawrence's "poppy"—like many of his male characters—falls in its "pride"/prime (*IR* 212).

Lawrence also grounds his review of "German Books" in a critique of Gustave Flaubert, though again without conceding the possibility of any irony in Mann's characterisation of Aschenbach, not least by naming him Gustav.[21] Lawrence returns to Flaubert almost as obsessively as Aschenbach to the youthful Tadzio in Mann's novella, mentioning Flaubert five times during his short review, with the first reference as early as line 10 and the last only five lines from the end. Initially, his criticism reads like a riposte to Hueffer, who had urged him that a novel "*must* be impersonal, like Turgenev or Flaubert" (*IL* 178, Lawrence's emphasis). Two years later, in June 1912, soon after the novel had finally been published by Garnett, Lawrence was still writing that he "suffered badly from Hueffer re Flaubert and perfection" (*IL* 417). In "German books" a critique of Flaubertian form crystallises around the use of "Leitmotiv", and Lawrence provides what Neil Reeve and John Worthen credit as his "own, fairly accurate translation of part of an address by Mann to the Literary Historical Society of Bonn, given in 1906" (*IR* 488):

> In writing of the Leitmotiv and its influence, [Mann] says: "Now this method alone is sufficient to explain my slowness. It is the result neither of anxiety nor indigence, but an overpowering sense of responsibility for the choice of every word, the coining of every phrase ... Can one know before-hand whether a sentence, or part of a sentence may not be called upon to appear again as motiv, peg, symbol, citation or connection? And a sentence which must be heard twice must be fashioned accordingly ... So every point becomes a standing ground, every adjective a decision, and it is clear that such work is not to be produced off-hand". (*IR* 208)

From this description, Lawrence extrapolates that Mann forced his art— "He forced himself to write, and kept himself to the work"—in other words, this is not an art that flowers organically. Worse still his art is "parasit[ic]", based as it is on endurance and suffering, so that "it seems, the artist has absorbed the man, and yet the man is there, like an exhausted organism on which a parasite has fed itself strong" (*IR* 209). This is one of several striking parallels between Lawrence's review of "German Books" and Nietzsche's *The Case of Wagner*, in which Nietzsche describes the Wagnerian conception of love as "no more than a refined form of *parasitism*, a making one's nest in another's soul and sometimes even in another's flesh—Ah! and how constantly at the cost of the host!" (Nietzsche 1911: 8).[22]

The Case of Wagner—in which the word "case" bears the double meaning of a legal or moral investigation and a medical condition—also observes the malign influence of Flaubert: "Would you believe it that Wagner's heroines one and all … are almost indistinguishable from Mdme. Bovary!" For Nietzsche, too, decadence coheres around the pernicious practice of leitmotif:

> How is *decadence* in *literature* characterised? By the fact that in it life no longer animates the whole. Words become predominant and leap right out of the sentence to which they belong, the sentences themselves trespass beyond their bounds, and obscure the sense of the whole page, and the page in turn gains in vigour at the cost of the whole,—the whole is no longer a whole. (Nietzsche 1911: 28)

Lest there is any doubt that Nietzsche is referring to leitmotif he makes this plain:

> Once more let it be said that Wagner is really only worthy of admiration and love by virtue of his inventiveness in small things, in his elaboration of details,—here one is quite justified in proclaiming him a master of the first rank, as our greatest musical *miniaturist* who compresses an infinity of meaning and sweetness into the smallest space. His wealth of colour, of chiaroscuro, of the mystery of a dying light, so pampers our senses that afterwards almost every other musician strikes us as being too robust. (Nietzsche 1911: 21)

But Nietzsche goes on to condemn the perceived effeminacy and effeminising effects of Wagner's music, while Lawrence refrains from commenting directly on the homoeroticism of Mann's novella, insisting that "Aschenbach loves the boy—but almost as a symbol. In him he loves life and youth and beauty, as Hyacinth in the Greek myth" (*IR* 210).[23] This is not an aspect of Mann, or even of Wagner, that seems to trouble him in 1913; and a few months after reviewing *Death in Venice*, Lawrence ponders, "why nearly every man that approaches greatness tends to homosexuality." (*2L* 115).[24] Nietzsche, on the other hand, finally equates Wagner's sickness with homosexuality in his Postscript to *The Case of Wagner*:

> Never on earth has there been such a connoisseur of paltry infinities, of all that thrills, of extravagant excesses, of all the feminism from out the vocabulary of happiness! My friends, do but drink the philtres of this art! Nowhere will ye find a more pleasant method of enervating your spirit, of forgetting your manliness under a rosebush. (Nietzsche 1911: 40)

The allusion here to the love potion that precipitates the adulterous love of *Tristan und Isolde* hints at another kind of forbidden love that began to permeate Wagnerian discourses at the beginning of the twentieth century. Hans Fuchs published a study of *Wagner and Homosexuality* in 1903 and an erotic Wagnerian novel *Eros zwischen euch und uns* (*Eros between you and us*) in 1909—the same year that the composer Alban Berg wrote from the Bayreuth Festival of "the ghastly horde of Wagnerian homosexuals" (qtd. Morris 2002: 271). Mitchell Morris posits an appeal of Wagnerian opera deriving from its liminality and transgressiveness, citing a patient of Richard von Krafft-Ebing's who claimed that "I passionately love music, and am an enthusiastic devotee of Richard Wagner's, which partiality I have noticed most homosexuals have; I find that this music corresponds so precisely to our natures" (Morris 2002: 271).

Although such associations do not seem to find their way into Lawrence's *The Trespasser*, the thwarting of Siegmund's passion by Helena's shivering coldness (see, for example *T* 63) can be read, in the light of Helen Corke's own accounts of her real-life story in *Neutral Ground* and *In Our Infancy*, as relating to her own resistance of normative heterosexuality.[25] Even in "The Cornwall Writing" of 1911–1912 she records her "struggle" to "fight with the demands of [HBM's] desire" and his "bitter" allegations that she is "cruel" in her resistance of his desire: "This *is* the tragedy" (*T* 317, original emphasis). As Lawrence became sexually interested in Helen, he described her lack of response in comparable terms, rewriting her poem "Fantasy" about a dreamy "ghost land" (*Poems* 861–862) as "Coldness in Love", in which "all evening long you were cold, / And I was numb with a bitter, deathly ache" (*Poems* 63). In *The Trespasser*, themes of coldness and whiteness are set against motifs of pulsing blood and sunshine as a lurking threat that is glimpsed by Siegmund: "under all, was this deep mass of cold, that the softness and warmth merely floated upon" (*T* 89). This coldness finds its apotheosis in *Women in Love* (1920), in the frozen death of Gerald Crich, who, like Lawrence's Siegmund and Wagner's Tristan, seeks death, and crucially, too, he resists Birkin's openness to "another kind of love" (*WL* 481) that runs counter to a narrative of heterosexual couples.[26] As I discuss further in Chap. 5, Gerald is a more fully realised version of Tristan, in Lawrence's continuing critique of a culture that seeks to dissolve the boundaries between self and other, in love and death; but already in *The Trespasser*, he was searching for "progressive" forms to mitigate against Wagnerian decadence (*IR* 204).

Towards Modernist Musicality

Wagner's music is often associated with conflagration; from the all-consuming passion of *Tristan und Isolde* to the fire that consumes Valhalla at the end of the *Ring* cycle. The theme of coldness in *The Trespasser* is therefore introduced by a reference to the music of Debussy's opera *Pelléas et Mélisande* (1902), which Siegmund considers "cold" (*T* 52). Siegmund "struggled" to explain his feeling, although numerous references to "cold" in the libretto are reinforced by music that seems cold in comparison to the passion that Lawrence has attributed to Wagnerian opera. This is an opposition perceived by Robin Holloway, who argues that "the subject of *Tristan und Isolde* is Passion, or rather as Mann put it, 'sensuality, enormous sensuality … sensuality unquenchable by any amount of gratification', whereas the subject of *Pelléas et Mélisande* is loneliness, lack of connection—in the end a frigid nihilism" (Holloway 1979: 61). This seems at once to describe Gerald's frozen death in *Women in Love*, while also pointing to "The Poetry of the Present", in which Lawrence exhorts: "Give me the still, white seething, the incandescence and the coldness of the incarnate moment" (*Poems* 646). To what extent, then, does the perceived coldness of Debussy's music provide a counterpoint to Wagnerian passion in the evolution of Lawrence's style?

When Thomas Beecham revived *Pelléas* at Covent Garden in 1910, it was received as a favourable contrast to recent productions there by Wagner's heir Richard Strauss. Lawrence had seen Strauss's *Elektra* there in March 1910 and judged it (in similar terms to Nietzsche's criticism of Wagnerian "colour" and "inventiveness", quoted above) as having "a great deal of sensuous colour, but it is all abstract, impersonal in feeling, not the least sensual. One tires of it … It is emotionally insufficient, though splendid in craftsmanship" (*STH* 147). According to one contemporary reviewer, *Pelléas* "came along at the right moment: blood and thunder had exhausted [Strauss's] appeal; there was something akin to an unspoken demand for a work of pure beauty. London responded immediately; a large gathering assembled to hear Debussy's masterpiece" (qtd. Abbate and Parker 2012: 432). Lawrence's muted tones in *The Trespasser* mark a corresponding contrast with the perceived "blood and thunder" of Wagner, as well as with Strauss.

Debussy regarded Wagnerian leitmotif in comparable terms to Nietzsche. Writing of his own opera, Debussy insisted that:

> If in Pelléas symphonic development does not, on the whole, find much of a place, it is a reaction against that pernicious neo-Wagnerian aesthetic which claims to render simultaneously the feelings expressed by the character and the inner thoughts which motivate him ... That is why there is no "guiding thread" in Pelléas and why the characters are not subjected to the slavery of the "leit-motif" ... Notice that the motif which accompanies Mélisande is *never* altered ... Emphasis must be laid on the simplicity in Pelléas—I spent 12 years removing anything *parasitic* that might have crept into it ... (Nichols and Langham Smith 1994: 185–186, Debussy's emphases)

In other words, Debussy viewed the Wagnerism of his early years as a sickness which he struggled to shed, later recalling: "1889: A marvellous year! I was full of the Wagnerian madness" (Lesure and Langham Smith 1977: 167). He had fallen for *Tristan und Isolde* on a first hearing in 1880, when he promptly purchased and attempted to memorise the score, and his first and only opera completed 12 years later self-consciously refers to *Tristan*. For example, when Mélisande says, "Mais je suis triste" (Act IV, Scene 4), Debussy uses the word "triste" (sad) as an opportunity to quote Wagner's Tristan chord: but as Arthur Wenk argues, Debussy does something very different with the chord, using it to indicate stasis rather than development: "The half-diminished seventh, or Tristan, chord takes on a referential significance in place of functional harmonic significance. Debussy isolates this harmony as a sound symbol, attenuating or even breaking the bonds of harmonic progression" (Wenk 2017: n.p.). To reiterate Debussy's own explanation, we should "Notice that the motif which accompanies Mélisande is *never* altered".

The spatialisation of music associated with Debussy's music often draws comparisons with the techniques of impressionist painting, but for Theodor Adorno this represents a desire to withdraw from the becoming that all music presupposes:

In Debussy the individual timbre complexes were still mediated with each other through the Wagnerian "art of transition": The sound is not delimited; rather, each note shoots beyond its own limits. Through this swimming of notes into one another, the music produces something like a sensual infinity. By the same procedure in impressionist paintings, that is, through the dynamic effect of the juxtaposition of spots of color—the technique that music absorbed—luminous effects are materialized. (Adorno 2006: 141)

Similar effects are at work in the descriptive passages of *The Trespasser*, in which Jane Heath perceives "a voluminous sense of atmosphere, of sky, wind, cloud and mist and a sense of place" (Heath 1995: 321). For instance, "As the sun set, the fog dispersed a little. Breaking masses of mist went flying from cliff to cliff, and far away beyond the cliffs the western sky stood dimmed with gold" (*T* 61). This is the same scene, discussed above, that prompts Siegmund to describe the sunset as a symphony.

For Adorno, however, such effects "degrade music to a parasite of painting" (Adorno 2006: 143). The reference to parasitic art leads once again to Nietzsche, who is indeed quoted and disputed by Adorno in a footnote concerning "Nietzsche's concept of musical progress" (Adorno 2006: 184 n. 3). Adorno also differed with Nietzsche on the latter's strong emphasis on dance: "Real dance, in contradistinction to mature music, is a temporarily static art, a turning in circles, movement without progression. It was in consciousness of this that the sonata form transcended the dance form, at once conserving it and abolishing it" (Adorno 2006: 143). But for Lawrence, who aligned more closely with Nietzsche than with ideas of sonata form espoused by Hueffer, the stasis evoked by the music of Debussy, including his dance music for the Ballets Russes, suggested a way to resist a drive towards resolution. In this sense, the "progressiveness" that Lawrence admired in *The Trespasser* represented a turn from the temporal to the spatial, that he would pursue in *The Rainbow*. While *The Rainbow*, like *The Trespasser*, has a triple time scheme that renders three generations successively, there is still no sense of three movements in a sonata. Instead, as I argue in Chap. 4, *The Rainbow* is conceived spatially around arches and a "widening circle" (the title of two chapters), and has key scenes explicitly rendered through the music of dance.

Coda

In the meantime, *Sons and Lovers* intervened as Lawrence's first major success. In striving towards the "impersonality" that Hueffer advocated, Lawrence's third novel eschews the musicality of its predecessors—and its successors—and so Martin's comparison of *Sons and Lovers* to Wagner's *Siegfried* as part of a Lawrentian *Ring* cycle (Martin 1982: 178) seems difficult to justify. In *Sons and Lovers*, a relative scarcity of allusions to music may be governed by a temporary change to a mostly "realist" mode of writing, which accompanies a rejection of the Wagnerian *Gesamtkunstwerk*.[27] Critics concede that the Wagnerism they attribute to *The Rainbow* is also less overt than in *The Trespasser*, with Hugh Stevens building on Martin's claim that Wagnerian motifs "were woven into Lawrence's own system so subtly as to be virtually invisible" to argue that they "echo unconsciously" (Stevens 2014: 613). Yet such descriptions, of invisible echoes, evoke a soundscape in *The Rainbow* more fundamental than any specifically Wagnerian motifs, akin to Lawrence's analogy of sound waves made visible in Chladni experiments that he uses to describe the "rhythmic form" he was after in *The Rainbow* (*2L* 184).

Recommended Listening

Bizet	*Carmen* (particularly "La Habañera")
Debussy	*Pelléas et Mélisande*
Wagner	*Siegfried* (particularly "Ride of the Valkyries"); *Tristan und Isolde* (particularly the Prelude and "Mild und leise", Isolde's final aria)

Notes

1. There is no record of any production/s of *Carmen* that Lawrence attended, but in *The White Peacock* he describes a performance by the Carl Rosa Opera Company at the Royal Theatre in Nottingham. As James Moran notes, it seems likely that Lawrence would have seen one of their performances there (Moran 2015: 91). Carl Rosa was the principal touring company in Britain and the first to perform *Carmen* in English: see http://www.carlrosatrust.org.uk/opera.html. John Worthen refers to a possible performance in Croydon (Worthen 1992: 439), drawing on Lawrence's letter of April 1911 (*1L* 247), but this post-dates the publication of *The White Peacock*.

2. Elgin W. Mellown, on the other hand, construes "References to opera and ballet, as well as to symphonic music … [as] particularly significant social markers" that Lawrence self-consciously exploited as cultural currency (Mellown 1997: 50). On closer examination of Lawrence's work and in light of more recent studies of the role of music in literary modernism,

Mellown's reading of Lawrence as an equivalent of "Forster's Leonard Bast" misunderstands his proto-modernist project.

3. Greiffenhagen's painting made such a profound impression on Lawrence that he made four copies of it, including one for his fiancée Louie Burrows (*1L* 234). For further discussion see Worthen 1992: 284–286 and Stewart 1997–1998.

4. For libretto see https://archive.org/stream/carmenoperainfou1875bize/carmenoperainfou1875bize_djvu.txt

5. E.M. Forster urged a friend to read "A Poem of Friendship", writing that "The whole book is the queerest product of subconsciousness I have yet struck ... he has not a glimmering from first to last of what he is up to" (Lago and Furbank 1985: 11). However, Lawrence may have been influenced by a similarly homoerotic bathing scene in Forster's novel *A Room with a View* (1908). There are further parallels between the two novels in that Lettie, like Lucy Honeychurch, plays composers to suit her mood: "When she was angry she played tender fragments of Tchaïkowsky, when she was miserable, Mozart" (*WP* 25). In an earlier draft, "When she was angry she played Beethoven" (*WP* 359 n. 25:32), which is directly comparable to Lucy.

6. For instance, the narrator of Mérimée's novella is described as "singing in the style of bored Parisian flâneurs" (Mérimée 2008: 50), while Cyril retreats to London where he "loved to move in the aimless street's procession, watching the faces come near to me" (*WP* 264). Lawrence mentions Mérimée's *Lukis* (*WP* 118) and *Colombo* in *Sons and Lovers* (*SL* 174), and it is likely that he also read *Carmen*. For instance, Judith Ruderman suggests parallels between Lawrence's late novella *The Virgin and the Gipsy* and Mérimée's "conflation of gypsies, blackness, femaleness, and Jewishness in a quadruply powerful simplification of otherness" (Ruderman 2003: 58).

7. Mellown fails to perceive this, writing instead that "Whether intentional or not, Lawrence's attitude is almost identical to that of Forster's Philip Herriton, the proper Englishman who overcomes the handicap of his nationality and social difference" (Mellown 1997: 52).

8. Although Bizet was almost universally criticised by his contemporaries for Wagnerite tendencies—and his letters do reveal his enthusiasm—subsequently critics have recognised that of all the French composers of the nineteenth-century Bizet was "the least influenced by the master of Bayreuth" (Klein 1947: 50).

9. See also the interesting discussions of Wagnerism in *The Trespasser* by Hinz (1971) and Kestner (1977).

10. For instance, Blissett argues that d'Annunzio is "the important influence and analogue" for *The Trespasser*, claiming that although "The evidence of Lawrence's familiarity with D'Annunzio dates from after *The Trespasser* ... most of his early reading is undocumented" (Blissett 1966: 26–27).

11. Jessie Chambers confirms "we heard *Tannhäuser*" (Chambers 1980: 109), but there is no other mention of *Lohengrin*.

12. See Helen Corke's autobiographical writings in the appendices to the Cambridge Edition of *The Trespasser*: "From 'The Letter': The Diary of Helen Corke (written 5 September 1909——8 May 1910) (Appendix 1, *T* 281–292); "The Freshwater Diary (written 1909–1910), by Helen Corke (Appendix 2, *T* 293–301); and "From 'The Cornwall Writing' (written 1911–1912) by Helen Corke" (Appendix 3, *T* 301–318).

13. For a discussion of Wagner's music as a cause of "neurasthenia" see Kennaway 2012: 70–73.

14. http://www.bbc.co.uk/programmes/articles/1sgMxZvFzHQG3Y1Hkt Mfg6w/history-of-the-proms

15. Following the pioneering essay by Stang and Smith (1989), see more recent essays on Hueffer and Wagner by Wrenn (2014) and Lockyer (2014).

16. Hueffer's letter has been lost, but his account appears in *Mightier Than the Sword*, where he describes it "as a thoroughly bad hybrid book and I told him so" (qtd. *1L* 178) and another letter on the subject is published in *8L* 2–3.

17. A certain amount of snobbery is evident in assessments of Lawrence's musical appreciation, which I hesitate to attribute to Hueffer. Elliott Zuckerman, for example, emphasises the class dimensions of Aestheticism, concluding that due to his "pedigree, fashionable Wagnerism suited the talent of Lawrence no more naturally than, say, illustrations by Beardsley would suit *Sons and Lovers*" (Zuckerman 1964: 127).

18. It is not clear which symphony Siegmund is referring to here. Beethoven weaves many scenes from nature into his so-called *Pastoral Symphony* (No. 6) and perhaps Siegmund perceives a rendering of sunset in the fifth and final movement's afterglow following the storm depicted in the fourth movement. There is also a setting by Beethoven (op. 108 no.2) of a Scottish song called "Sunset".

19. Liszt quoted http://www.musicwithease.com/lohengrin-music.html

20. Beardsley's style of drawing is referenced in *The White Peacock* (WP 159).

21. Usually Gustav is taken to refer to Gustav Mahler, but Clayton Koelb also points to Flaubert, noting too that the surname "Aschenbach literally means 'Ashbrook', and it carries connotations of exhausted fires, of a stream gone dry, and of the aftermath of cremation" (Koelb 2004: 96).

22. Bruce Steele notes that "It is likely but not certain that DHL also read *The Case of Wagner*, trans. Oscar Levy (1888)" (*STH* 255 n. 7:2).

23. But see the contrary reading of Barry J. Scherr (who also cites Jonathan Dollimore) that "Clearly Lawrence, after reading Mann's 'unwholesome', homoerotic *Death in Venice*, was angered by this 'aesthetic' idealization of homosexual-pederastic lust in which formal perfection disguises 'decadent' homosexual desires" (Scherr 2004: 173).

24. Lawrence's views about homosexuality are subject to much critical debate, not least because of a subsequent letter condemning "men loving men" as "something almost unbearable to me" (*2L* 320).

25. See also Helen Baron's article concluding that Corke's writing provides "first-hand evidence of ambivalent gender identity and the confident lesbian lifestyle" (Baron 2007: 39). Baron also cites Garnett's opinion that rejections of Corke's manuscript of *Neutral Ground* were unsurprising as "publishers are shy of a study of the 'intermediate type'" (Baron 2007: 33). Although as Howard J. Booth has commented to me, a more nuanced reading of *Neutral Ground* might suggest asexuality.

26. At the end of the novel, Gerald's frozen body accuses Birkin, who as Vincent Sherry points out: "can be heard defending against the homoerotic attachment to Gerald, which has run as a narrative parallel in the novel to the straighter line development of his romantic union with Ursula. Where the queer interest associated with decadence has been sidelined by the plot, it is emerging again at the end in a poetry whose contorted form reflects all of the pressure that the ideology of the romantic plot has brought to bear on the sensibility of decadence" (Sherry 2015: 146).

27. There may also be a biographical reason for the silence of the Morel family piano. Lawrence's sister Ada writes that "Until the death of Ernest, Mother always took part in our games and joined in our songs. He had been the life and soul of them. After he died she would stay in the kitchen in her rocking chair, pretending to read. We knew where her thoughts were, and it always cast a shadow over the fun" (Lawrence and Gelder 1966: 43).

REFERENCES

Abbate, Carolyn, and Roger Parker. 2012. *A History of Opera: The Last Four Hundred Years*. Harmondsworth: Penguin.

Adorno, T.W. 2006. *The Philosophy of New Music*. Trans. Robert Hullot-Kentor. Minneapolis/London: University of Minnesota Press.

Baron, Helen. 2007. Helen Corke's Autobiography, Part II. *Journal of D.H. Lawrence Studies* 1 (2): 23–39.

Begam, Richard, and Matthew Wilson Smith, eds. 2016. *Modernism and Opera*. Baltimore: Johns Hopkins University Press.

Bell, Michael. 1992. *D.H. Lawrence: Language and Being*. Cambridge: Cambridge University Press.

Black, Michael. 1986. *D.H. Lawrence: The Early Fiction*. Cambridge: Cambridge University Press.

Blissett, William. 1966. Lawrence, D'Annunzio, Wagner. *Wisconsin Studies in Contemporary Literature* 7 (1): 21–46.

Bynner, Witter. 1953. *Journey with Genius: Recollections and Reflections concerning the D.H. Lawrences.* London/New York: Peter Nevill.

Chambers, Jessie [E.T.]. 1980. *D.H. Lawrence: A Personal Record.* Cambridge: Cambridge University Press.

Corke, Helen. 1971. D.H. Lawrence: The Early Stage. *D.H. Lawrence Review* 4 (2): 111–121.

———. 1974. The Writing of *The Trespasser. D.H Lawrence Review* 7 (3): 227–239.

Curtiss, Mina. 1958. *Bizet and His World.* New York: Alfred A. Knopf.

Delany, Samuel R. 1996. *Longer Views: Extended Essays.* Hanover/London: Wesleyan University Press.

Deutsch, David. 2015. *British Literature and Classical Music: Cultural Contexts 1870–1945.* London: Bloomsbury.

Draper, R.P. 1986. *D.H. Lawrence: The Critical Heritage.* London/New York: Routledge and Kegan Paul.

Fillion, Michelle. 2010. *Difficult Rhythm: Music and the Word in E.M. Forster.* Urbana/Chicago/Springfield: University of Illinois Press.

Fisher, Burton D. 2017. *Wagner's The Ring of the Nibelung.* Boca Raton: Opera Journeys.

Galbo, Joseph. 2017. A Decadence Baedeker: D'Annunzio's *The Triumph of Death. The European Legacy* 22 (1): 49–67.

Heath, Jane. 1995. Helen Corke and D.H. Lawrence: Sexual Identity and Literary Relations. *Feminist Studies* 11 (2): 317–342.

Hinz, Evelyn J. 1971. The Trespasser: Lawrence's Wagnerian Tragedy and Divine Comedy. *D.H. Lawrence Review* 4 (2): 122–141.

Holloway, Robin. 1979. *Debussy and Wagner.* London: Eulenburg Books.

Jameson, Fredric. 2013. Wagner as Dramatist and Allegorist. *Modernist Cultures* 8 (1): 9–41.

Kennaway, James. 2012. *Bad Vibrations: The History of the Idea of Music as a Cause of Disease.* Farnham: Ashgate.

Kennedy, Michael. 1987. *The Oxford Dictionary of Music.* Oxford: Oxford University Press.

Kestner, Joseph. 1977. The Literary Wagnerism of D.H. Lawrence's *The Trespasser. Modern British Literature* 2: 123–138.

Klein, John W. 1947. Bizet and Wagner. *Music and Letters* 28 (1): 50–62.

Koelb, Clayton. 2004. Death in Venice. In *A Companion to the Works of Thomas Mann,* ed. Herbert Lehnert and Eva Wessell, 95–113. Rochester/Woodbridge: Random House.

Lago, Mary, and P.N. Furbank, eds. 1985. *The Letters of E.M. Forster: Vol. 2 1921–1970.* London: HarperCollins.

Lawrence, Ada, and G. Stuart Gelder. 1966. *Young Lorenzo: Early Life of D.H. Lawrence.* New York: Russell & Russell.

Leavis, F.R. 1962. *D.H. Lawrence: Novelist*. London: Chatto & Windus.

Lesure, François, and Richard Langham Smith, eds. 1977. *Debussy on Music*. New York: Alfred A. Knopf.

Lockyer, Rebekah. 2014. Ford Madox Ford's Musical Legacy: *Parade's End* and Wagner. *Forum for Modern Language Studies* 50 (4): 426–452.

Maehder, Jürgen. 2011. A Mantle of Sound for the Night: Timbre in Wagner's *Tristan und Isolde*. In *Tristan und Isolde*, ed. Arthur Groos, 95–119. Cambridge: Cambridge University Press.

Mann, Thomas. 2003. *Death in Venice, Tonio Kröger, and Other Writings*. Ed. Frederick A. Lubich. New York: Continuum.

Martin, Stoddard. 1982. *Wagner to "The Waste Land": A Study of the Relationship of Wagner to English Literature*. London: Macmillan.

McClary, Susan. 1991. *Feminine Endings: Music, Gender and Sexuality*. Minneapolis: University of Minnesota Press.

Mellown, Elgin W. 1997. Music and Dance in D.H. Lawrence. *Journal of Modern Literature* 21 (1): 49–60.

Mérimée, Prosper. 2008. *Carmen, and Other Stories*. Trans. Nicholas Jotcham. Oxford: Oxford University Press.

Mizener, Arthur. 1971. *The Saddest Story: A Biography of Ford Madox Ford*. London: Harper & Row.

Moran, James. 2015. *The Theatre of D.H. Lawrence*. London/New York: Bloomsbury.

Morris, Mitchell. 2002. Tristan's Wounds: On Homosexual Wagnerians at the Fin de Siècle. In *Queer Episodes in Music and Modern Identity*, ed. Sophie Fuller and Lloyd Whitesell, 271–291. Urbana/Chicago: University of Illinois Press.

Nichols, Roger, and Richard Langham Smith. 1994. *Claude Debussy: Pelléas et Mélisande*, Cambridge Opera Handbooks. Cambridge: Cambridge University Press.

Nietzsche, Friedrich. 1911. *The Case of Wagner*. Trans. Anthony M. Ludovici. Edinburgh/London: T.N. Foulis. Project Gutenberg. http://www.gutenberg.org/files/25012/25012-pdf.pdf

Nowinski, Judith. 1970. Sense and Sound in Georges Bizet's *Carmen*. *The French Review* XLIII (6): 891–900.

Roberts, David. 2011. *The Total Work of Art in European Modernism*. Ithaca: Cornell University Press and Cornell University Library.

Ruderman, Judith. 2003. An "Englishman at Heart"? Lawrence and the National Identity Debates. In *D.H. Lawrence: New Worlds*, ed. Keith Cushman and Earl G. Ingersoll, 50–67. Madison/London: Fairleigh Dickinson University Press.

Saunders, Max. 2012. *Ford Madox Ford: A Dual Life, Volume I: The World Before the War*. Oxford: Oxford University Press.

Scherr, Barry J. 2004. *D.H. Lawrence Today: Literature, Culture, Politics*. New York: Peter Lang.

Shaw, Bernard. 1986. *Major Critical Essays*. Harmondsworth: Penguin.

Sherry, Vincent. 2015. *Modernism and the Reinvention of Decadence*. Cambridge: Cambridge University Press.

Stang, Sondra J., and Carl Smith. 1989. "Music for a While": Ford's Compositions for Voice and Piano. *Contemporary Literature* 30 (2): 183–223.

Stevens, Hugh. 2014. From *Genesis* to the *Ring*: Richard Wagner and D.H. Lawrence's *Rainbow*. *Textual Practice* 28 (4): 611–630.

Stewart, Jack. 1997–98. Landscape Painting and Pre-Raphaelitism in *The White Peacock*. *D.H. Lawrence Review* 27 (1): 3–25.

Sutton, Emma. 2002. *Aubrey Beardsley and British Wagnerism in the 1890s*. Oxford: Oxford University Press.

Wenk, Arthur. 2017. *Debussy's Prism*. http://www.arthurwenk.ca/PDF%20Files/Debussy's%20Prism.pdf

Worthen, John. 1992. *D.H. Lawrence: The Early Years 1885–1912*. Cambridge: Cambridge University Press.

———. 2005. *D.H. Lawrence: Life of an Outsider*. London: Allen Lane.

Wrenn, Angus. 2014. Wagner's *Ring* Cycle and *Parade's End*. In *Ford Madox Ford's Parade's End: The First World War, Culture, and Modernity*, ed. Ashley Tranter and Rob Hawkes, 67–80. Amsterdam/New York: Rodopi.

Zuckerman, Elliott. 1964. *The First Hundred Years of Wagner's "Tristan"*. New York/London: Columbia University Press.

CHAPTER 4

"Between Heaven and Earth": Space, Music, and Religion in *The Rainbow*

Introduction

Although *Sons and Lovers* (1913) was his first major critical success, Lawrence soon became dissatisfied by its form, which was rooted in the visual realism of nineteenth-century art and literature.[1] He declared that his next novel would be "quite unlike *Sons and Lovers*, not a bit visualised" (*1L* 526), and instead proposed an acoustic model of "rhythmic form" (*2L* 184). In his analogy of the Chladni patterns of sound waves on a vibrating plate of sand (illustrated in Fig. 1.2), Lawrence explained: "Again I say, don't look for the development of the novel to follow the lines of certain characters: the characters fall into the form of some other rhythmic form, like when one draws a fiddle-bow across a fine tray delicately sanded, the sand takes lines unknown" (*2L* 184).[2] This technique is exemplified in "The Cathedral" chapter of *The Rainbow* (1915) by Will Brangwen's experience of "perfectly proportioned space and movement … and passion surging its way in great waves to the altar" (*R* 188).[3] These "great waves" of musical "silence" (reinforced by the rhythmic repetition of the words "silence" and "hush" in this extended passage on pages 187–188) resemble sound waves, since in Chladni figures (illustrated in Fig. 1.1), the lines in the sand gather at the still points between areas of the plate which vibrate to the frequency of the fiddle-bow.

The recurrent use of stillness and silence in *The Rainbow* is intrinsically musical and spatial, as the examples in this chapter will show, forming

© The Author(s) 2019
S. Reid, *D. H. Lawrence, Music and Modernism,*
Palgrave Studies in Music and Literature,
https://doi.org/10.1007/978-3-030-04999-7_4

patterns within the text, like a musical composition that exists in "the space between the notes".[4] Suspensions in time, enacted through Will's experience of "timeless ecstasy"—"There his soul remained, at the apex of the arch, clinched in the timeless ecstasy, consummated" (*R* 188)—are reinforced throughout the novel by the spatial imagery of the arch, in ways that parallel a spatial turn in music. This chapter explores how a range of musical developments, extending from Richard Wagner to Arnold Schoenberg, may have influenced Lawrence's idea of "rhythmic form" and the patterning of his text as a "widening circle" (the title of chapters X and XIV) rather than a linear progression.[5]

Schoenberg described his radical 12-tone compositional method, in similar terms to Lawrence's analogy of Chladni figures, as a relationship of vibrations in which: "There is no absolute down, no right or left, forward or backward. Every musical configuration, every movement of tones has to be comprehended primarily as a mutual relation of sounds, of oscillatory vibrations, appearing at different places and times" (Berry 2008: 100). Schoenberg directly explored the spatialisation of music in his unfinished oratorio *Die Jakobsleiter* (begun in 1912), which opens with the archangel Gabriel's announcement: "Right or left, forward or backward, uphill or downhill—you must go on. Do not ask what lies in front or behind. It must be hidden; you ought to forget, you must forget, so that you can fulfil your task!" (qtd. Auner 2003: 144). These words find an echo in Schoenberg's law of "unity of musical space" that is also prefigured in the oratorio's opening music by repetition and counterpoint of the six tones of a hexachord played by different instruments.[6] The opening pages of *The Rainbow* emphasise a similar spatial relativity between land and sky, front and back, near and far, reinforced by rhythm and repetition. The unnamed Brangwen men work to the "beats and pulses" of nature and the human body (a sort of *musica instrumentalis* or music perceptible through the senses in Boethius's terms), while the women aspire to knowledge perceptible in the mind (a sort of *musica humana*): "They were aware of the lips and the mind of the world speaking and giving utterance, they heard the sound in the distance, and they strained to listen" (*R* 10).[7] Their vicar suggests the possibility of a bridge to a spiritual world of "higher being" expressed in a "magic language" (*R* 11), and which is ultimately envisioned by Ursula Brangwen as a rainbow "fitting to the over-arching heaven" (*R* 459). Both *Die Jakobsleiter* and *The Rainbow* thus explore the threshold "between heaven and earth" (*R* 10), while also challenging the perceived limits of music and language, in ways I compare at the end of this chapter.

Lawrence and Schoenberg shared a cultural heritage that reached back through expressionism and impressionism to a spatial turn in music and the European arts more generally, in which Wagner is an important precursor (Johnson 2010: 111). Wagnerism is a formative current in *The Rainbow*, as it was in *The Trespasser*, except that Lawrence has learned to resist and refine this influence within a "rhythmic form" that is wholly his own. The first part of this chapter considers *The Rainbow*'s widening trajectory from inner to outer worlds in the context of Wagner's final opera *Parsifal* (1882), positing the novel as a sort of anti-*Parsifal*. Lawrence's thinking about the role of music in the arts thus owes something to Wagner but is also mediated through other writers and composers. Thomas Hardy, Friedrich Nietzsche, Claude Debussy, and Schoenberg offered various models for negotiating a course between Romanticism and realism, spirituality and materialism, towards a modernism that brings together the putatively sacred and profane. Cumulatively, this chapter argues that the "rhythmic form" of *The Rainbow* establishes patterns of repetition and stasis to render a prose that is not only musical but hymn-like, drawing on the biblical rhythms of the "Song of Songs" and the non-conformism of William Blake.[8]

WAGNER, *PARSIFAL*, AND THRESHOLDS

The "mythic dimension" of *The Rainbow* (Becket 2002: 50; see also Bell 1992: 76–92), combined with its over-arching imagery of the rainbow, has inevitably attracted comparison with Wagner's *Das Rheingold* (Martin 1982; Whelan 1988; Stevens 2014), since both works culminate with a symbolic rainbow bridge between worlds.[9] But in several ways, *The Rainbow* critiques Wagnerian motifs and notions of "endless melody" that tend towards a submergence of the individual self within the universal (as discussed above in relation to *The Trespasser*). For example, Will's "ecstatic" experience of timeless "oneness" in Lincoln Cathedral is questioned, both by Anna's conflicting experience of being "silenced rather than tuned to the place" (*R* 188) and by his own subsequent deflation. Will's Dionysian "ecstasy" (a word reiterated ten times in *R* 186–188) needs to be shaped by Apollonian rationality in a similar way to Nietzsche's perception of artistic unity in *The Birth of Tragedy from the Spirit of Music* (1872). Lawrence's great novel about the marriage of "opposites, not complements" (*R* 157) thus speaks to the role of the artist as well as to the relationship between men and women.[10]

For Will leaving the cathedral is an awakening. While inside the sacred space, he perceives the altar as a "mystic door, through which all and everything must move on to eternity", but afterwards:

somehow, sadly and disillusioned, he realised that the doorway was no doorway. It was too narrow, it was false. Outside the cathedral were many flying
spirits that could never be sifted through the jewelled gloom. He had lost
his absolute.

He listened to the thrushes in the garden, and heard a note which cathe-
drals did not include: something free and careless and joyous. (*R* 191)

The "music" of nature returns Will to the everyday world after his ecstatic
experience, unlike Wagner's Tristan and Isolde, who continue to crave the
night (as a metaphor for death), or the progressive retreat from the material world enacted during *Parsifal*.

In Act I of *Parsifal*, Gurnemanz's pronouncement—"You see, my son,
here time becomes space"—marks the opera's transition from the natural
world of the forest to the spiritual enclosure of the Castle of the Grail. For
many musicologists, *Parsifal* signifies a turning point in music, with Julian
Johnson, for example, tracing a direct line of influence from this "threshold" moment in Wagner's final opera to the preoccupation of Mahler and
Schoenberg with the "displacement" of "linear progress of musical time
... by an exploration of musical space" (Johnson 2010: 111). But although
"The Cathedral" chapter in *The Rainbow* marks a spatial turn—"Away
from time, always outside of time! ... only perfectly proportioned space
and movement" (*R* 187–188)—the text avoids treating this as a threshold
moment, through Will's realisation that "the doorway was no doorway"
(*R* 191) and by pursuing ever widening circles thereafter.

Wavering on the threshold of religious orthodoxy, Will represents a
transitional figure between Romantic and modernist attitudes towards the
church and is thus a close relation, as Pericles Lewis remarks, to the eponymous hero of Hardy's final novel *Jude the Obscure* (Lewis 2010: 17). While
the Romantics stood outside the church door seeking consolation in
nature (as exemplified by Wordsworth's "Tintern Abbey") and their modernist successors treated the church with "bemused detachment", Will
Brangwen and Jude Fawley venture inside, "still hop[ing] for some meaning and guidance" (Lewis 2010: 4, 17–18). Even Will's apprehension of
the natural world as "the whole blue rotonda of the day" (*R* 191) echoes
the "dome" of the cathedral (*R* 188) and, like Jude the stone mason, Will
tends to the fabric of the church: "He looked after the stone and wood-
work, mending the organ and restoring a piece of broken carving, repair-
ing the church furniture. Later, he became choir-master also" (*R* 191).[11]

Significantly Will also makes music, which is represented as the life-blood of the church building: "The sound of the organ seemed to belong to the very stone of the pillars, like sap running in them" (*R* 337). Music is thus rendered as a vivifying force and a link with nature that recognises the world beyond the church walls and points forward to the novel's displacement of "the old church-tower standing up in hideous obsoleteness" in Ursula's concluding vision of the rainbow as "the earth's new architecture" (*R* 458–459). Far from retreating from the world, and from life, the widening circles of *The Rainbow* thus take an opposite trajectory from *Parsifal*, in which the "expanded tonality" announced in the Prelude to Act III culminates in deeper withdrawal into the mystical interior of the Castle of the Grail (Kinderman 2005b: 161). The original stage design for the last scene of *Parsifal* resembles the dome of a vast cathedral (illustrated in Fig. 4.1). In moving outwards from the cathedral depicted at the novel's centre (in the 7th of its 16 chapters), *The Rainbow* represents a sort of anti-*Parsifal*, even as it absorbs and responds to some of *Parsifal's* musical innovations.[12]

Fig. 4.1 Stage design for the temple of the Grail in Wagner's *Parsifal*, Bayreuth (1882) © Alamy

In the first half of 1914, *Parsifal* was performed in more than 50 theatres around the world, including its London premiere on 2 February 1914 (Beckett 1981: 93–95).[13] Prior to that, it was performed only in Wagner's *Festspielhaus* in Bayreuth, which had become a site of quasi-pilgrimage for many writers, composers, and artists.[14] *Parsifal* had already begun to influence a spatial and spiritual turn in the early twentieth-century arts, which Lawrence experienced through a variety of secondary sources; notably Nietzsche's polemical *The Case of Wagner* (1888), George Moore's novel *Evelyn Innes* (1898), and Debussy's opera *Pelléas et Mélisande* (1902). Nietzsche broke with Wagner over his perceived decadence (as discussed in Chap. 3), culminating with *Parsifal*, in which he accused Wagner of sinking down "helpless and broken before the Christian cross".[15] Other critics, however, have noted the opera's ambivalence towards Christianity, exemplified by Wagner's declared intent, in *Religion and Art* (1880), "to rescue the essence of religion by perceiving its mythical symbols" (qtd. Kinderman 2005a: 1–2); an aim which has some resonance with Lawrence's re-framing of "the religious effort of Man" (*STH* 59). Lawrence's novel straddles both sides of the Nietzsche/Wagner divide, since *The Rainbow* is both counter-Wagnerian and counter-biblical.[16]

The Rainbow also takes a counter-stance to Moore's *Evelyn Innes* (mentioned in Lawrence's letters of 1909–1910 [*1L* 142, 154]), in which the eponymous Wagnerian diva leaves both her lover and her promising stage-career in shame at the prospect of portraying the penitent sinner Kundry in *Parsifal*; she then spends much of the sequel, *Sister Teresa* (1901), in a nunnery deciding whether to take the veil. Like Wagner's Kundry, Evelyn embraces renunciation and is effectively silenced (Kehler 2012: 160). By contrast, *The Rainbow* attempts to do its "work for women, better than the suffrage" (*1L* 490) and it is the women in the novel who primarily challenge conventional religious and cultural mores (Fernihough 2000: xiv). And yet, at the same time, *The Rainbow* also responds to important developments in music prompted by *Parsifal*, regarding the creation of spatial effects and de-emphasising the perceived linearity of time.

The idea of a threshold between two worlds is figured in *The Rainbow*'s recurrent imagery of arches, doorways, and rainbows, and is explicitly related to characterisation and the notion of "becoming"; for instance, when the narrator says of Anna that "She was a door and a threshold, she herself. Through her another soul was coming, to stand upon her as upon the threshold, looking out, shading its eyes for the direction to take" (*R* 182). This brief example suggests the cyclical repetition within the novel's narrative scheme, but its language also uses techniques to withhold temporal progression and delay resolution, exemplified through use of repetition ("threshold" twice) and the rhythmic pauses enacted by the punctuation.[17] Experiments with musical form in the period 1880–1920 also sought to counteract the linear progress of time in remarkably similar ways, notably in Mahler's use of what Adorno termed "suspensions" (Adorno 1996: 41)[18] and Debussy's use of the sinuous *arabesque* to "prolong emotion" (as Mallarmé said of Debussy's orchestral setting of his poem in *Prélude á l'après-midi d'un faune* [qtd. Walsh 2018: 97]).

In *Study of Thomas Hardy*, Lawrence wrote that "It seems to me as if a man, in his normal state, were like a palpitating leading-shoot of life, where the unknown, all unresolved, beats and pulses, containing the quick of all experience, as yet unrevealed, not singled out" (*STH* 34). These "unresolved ... beats and pulses"—in their musical sense[19]—evoke the resistance to resolution that characterised the modernist music of Mahler's epic symphonies and Debussy's sinuous melodies.[20] The opening pages of *The Rainbow* immediately extend the various meanings of "beats and pulses" (physical, poetic, and musical) to reveal patterns of behaviour that poetry and music are well placed to delineate through techniques of rhythm and repetition. The celebrated opening paragraphs "pulse" with the rhythms of the Brangwens' farm, underscored by threefold repetition of the word within a single sentence: "the cows yielded milk and pulse against the hands of the men, the pulse of the blood of the teats of the cows beat into the pulse of the hands of the men" (*R* 10). The visceral renditions of "pulse" and "beat" bring poetic language down to earth, countering the "bodyless" transcendence of Romantic poetry of which Lawrence complained in the *Study* (*STH* 71; see also Worthen 2014: 24–25). From the outset, *The Rainbow* thus erects a tension or dissonance between two worlds, "between heaven and earth" (*R* 10), but also between the putatively "high" and "low" in art. This dissonance resounds with musical notions of the threshold (introduced by *Parsifal*) and the role of the artist in negotiating this threshold. *Parsifal* was thus one source of inspiration for those like Schoenberg, who regarded "the artist as a kind of threshold" or mediator between the material and spiritual worlds (Johnson 2010: 111–117), as exemplified by the figure of the Chosen One in *Die Jakobsleiter*.[21] But there were other musical models that sought to dissolve the threshold between the sacred and the profane, notably in the biblical example of the "Song of Songs" adapted in *The Rainbow* and in the music of Debussy.

THE SACRED AND THE PROFANE: SOLOMON AND DEBUSSY

The opening pages of *The Rainbow* combine "almost biblical rhythms" (Kinkead-Weekes 2001: 385) with a sexualisation of language that likens the fertile earth to the sexual human body ("intercourse", "nakedness", "inter-relations", "body", "open", "smooth", "supple", "desire").[22] The punctuation contributes to a surging rhythm of long sentences, which could be presented as stanzas of free verse or song (where line breaks accord with pauses in punctuation):

> They knew the intercourse between heaven and earth,
> sunshine drawn into the breast and bowels,
> the rain sucked up in the daytime,
> nakedness that comes under the wind in autumn,
> showing the birds' nests no longer worth hiding.
>
> Their life and inter-relations were such;
> feeling the pulse and the body of the soil,
> that opened to their furrow for the grain,
> and became smooth and supple after their ploughing,
> and clung to their feet with a weight that pulled like desire,
> lying hard and unresponsive when the crops were to be shorn away. (*R* 10)

Described by Mark Kinkead-Weekes as a "choric prelude" (R xxxiv) and by Adam Thorpe as a "pastoral hymn" (Thorpe 2003: n.p.), Lawrence's frank celebration of the fecundity of nature is at once sacred and profane, corresponding with the sexuality that caused the biblical fall.[23] One musical source for this is the "Song of Songs"—the "most erotic of biblical texts" (Wright 2000: 211)—that Lawrence discusses in *Study of Thomas Hardy* and a second is provided by Debussy's *Danses sacrée et profane* (1904), which impressed Lawrence in 1910.[24]

In the *Study*, Lawrence invokes the "Song of Songs" when he likens Solomon's "physical contact" with the Shulamite woman to "God come close" (*STH* 61). Since this passage traces a "threefold utterance" encompassing David, Solomon, and Job, Kinkead-Weekes perceives that these biblical stories shape three "testaments" of the Brangwen saga (Kinkead-Weekes 1968: 384). However, the *Study* specifically identifies the "Song of Songs" as "religious art" in a threefold relationship of "religion, religious art, and tragic art" (*STH* 61–62). The importance of "religious art" is reinforced in the *Study*'s concluding vision of "the supreme art", which draws on the language and biblical rhythm of the "Song of Songs" in a celebration of the erotic union of "male and female":

> But when the two [clasp] hands, a moment, male and female, [clasp] hands and are one, the poppy, the gay poppy flies into flower again; and when the two fling their arms about each other, the moonlight runs and clashes against the shadow, and when the two toss back their hair, all the larks break out singing, and when they kiss on the mouth, a lovely human utterance is heard again—and so it is. (*STH* 128)

Song is married with the visual imagery of "the gay poppy", "moonlight", and "shadow", reinforced by the poetic repetition of key words, such as "hands" and "two" (balanced with the single instance of "one", which perfectly reflects the symmetry of "two-in-one") and the rhythm of many clauses in a single sentence. The "clash" of moonlight and shadow here anticipates the dissonance of a series of moonlit scenes in *The Rainbow* (and subsequently in *Women in Love*), to which I will return below (and in Chap. 5), but first I will underline the biblical themes that carry across from the *Study*'s "Amen" ending—"and so it is"—into Lawrence's notion of erotic love.

Lawrence's essay "Love" (1917) reiterates the theme of balance between opposites developed in *Study* and *The Rainbow* by using an intensified reference to Song of Solomon ii. 16, "My beloved is mine and I am his" (qtd *RDP* 393), to assert that "Sacred love and profane love, they are opposed and yet they are both love ... I am in the beloved also, and she is in me" (*RDP* 9). The examples of unbalanced love that Lawrence chooses here are "Tristan and Isolde"—"This is the profane love, that ends in flamboyant and lacerating tragedy when the two which are so singled out are torn finally apart by death"—and St. Francis of Assisi and his follower St. Clare—whose "sacred love ends in a poignant yearning and exquisite submissive grief" (*RDP* 10–11). Respectively, these two types of love represent "tragic art" and "religion", which leaves the third category that Lawrence suggested in the *Study*, namely "religious art" (*STH* 61–62), which he now describes as "two in one, always two in one—the sweet love of communion and the fierce, proud love of sensual fulfilment, both together in one love. And then *we* are like a rose" (*RDP* 11, my emphasis). Lawrence thus modifies the opening line of the "Song of Songs", in which the beloved declares "I am the rose of Sharon", to render his idea of "religious art" as a bridge between heaven and earth.[25]

Debussy provided another model of the proximity of music and nature that challenged the relationship between the sacred and profane. Hearing Debussy's *Danses sacrée et profane* prompted Lawrence to write "I love Debussy" (*IL* 205) in a letter inscribed on the back of the concert programme.[26] The melodic line of the first "sacred" dance exhibits an almost medieval spirituality, which has some affinities with plainchant, as Mark DeVoto remarks, while the second is "profane" only in the sense of evoking a love of nature and of earthly existence (DeVoto 2004: 169, 174). For Debussy:

> Music is the art that is in fact closer to Nature … [painters and sculptors] can capture only one of its aspects at a time, preserve only one moment. It is the musicians alone who have the privilege of being able to convey all the poetry of night and day, of earth and sky. Only they can recreate Nature's atmosphere and give rhythm to her heaving breast. (Qtd. Simeone 2003: 111)

His music reflects a conception of melody that "results from a multiplicity of simultaneous lines", inspired by naturally occurring forms such as leaves and vines (Potter 2003: 144) as well as by the polyphonic patterns of Gregorian chant (Tresize 2003: 252). The confluence of music and dance in Debussy is also pertinent here, for instance, in his development of the *arabesque* (most famously in the introduction to *Prélude a l'après-midi d'un faune*) as an undulating form that plays with space and time in ways that mimic its use in dance (Potter 2003: 144). This suggests another way of approaching the dance scenes in *The Rainbow*, which are not usually considered in terms of a musical dimension. Specifically, I will consider the extent to which such scenes evoke the rhythmic patterns of Debussy's "dance" music.

In the corn-stacking scene of Chapter IV, several types of rhythm are in play as Will and Anna perform a sort of nature or fertility rite (Mester 1997: 106; Poplawski 1993: 113):[27]

> The rhythm of the work carried him away again, as she was coming near.
> They worked together, coming and going, in a rhythm, which carried their feet and their bodies in tune … She hesitated, set down her sheaves, there was a swish and hiss of mingling oats, he was drawing near, and she must turn, again. And there was the flaring moon laying bear her bosom again, making her drift and ebb like a wave. (*R* 114)

Their movements can be construed as a dance of opposites (Kinkead-Weekes 1992; Poplawski 1993), but the language of the text is also musical. Anna and Will move to a rhythm, and their bodies are "in tune"; they are accompanied by the onomatopoeic "swish and hiss of mingling oats", the mingled noises suggestive of chords and harmonies; and their movements form wave-like patterns like the Chladni figures that exemplify Lawrence's idea of "rhythmic form" (*2L* 184). The rhythm is at once universal—influenced by the moon and evocative of an unheard music of the spheres—and increasingly erotic. Initially, the narrative emphasises the "space between them"—like the lines the fiddle-bow leaves in the sand-tray—but this collapses as the rhythm intensifies:

> Why was there always a space between them, why were they apart? Why, as she came up from under the moon, would she halt and stand off from him? Why was he held away from her? His will drummed persistently, darkly, it drowned everything else.
>
> Into the rhythm of his work there came a pulse and a steadied purpose. He stooped, he lifted the weight, he heaved it towards her, setting it as in her, under the moonlit space. And he went back for more. Ever with increasing closeness he lifted the sheaves and swung striding to the centre with them, ever he drove her more nearly to the meeting, ever he did his share, and drew towards her, overtaking her. There was only the moving to and fro in the moonlight, engrossed, the swinging in the silence, that was marked only by the splash of sheaves, and silence, and a splash of sheaves. And ever the splash of his sheaves broke swifter, beating up to hers, and ever the splash of her sheaves recurred monotonously, unchanging, and ever the splash of his sheaves beat nearer. (*R* 115)

The insistent repetition of "why" four times at the beginning of this passage builds a sense of "drum[ming]", "puls[ing]" and "beating", before these musical terms are introduced. The movement "to and fro in the moonlight" resembles a duet between "the splash of his sheaves" and the "splash of her sheaves". The repetition of "splash of sheaves" (note also the internal repetition of "sh", as in hush or the sound of the sea) five times in the final two sentences of this extract, interposed between silences, underlines the "monotonously, unchanging" motion of the pair. Movement here is like a form of stasis: a movement around a fixed point "where infinite motion becomes rest", as described in *Study*, "beyond change or motion, beyond time or limit" (*STH* 54–55).[28] Will and Anna thus perform figures of the *arabesque* in spatial and musical terms, while

Lawrence's rhythmic use of silence also has parallels with Debussy, who wrote of his own work that "Silence is a beautiful thing ... the empty bars in *Pelléas* [*et Mélisande*] are evidence of my love of this sort of emotional expression" (qtd. Orledge 1982: 204).

The modified repetition of "moon"/"moonlit"/"moonlight" combined with stasis evokes the stillness of Debussy's well-known Prelude for piano titled "Clair de lune" (1890), as well as his moonlit opera *Pelléas et Mélisande*. But the repeated word "splash" also evokes the sound of water, and an ominous threat of "drown[ing]", which becomes more pronounced in a later moonlit dance scene between Ursula and Skrebensky in which a sense of the oceanic oscillates between eroticism and erasure:

> The music came in waves. One couple after another was washed and absorbed into the deep underwater of the dance ...
>
> They were both absorbed into a profound silence, into a deep, fluid, underwater energy that gave them unlimited strength. All the dancers were waving intertwined in the flux of music. Shadowy couples passed and re-passed before the fire, the dancing feet danced silently by into the darkness, it was a vision of the depths of the underworld, under the great flood.
>
> There was a wonderful rocking of the darkness, slowly, a great, slow swinging of the whole night, with the music playing lightly on the surface, making the strange, ecstatic rippling on the surface of the dance, but underneath only one great flood heaving slowly backwards to the verge of oblivion, slowly forward to the other verge, the heart sweeping along each time, and tightening with anguish as the limit was reached, and the movement, at crisis, turned and swept back. (*R* 295–296)

The waves and ripples are another example of Chladni patterns, which here are directly associated with sound waves: "The music came in waves". The psychological depths stirred by this "underwater music" may owe something to Wagner's Rhine music in the *Ring* (Stevens 2014: 621–625), but the play on surface and depth also chimes with Debussy's "La cathédrale engloutie", from Book I of his piano *Preludes* (1909–1910). This piece recreates the Breton legend of Ys, in which a submerged cathedral mystically emerges from the sea emitting sounds of church bells, chanting and organ music, evoking a soundscape in some ways reminiscent of *The Rainbow*. Described by Debussy as "profondement calme", his Prelude resonates with the "hushed" music of Lawrence's cathedral (*R* 187), and the "shadowy atmosphere" of the church where Will "liked to sink himself in its hush as a stone sinks into water":

He loved to light the candles at the organ, and sitting there alone in the little glow, practise the hymns and chants for the service. The whitewashed arches retreated into darkness, the sound of the organ and the organ-pedals died away upon the unalterable stillness of the church, there were faint, ghostly noises in the tower, and then the music swelled out again, loudly, triumphantly. (*R* 192)

If Lawrence's play on surfaces seems impressionistic—as Debussy's music is sometimes perceived to be (Simeone 2003: 101–116)—this is counterpointed by expressionist depths at "the verge of oblivion" (Stewart 1999: 64–66). In a comparable way, Debussy's depictions of water can be terrifying and often cosmic, in ways that exceed impressionism, as Stefan Jarociński observes of his symphonic sketches *La mer* (qtd. Tresize 1994: 41). Indeed, the boundaries between impressionism and expressionism seem permeable, or at least overlapping, since features of both have been ascribed to Lawrence and Debussy.

Musical Expressionism

In *Concerning the Spiritual in Art* (1911), his manifesto for expressionist art, Kandinsky praised Debussy's ability to "create a spiritual impression, often taken from nature, but embodied in purely musical form" (Kandinsky 1977: 16). Kandinsky would subsequently sense a deeper kinship with Schoenberg—as evidenced by his series of sketches and paintings inspired by hearing Schoenberg's music in 1911 and their correspondence thereafter[29]—but his appreciation of both Debussy and Schoenberg brings them into closer proximity than their labelling (respectively) as "impressionist" and "expressionist" might imply. In fact, there are some striking parallels in that both tuned their musical voices by setting the poetry and prose of decadent and symbolist writers, including Maurice Maeterlinck (Schoenberg intended to extend his tone poem of *Pelléas et Mélisande* into an opera).[30] Their ability to find music in prose is also notable, with Schoenberg's *The Theory of the Text* (1912) insisting that "the outward correspondence between music and text ... is far less important than the more ineffable 'inward' correspondence" (Frisch 2010: 15–16); an idea that links both with Kandinsky's idea of "das innerer Klang" (inner sound) and with Lawrence's idea of "rhythmic form" (*2L* 183).[31] In this regard, all three may have been influenced by Chladni, as a German physicist, musician, and founder of modern acoustics, who "greatly influenced Goethe and the German Romantics" (Elder 2008: 27).

The German expressionists were early precursors of inter-arts modernism in the pre-war period that Lawrence portrays in *The Rainbow* and so several critics have already argued for a shared "response to the zeitgeist" (Stewart 1980: 297).[32] Tony Pinkney makes a bold claim for *The Rainbow* as "Britain's first (and best) Expressionist" novel (Pinkney 1990: 75), although he and others, notably Jack Stewart, focus primarily on the visual arts of expressionism. And yet Stewart's frequent use of musical terms to argue that "the new *key* of symbolic *resonance* [in *The Rainbow* and *Women in Love*], requires reorientation to the visual dimensions of Lawrence's language" (Stewart 1999: 6, my emphasis), indicates that a further reorientation towards music is required; a direction which Joyce Wexler also implies by pointing out that music was regarded by the expressionists as the least material and therefore the most spiritual of the arts (Wexler 2016: 65). As Kandinsky wrote in 1911: "the various arts are drawing together. They are finding in Music the best teacher. With few exceptions music has been for some centuries the art which has devoted itself not to the reproduction of natural phenomena, but rather to the expression of the artist's soul, in musical sound" (Kandinsky 1977: 19). This linkage between music and spirituality is highly suggestive for an approach that explores the musical implications of the "almost biblical rhythms" that Kinkead-Weekes (2001: 385) has perceived in *The Rainbow*.

Carl Krockel has recognised the relevance of expressionist music (albeit without considering the spiritual aspects) in his allusion to "Schoenbergian" qualities in some "dissonant 'ostinato' sections" in *The Rainbow* (Krockel 2007: 122). But these musical terms have much wider application than Krockel's brief discussion can convey. Ostinato pertains to repetition in music, which is certainly a feature of Lawrence's language throughout *The Rainbow*, as examples throughout this chapter have shown. The novel's thematic development of the dissonance of unresolved opposites (including the Dionysian and the Apollonian) may also owe something to a shared legacy of Nietzschean thought.[33] In his *Theory of Harmony* (1911), and his music composed around this time, Schoenberg was already developing ideas about the "emancipation of dissonance", which would overturn the rule of consonance—or resolution of tension—that had characterised classical music for centuries (Harrison 1996: 18–19). This theory also connects with ideas about musical space, which Krockel considers in his comparison of Lawrence's short story "The Prussian Officer" (1914)—in which the orderly feels that he will "fall through the everlasting lapse of space" (*PO* 20)—with the ending of Schoenberg's one act opera *Erwartung* (Op. 17, 1909), noting that "Instead of following Wagner's conclusion with the traditional resolution of tonality of *Tristan und Isolde*, each group of instruments in *Erwartung* moves up and down the chromatic scale to saturate the musical space, expressing the woman's madness" (Krockel 2007: 109–110). Subsequently, Schoenberg extended his exploration of musical space in *Die Jakobsleiter*, in ways that correspond with Lawrence's views on "rhythmic form" and how the individual passes through "allotropic states ... of the same radically-unchanged element. (Like as diamond and coal are the same pure single element of carbon)" (*2L* 183–184). Notably, the figure of the Chosen One is singled out in the libretto of *Die Jakobsleiter* as being "like the bright rock crystal, further than coal is from diamonds" (qtd. Auner 2003: 146). At one extreme, *The Rainbow* aspires to the transcendent music of the heavens in ways that resemble Schoenberg's project in *Die Jakobsleiter*.

SACRED SONGS: LAWRENCE AND SCHOENBERG

In *Study of Thomas Hardy*, Lawrence's assertion of the "Song of Songs" as "religious art" (*STH* 61) precedes a discussion of artists whose paintings seem to "sing", as "A bird in spring sings with the dawn, ringing out, out from the moment of consummation in wider and wider circles. Dürer, Fra Angelico, Botticelli all sing of the moment of consummation, some of them marvelling and lost in the wonder at the other being ... Raphael too" (*STH* 71). Paintings that sing may recall Kandinsky (described by Michael Sadler as "painting music" [Kandinsky 1977: xix]), but Lawrence's return to medieval art through song also bears comparison with the preoccupation of contemporary composers with the sacred music of Palestrina (Garratt 2004). Lawrence may have gleaned something of this interest from reading *Evelyn Innes*, in which Moore sets up the perceived purity of Palestrina's church music as a somewhat misleading contrast with the worldly "decadence" of Wagnerian opera; in fact, Wagner conducted a performance of a Palestrina *Stabat Mater* on Palm Sunday in 1848 and may have carried some influences into works such as *Lohengrin* (1850). Furthermore, Wagner's interest in Palestrina may have partly inspired Schoenberg, as well as Debussy (whose *Danse sacrée*, among other of his works, draws on plainchant).

Fra Angelico's painting *The Last Judgement* (c. 1451) plays an important structural role in *The Rainbow*; as Jeffrey Meyers has argued, its "paradisal angels, which link the generations of Brangwens, symbolise a quest for the connection between the material and spiritual worlds and helps the characters develop a 'visionary awareness'" (Meyers 1975: 2). Meyers's description draws attention to synergies with Schoenberg's *Die Jakobsleiter*, in the figuring of angels as a musical threshold between heaven and earth, but these intensify if we also consider the importance of music in the responses of Will and Anna to Fra Angelico's painting. For Will, "the singing process to paradise on the one hand, the stuttering descent to hell on the other, completed and satisfied him. He did not care whether or not he believed in devils or angels. The whole conception gave him the deepest satisfaction, and he wanted nothing more" (*R* 259). Even the usually rational Anna is enraptured by "The beautiful, innocent way in which the Blessed held each other by the hand as they moved towards the radiance, the real, real, angelic melody, made her weep with happiness" (*R* 166–167). Since three generations of Brangwens ascend through Ursula to an anticipation of "a man created by God" (*R* 457)—akin to the Chosen One in Schoenberg's *Die Jakobsleiter*, both as a higher being and as a vehicle for the artist—I would question whether *The Rainbow* depicts three "testaments" of the Bible (per Kinkead-Weekes 1968: 384), or whether the novel more closely resembles a sort of oratorio or "the singing process to paradise" that Will Brangwen admires (*R* 259).

There are important parallels, but also differences, between Lawrence's project in *The Rainbow* and that of Schoenberg's *Die Jakobsleiter*, in which he sought to render "oratorio that becomes visible and audible. Philosophy, religion, that are perceived with the artistic senses" (qtd. Johnson 2010: 119). As Julian Johnson argues: "*Die Jakobsleiter*, despite remaining an incomplete fragment, is Schoenberg's most sustained and single-minded exploration of the idea of the threshold. As its title suggests, it thematises the notion of a liminal space by means of the reference to Jacob's dream-vision of a staircase joining heaven to earth, which the angels ascend and descend between the two (*Genesis* 28: 10–17)" (Johnson 2010: 114). Intriguingly, the manuscript version of *The Rainbow* also adapted the biblical story of Jacob's Ladder, in a draft passage from "The Cathedral" chapter in which:

> [Anna] dreamed of the angels, who went in shadow by day, at night in flickering flames. They flickered on the outer circle of the Most High like altar flames, they quivered in flames of praise. And she knew in her dream, that beyond these the fiery, stately Archangels, and beyond these were the fiercely bright circle of the Cherubim, the Innermost, palpitating to the awful brightness of the Presence, absorbed in their wonder of praise. (*R* 592)

The spatial imagery in Lawrence's draft is oddly circular compared to the biblical image of a stairway to heaven, and seems instead to adapt a detail from *The Last Judgement* (illustrated in Fig. 4.2), known as the caròla of the saints, in which the saints and angels dance in a circle during "the singing

Fig. 4.2   Detail from Fra Angelico, *The Last Judgement* (c. 1451) © Alamy

process to heaven" (as Will describes this scene [R 259]). In turn, Fra Angelico's imagery resonates with the following "verses from a [medieval] sacred laud" (Supino 1902: 79):

Una rota si fa in cielo
De tutti I Santi in quel zardino,
Là ove sta l'amor divino
Che s'infiamo de l'amore.

In quella rota vano I Santi
Et li Angioli tutti quanti;
A quello Sposo van davanti:
Tutti danzan per amore.

[In Paradise that garden lies
Where love divine eternal shines,
And holy saints carolas weave,
Their souls inflamed with sacred love.

The Saints in that bright joyous ring,
With Angels fair of all degrees,
Before the Bridegroom graceful move
And weave the dance of sacred love.]

There are no circles or flames in the biblical story of Jacob's Ladder, and perhaps for such reasons Lawrence excised Anna's dream from his text. The final version of "The Cathedral" chapter consolidates spatial imagery of stone leaping upwards towards the heavens, modified by arches which rise but also return to earth: "The far-off clinching and mating of the arches, the leap and thrust of the stone, carrying a great roof overhead, awed and silenced her" (R 188). Ultimately, the verticality of columns and stairways is superseded by the novel's closing vision of a rainbow forming in the space "between heaven and earth" established in its opening pages (R 10). However, the novel's conclusion makes a final oblique reference to Jacob's Ladder, when Ursula reflects on "How long, how long had she fought through the dust and obscurity for this new dawn?" (R 457); the biblical text being "Your descendants will be like the dust of the earth, and you will spread out to the west and to the east, to the north and to the south. All peoples on earth will be blessed through you and your offspring" (Genesis 28: 14).

As descendants of Jacob, the Brangwens struggle with the material and spiritual problems of modernity in strikingly similar ways to those envisaged by Schoenberg in *Die Jakobsleiter*. As Schoenberg wrote to the poet Richard Dehmel in 1912, imploring him to write the libretto:

> For a long time I have been wanting to write an oratorio on the following subject: modern man, having passed through materialism, socialism, and anarchy and, despite having been an atheist, still having in him some residue of ancient faith (in the form of superstition), wrestles with God (see also Strindberg's *Jacob Wrestling*) and finally succeeds in finding God and becoming religious. Learning to pray! (qtd. Auner 2003: 119)

As Lawrence completed the final version of *The Rainbow*, he was wrestling with angels and demons of his own. In January 1915, he wrote to E.M. Forster (referring again to the "Song of Songs"): "I want somebody to come and make a league with me, to sing the Chanson des Chansons—das Hohe Lied—and to war against the fussy Mammon" (*2L* 262). Another "very angelic letter" (also to Forster) invoked Fra Angelico as an artist who attempted "a conception of the Whole: as Plato tried to do, and as the mediaeval men—as Fra Angelico—a conception of the beginning and the end, of heaven and hell, of good and evil flowing from God through humanity as through a filter, and returning back to god as angels and demons" (*2L* 266–267). Lawrence's conception here is close to the response of his characters in *The Rainbow* to Fra Angelico's *Last Judgement*, and he seems as nostalgic for a sense of being "complete" as Will Brangwen (*R* 259).

Lawrence's interest in Fra Angelico was "lodged", according to T.R. Wright, by his reading of Katharine Jenner's *Christian Symbolism* (Wright 2000: 87)—although Lawrence's reference to Plato (as above *2L* 262) is another source for the angelic notion of "two-in-one" that infuses both the *Study* and *The Rainbow* (*STH* 128).[34] Lawrence's emphasis on "the singing process" (*R* 259) and "angelic melody" (*R* 167) is more mysterious, however, particularly when read alongside this passage from the *Study*:

> And since the beginning, the reaction has become extended and intensified, what was one great mass of individual constituency has stirred and resolved itself into many smaller, characteristic parts, what was an utter, infinite neutrality has become evolved into still rudimentary, but positive, orders and species. So on and on till we get to naked jelly, and from naked jelly to

enclosed and separated jelly, from homogenous tissue to organic tissue to organic tissue, on and on, from invertebrates to mammals, from mammals to man, from man to tribesman, from tribesman to me: and on and on, till, in the future, wonderful, distinct individuals, like angels, move about, each one being himself, perfect as a complete melody or a pure colour.

How one craves that his life should be more individual, that I and you and my neighbour should each be distinct in clarity from each other, perfectly distinct from the general mass. Then it would be a melody if I walked down the road, if I stood with my neighbour it would be a pure harmony. (*STH* 42–43)

There are synergies here with Kandinsky's ideas about music as colour, which were shared to some extent by Schoenberg in their correspondence on the subject and reflected in "Farben" ("Colours"), one of his *Five Pieces for Orchestra* (Op. 16, 1909).[35] But these ideas, in their turn, were influenced by Balzac and, directly and indirectly, by Swedenborg's eight-volume interpretation of the Bible *Arcana Celestia* (1749–1756). Balzac's novel *Séraphita* (1834)—about a sex-changing angel who takes shape on earth as both Séraphita and Séraphitus, but finally transcends human form and ascends to heaven through the power of prayer—inspired Schoenberg's oratorio; specifically the final chapter which concludes: "Light gave birth to melody, and melody to light; colors were both light and melody; motion was number endowed by the Word; in short, everything was at once sonorous, diaphanous, and mobile; so that everything existing in everything else, extension knew no limits, and the angels could traverse it everywhere to the utmost depths of the infinite" (qtd. Johnson 2010: 113).

Balzac's melding of light and colour with melody has marked resonances with the passage from *Study* quoted above, which carries over into the imagery of *The Rainbow*, including Ursula's perception of "the hovering colour" as she witnesses "a rainbow forming itself" (*R* 458). The end of *The Rainbow* provides a final example of the suspension of temporal development, marked by unresolved verb tenses ("colouring", "forgetting", "hovering", "forming"), the anticipation of a man who "should come from the Infinite" / "would come out of Eternity", and Ursula's apprehension "of that vaster power in which she *rested* at last" (*R* 457–458, my emphasis). All sound has been suspended too: "In the still, silenced forms of the colliers she saw a sort of suspense, a waiting in pain for the new liberation" (*R* 458). These pages represent a sort of silent anti-hymn that disavows the soul-destroying materialism of industrialisation and seeks to bring a new heaven down to earth.

The end of *Die Jakobsleiter* enacts a similar suspension of reality via a floating soundscape that transcends language. As Schoenberg's pupil, Winfried Zillig, enthusiastically proclaimed:

> Strangely enough, the conclusion of the 'Jacob's Ladder' fragment is one of the most impressive endings in the whole of Occidental music. Schoenberg's invention of sounds floating in space does in fact lead to new regions. The enchantment is complete despite the fragmentary character. Indeed, one cannot help thinking that this strange and unique enchantment arises directly from the work's unfinished state; for such a work, given its intellectual premise, can provide only an incomplete answer in view of mankind's limitations when facing the eternal. (Qtd. Berry 2008: 94)

In Schoenberg's case, he was inspired by a scene at the end of Balzac's novel in which "The last hymn was not uttered in words, nor expressed by gestures, nor any of the signs which serve men as a means of communicating their thoughts, but as the soul speaks to itself; for at the moment when Seraphita was revealed in her true nature, her ideas were no longer enslaved to human language" (qtd. Johnson 2010: 112). A tension between music and language is associated here with a mystic domain that exceeds the constraints of realism and informs the modernist experimentation of Lawrence as well as Schoenberg.

Lawrence read several of Balzac's "realist" novels (he cites *Eugénie Grandet* among others in *1L* 98–99), and although he never mentions *Séraphita*, it seems highly likely that he would at least have known of it.[36] His early mentors in London, Pound and Yeats, were strongly influenced by both Balzac and Swedenborg (Surette 1994: 129–130), and, like Yeats, Lawrence may have absorbed some Swedenborgian theory indirectly through Blake.[37] In this respect, a reference in Lawrence's first novel *The White Peacock* (1911) seems indicative: when Lettie Beardsall "played Handel in a manner that suggested the plains of Heaven in the long notes, and in the little trills as if she were waltzing up the ladder of Jacob's dream like the damsels in Blake's pictures" (*WP* 25). Lawrence retained a long-term admiration of Blake's paintings, writing in "Introduction to these Paintings" (1929) that "Blake is the only painter of imaginative pictures, apart from landscape, that England has produced" (*LEA* 194). He regrets "there is so little Blake", so he may not have known Blake's illustrations to his long poem, *Jerusalem*, and yet there are remarkable analogies between the closing scene of *The Rainbow* and Blake's "Plate 14: The Giant Emanation of Albion", which illustrates a woman beneath a rainbow and an angelic vision (see Fig. 4.3).

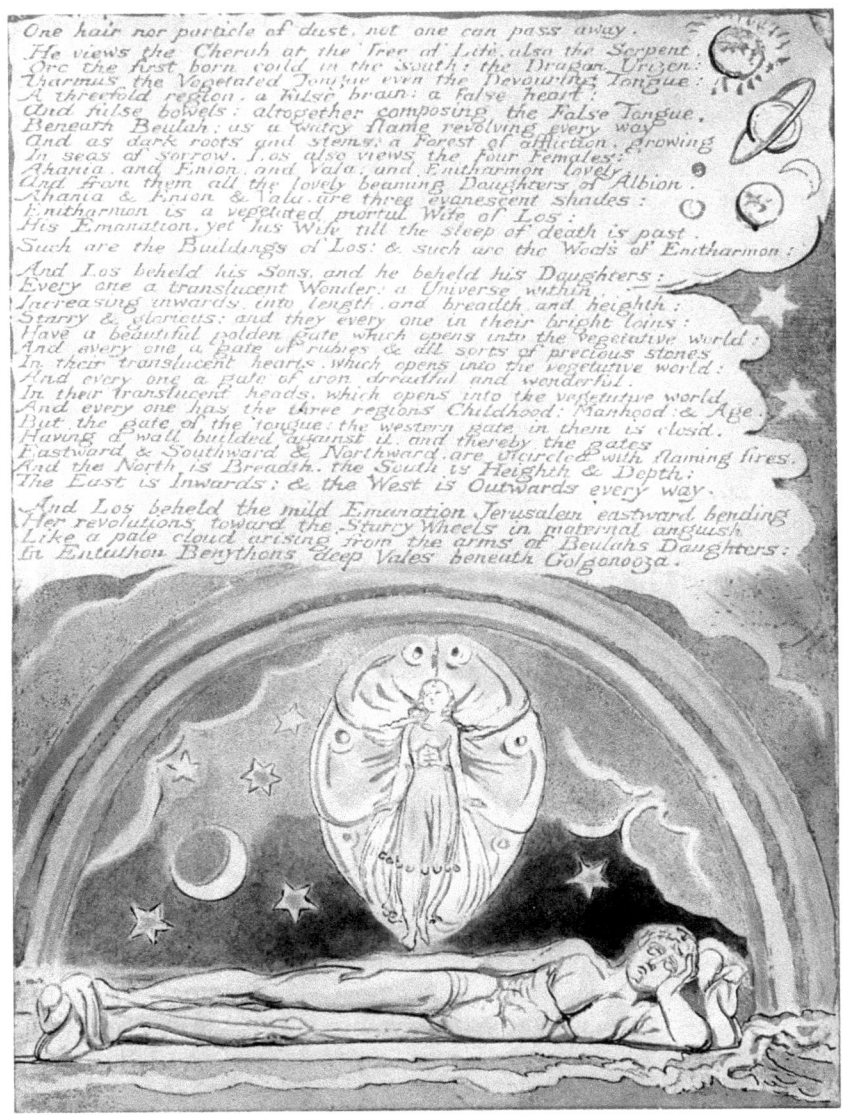

Fig. 4.3 William Blake, *Jerusalem*, Plate 14: The Giant Emanation of Albion
© blakearchive.org

Comparisons with Blake have faded into the history of Lawrence criticism, pushed into the background by a view of "high" modernism as a rupture with the past. This model is now being questioned, for instance, by Vincent Sherry, who argues persuasively that even the modernists who were most anxious to "make things new" owed an enormous debt to their Decadent forebears. Sherry perceives a legacy of "late" or "decayed" Romanticism that he traces back to Wordsworth's *Prelude* and his notion of "the spot of time" (Sherry 2015: 37), which, as I argued in Chap. 2, influenced the evolution of Lawrence's poetics. Given Lawrence's argument with Shelley in the *Study*, and his frequent references to various of the Romantic poets in his letters of 1912–1914, I would also argue for their importance in shaping Lawrence's "rhythmic form" in *The Rainbow*. The Keatsian lament that "Philosophy will clip an angel's wings" and science will "Unweave a rainbow" (Keats 1884: ll. 234, 237) speaks to the imagery of *The Rainbow*, and yet Lawrence also assimilated the emerging science of acoustics as a metaphor for the "rhythmic form" with which he developed his musical and mystical prose. In some respects, then, Blake is a more significant forebear, with his fluctuating interest in Swedenborgian theories and imagery.

Vivien de Sola Pinto noted Blakean parallels in Lawrence's increasingly combative attitude to society and his theory of creative destruction, which in *St. Mawr* (1925) "Fights, fights, fights to protect itself" (*SM* 80). He argues that Blake "is saying the same things in his most famous poem" (Sola Pinto 1969: 105):

> I will not cease from Mental Fight,
> Nor shall my Sword sleep in my hand:
> Till we have built Jerusalem,
> In Englands green & pleasant land.

Blake's vision in "And did those feet in ancient times" is comparable to the end of *The Rainbow*, which transposes Blake's "Dark Satanic Mills" to the "blackened hill" of a Nottinghamshire colliery town (*R* 458)—indeed Lawrence would later write an acerbic poem about "how much darker and more satanic they are now!" (*Poems* 543). Ironically, then, in March 1916, only four months after the banning and burning of *The Rainbow*—which was deemed unsuitable in a time of war—Hubert Parry was asked by Robert Bridges to set the words of Blake's poem, making it instantly famous as the hymn "Jerusalem".[38] Parry and Bridges, along with Hardy and Edward Elgar, were vice-presidents of the Fight for Right movement, formed in 1915 to reinforce British cultural values during the war (Heffer 2016: n.p.). When Parry became concerned about the jingoism of Fight for Right, he withdrew his tune from them (although some of this jingoism has persisted in the annual "Last Night of the Proms" in London, at which "Jerusalem" has become a staple). In the short term, however, the hymn became the anthem for the National Union of Women's Suffrage Societies and so "Jerusalem" did its work for the suffrage in ways that Lawrence's banned book could not.

Lawrence's hymn-like novel was received as an anti-hymn, which was deemed by the British establishment to come down on the wrong side of the threshold between materialism and spirituality. German expressionism did not survive the trauma of the war; many of its exponents were killed in combat, Kandinsky and Schoenberg parted ways as they developed new directions, and Schoenberg's *Die Jakobsleiter* remained unfinished. Lawrence did not write in the same style again, although he continued to negotiate a path between realism and Romanticism, in which the goal was to render the invisible somehow visible—and audible. In *Women in Love*, the concern with "real reality" intensified, in the words of Rupert Birkin, Lawrence's man "from the Infinite" (*R* 457):

> "We always consider the silver river of life, rolling on and quickening all the world to a brightness, on and on to heaven, flowing into a bright eternal sea, a heaven of angels thronging.—But the other is our real reality—"
> "But what other? I don't see any other," said Ursula.
> "It is your reality, nevertheless," he said; "that dark river of dissolution.—" (*WL* 172)

This is the quotation that inspired the title of a seminal study of Lawrence and English Romanticism by Colin Clarke (1969), in which he perceives a "downward rhythm" in *Women in Love*. In the next chapter, I will modify this thesis by arguing for a breaking down of rhythms and fragmenting of forms: there are no angels or rainbows in *Women in Love*, and the vibrations become more violent and threatening in a cosmos consuming itself with war. The space between heaven and earth was now occupied by Zeppelins, as Lawrence wrote in September 1915:

> It was like Milton – then there was a war in heaven. But it was not angels. It was that small golden Zeppelin, like a long oval world, high up. It seemed as if the cosmic order were gone, as if there had come a new order, a new heavens above us: and as if the world in anger were trying to revoke it. (*2L* 390)

Recommended Listening

Debussy	*Danses sacrée et profane, La cathédrale engloutie* (Book I of *Preludes*), *Prélude à l'après-midi d'un faune*
Palestrina	*Stabat Mater*
Parry	*Jerusalem*
Schoenberg	*Farben* (Op. 16, No. 3, *Five Pieces for Orchestra*), *Die Jakobsleiter, Seraphita* (Op. 22, No. 1, *Four Orchestral Songs*).
Wagner	*Parsifal* (particularly the transition music at the end of Act I and the unveiling of the Grail at the end of Act III), *Das Rheingold* (particularly the opening scene with the Rhine maidens and the final scene with the rainbow bridge)

Notes

1. The extent to which *Sons and Lovers* conforms to the realist mode has been a major area of critical concern. For example, Jack Stewart disputes whether "realism" is an "adequate term" to describe the metaphorical patterns in *Sons and Lovers* (Stewart 1999: 33), although for him the primary parallels remain in the visual arts of impressionism and expressionism. See also my discussion of Lawrence and realism in Reid 2018.

2. Since C.P. Ravilious (1973) first deciphered the riddle of the fiddle-bow and the sand-tray, many critics have noted Lawrence's analogy with Chladni's technique (Sagar 1980; Hyde 1990; Salter 2008), but for the most part without considering its musical implications or wider usage across the arts.

3. Lawrence thus invokes the "rhythms of architecture" that Ruskin famously described in "The Nature of Gothic", but we might also interpret this as a musical rhythm in light of Goethe's well-known maxim that "architecture is frozen music" (Ripley 1839: 282).

4. This oft-cited phrase has been variously attributed to Debussy, Mozart, and Ben Jonson, but certainly Debussy's music is noted for its use of silence, for example, see Orledge 1982: 204–205.

5. The cyclical development of *The Rainbow* is also widely interpreted as a function of Lawrence's rendering of myth, for example, in Bell 1992: 76–96.

6. Richard Taruskin provides a more technical description of how "different instruments enter in counterpoint with different orderings of the six tones of the hexachord, so calculated that after six such entries all six constituent tones are continuously present in the texture" (Taruskin 2010: 345).

7. As noted in my Introduction, there were three levels of music according to ancient Greek theory and later developed by Boethius. As Mark Evan Bonds explains, a "hierarchical distinction between the mind and the senses reveals itself with special clarity in the threefold classification of music in Boethius's *De institutione musica*. Two of the three categories he identifies are inaudible to the human ear: *Musica mundana*, the harmony of the spheres, imperceptible to humankind; *musica humana*, the harmony of the human soul, perceptible within the mind of the individual; *musica instrumentalis*, sounding music, perceptible through the senses" (Bonds 2014: 32). This distinction between mind and body, the heard and the unheard, resonates strongly with the opening pages of *The Rainbow* and provides a musical supplement to existing readings of the Brangwen women straining towards the social world.

8. See also Howard J. Booth's discussion of how *The Rainbow* is inflected by the religious language adapted by radical thinkers like Edward Carpenter. His quotation from Carpenter's poem "York Minster" resonates directly with my discussion of "The Cathedral" chapter: "The quaint barbaric tentative uncertain-toned Gregoric refrain, soaring, / Soaring, soaring, through the great desolate nave wandering" (qtd. Booth 2015: 26). On the "Song of Songs", see Baldanza 1961.

9. P.T. Whelan goes much further in arguing that "*The Rainbow* and *Women in Love* together form a sequence very similar to that of the four parts of the *Ring* cycle" (Whelan 1988: 175). E.M. Forster provides literary precedents of Wagnerian rainbows in Chapter 22 of *Howards End* and in his short story "The Celestial Omnibus" (1911).

10. George Hyde asserts that Chladni patterns also suggest how "a kind of silent 'Dionysiac' music … is given a provisional 'Apollonian' shape" (Hyde 1990: 58). For a book-length discussion of the influence of Nietzsche on Lawrence, see Milton 1987. Mark Kinkead-Weekes provides a succinct summary of Lawrence's thinking as he composed *The Rainbow*: "There is both Nietzsche and anti-Nietzsche in the argument that the individual will-to be-oneself-to-the-maximum, must also be able to put itself aside in order to give the maximum new life, secure in belief that the universe is governed by a great creative power" (Kinkead-Weekes 1996: 218–219).

11. Will Brangwen is based on Alfred Burrows, the father of Louie Burrows, a "church organist and teacher of wood carving" (Pinion 1978: 297). R. William Neville, the brother of Lawrence's friend George Neville, also became an organist, at Beauvale Methodist Church (Baron 1981: 4). There was also a fine organ at the Congregational Chapel in Eastwood, that Lawrence attended, installed in 1877: see http://www.hebdenbridge-history.org.uk/charlestown/eastwood/chapel.html

12. Stoddard Martin perceives that Lawrence's later novels *Aaron's Rod*, *Kangaroo* and *The Plumed Serpent* turn to "the Parsifalian [question] of

how a man loves another man" and "seek in various forms the ideal broth-
erhood" (Martin 1982: 177).

13. Until 1914, Wagner's specially constructed "Festspielhaus" (festival theatre) in Bayreuth, where *Parsifal* had its world premiere in 1882, staked its
claim to be the only space where Wagner's "Bühnenweihfestspiel" (stage-
consecrating festival play) could be performed.

14. Although Schoenberg argued for the limitation of performances outside
Bayreuth after the copyright expired, in the interests of Wagner's heirs, there
is no evidence that he ever visited (possibly due to financial constraints).

15. Lawrence's essay "Christs in the Tyrol" critiques "the monuments to physical pain ... found everywhere in the mountain gloom" (*TI* 44–45).

16. This is Robert Fraser's term for J.G. Frazer's *The Golden Bough* (qtd.
Wright 2000: 85). Wright goes on to discuss the important influence on
The Rainbow of Frazer's *The Golden Bough* (Wright 2000: 89–90).

17. My interpretation of "rhythmic form" thus extends to the fundamentals of
form in *The Rainbow* and I therefore disagree with Whelan's conclusion
that "the phrase 'rhythmic form' is used not in respect of the structure of
The Rainbow, but with reference to its characterisation" (Whelan 1988:
176). In my support, I would also cite Michael Bell's extended reading of
how "Lawrence's narrative language seeks to render the movements of
feeling, rather than ideas about feeling" (Bell 1992: 53).

18. Adorno explains that "Mahlerian suspensions tend to be sedimented as
episodes. These are essential to him: roundabout ways that turn out retro-
spectively to be the direct ones". His examples are "the 'Bird of Death'
passage before the entry of the chorus in the Second, the posthorn episode
in the Third, the episodes in the development sections of the first movements of the Sixth and Seventh, to the measures evoking spring in 'Der
Trunkene' in *Das Lied von der Erde*, and the passage marked *Etwas gehalten*
(somewhat restrained) in the Burlesque of the Ninth" (Adorno 1996: 41).

19. The pulse of a piece of music is sometimes described as its heartbeat; it is
the rhythm that makes us tap our feet.

20. For Mahler's contribution to musical modernism, see Albright 2004.
Albright notes, for example, how Mahler's symphonies "aspire to become
vehicles for the transmission of universal vibrations of human perception",
which suggests a shared zeitgeist with Lawrence, including shared
Nietzschean influences (Albright 2004: 6–7).

21. Schoenberg's *Moses und Aron* provides another important example of the
threshold between worlds, which has caused Adorno and others to consider
whether it is "an anti-*Parsifal* or a neo-*Parsifal*" (see Steinberg 2004: 222).

22. This passage is also influenced by Hardy as noted by Langbaum 1985: 73.

23. For a reading of *The Rainbow* and the biblical fall, see Burack 2000.

24. In a letter of December 1910, Lawrence referred to the Song of Solomon
in a flirtatious way to his fiancée Louie Burrows (*IL* 219): specifically, he

references *The Song of Songs. Translated from the Hebrew by Ernest Renan … Done into English by W. R. Thomas* (1895). Frank Baldanza recognises the importance of Hebrew texts in his analysis of Lawrence's use of parallelism in *The Rainbow*: "Hebrew poetry is, in essence, a series of parallel statements. This is exactly what Lawrence called 'slightly modified repetition'" (Baldanza 1961: 108). My intention here is to build from the poetic aspects of Lawrence's use of language towards an understanding of how he also challenged the boundaries of poetry and music.

25. T.R. Wright also discusses the "Song of Songs" in the context of Lawrence's essay "Love" (Wright 2000: 116).

26. Debussy's *Two Dances* were originally composed for harp and strings, but the concert programme indicates that the piano transcription was performed: "'Two Dances for Piano and Strings', Claude Debussy, (a) Danse Sacree (b) Danse Profane" (University of Nottingham, Manuscripts and Special Collections, La B 81).

27. Paul Poplawski's interesting analysis points to Lawrence's reading of Jane Harrison, to which I would add that Harrison also emphasised the role of music in ritual art. For instance, she writes: "It has often been noted that two, and two only, of our senses are the channels of art and give us artistic material. These two senses are sight and hearing" (Harrison 1948: 121). Her previous book *Themis* (1912) is more explicit about the interrelationship of dance and song.

28. Kirsty Martin interprets this scene in terms of her overall thesis of "rhythms of sympathy", in light of which she notes the repetition of "splash" as "a generic marker of the ballad form, a form which has been suggested to invoke ideas of community" (Martin 2013: 154–155). However, as I discuss in Chap. 1, Lawrence's adaptations of the ballad form also suggest a proximity to song.

29. For example, Kandinsky's *Impression III, The Concert* (1911), was a response to hearing Schoenberg's music. Some of Schoenberg's letters to Kandinsky are printed in Auner 2003.

30. Between 1880 and 1884, the young Debussy composed several songs for his mistress Marie Vasnier, which "enabled him to find his feet as a composer" (Walsh 2018: 29), while "close to 30 songs, all published posthumously, survive from Schoenberg's formative years through about 1900" (Frisch 2010: 15).

31. Kandinsky's "innerer Klang" literally translates as inner sound but is often given as "inner feeling" (Kandinsky 1977: 2), thus as with Lawrence's "rhythmic form" sound is a metaphor for, and means of revealing, feeling.

32. As Jack Stewart observes, "there is no evidence of [Lawrence's] conscious use of expressionist techniques" but, in any case, "'Influence' is too crude

a concept for Lawrence's response to the zeitgeist" (Stewart 1980: 297). Nietzsche was a formative influence that Lawrence shared with the German Expressionists, for whom *The Birth of Tragedy from the Spirit of Music* was a foundational text (Gray 2005: 39).

33. For the influence of Nietzsche on Schoenberg, see Harrison 1996: 47–48.

34. For a discussion of Lawrence's Platonic references to angels as two halves of a separated whole, see Reid 2013: 60–63.

35. Kandinsky may have been influenced by theosophist colour theories, for example, in *Thought-Forms* (1901), by Annie Besant and C.W. Leadbetter: see Enns 2013: 185–186.

36. Camille Paglia has also noted parallels in the attitudes of both writers, when she writes that "Seraphita chills sex and gender on Nordic ice. Body vs. mind, sensuality vs. abstraction: like D.H. Lawrence, Balzac diagrams the European cultural schizophrenia. Nature is in bondage to the seraph. The ice cracks and nature revives only when Seraphita weakens and dies" (Paglia 1990: 405–406). Paglia's references to ice bring to mind the final scenes of *Women in Love*, but her use of the term "diagrams" returns us to the Chladni patterns, with which this chapter commenced.

37. Emmanuel Swedenborg (1688–1772) was the author of an influential eight-volume, spiritual interpretation of the Bible titled *Arcana Celestia* (published 1749–1756).

38. *The Rainbow* was prosecuted under the Obscene Publications Act, with reference to evidence by hostile critics including James Douglas, who wrote that "A thing like *The Rainbow* has no right to exist in the wind of war" (qtd. Draper 1986: 94).

References

Adorno, Theodor W. 1996. *Mahler: A Musical Physiognomy*. Chicago/London: University of Chicago Press.

Albright, Daniel. 2004. *Modernism and Music: An Anthology of Sources*. Chicago/London: University of Chicago Press.

Auner, Joseph. 2003. *A Schoenberg Reader*. New Haven/London: Yale University Press.

Baldanza, Frank. 1961. D.H. Lawrence's Song of Songs. *Modern Fiction Studies* 7 (2): 106–114.

Baron, Carl. 1981. Editor's Introduction. In *A Memoir of D.H. Lawrence (The Betrayal)*, ed. G.H. Neville, 1–31. Cambridge: Cambridge University Press.

Becket, Fiona. 2002. *The Complete Critical Guide to D.H. Lawrence*. London/New York: Routledge.

Beckett, Lucy. 1981. *Richard Wagner: "Parsifal" (Cambridge Opera Handbooks)*. Cambridge: Cambridge University Press.

Bell, Michael. 1992. *D.H. Lawrence: Language and Being*. Cambridge: Cambridge University Press.

Berry, Mark. 2008. Arnold Schoenberg's "Biblical Way": From "Die Jakobsleiter" to "Moses und Aron". *Music & Letters* 89 (1): 84–108.

Bonds, Mark Evan. 2014. *Absolute Music: The History of an Idea*. Oxford: Oxford University Press.

Booth, Howard J. 2015. "At Last to Newness": *The Rainbow* and the Dream of a Better World. *Journal of D.H. Lawrence Studies* 4 (1): 19–44.

Burack, Charles M. 2000. The Religious Initiation of the Reader in D.H. Lawrence's *The Rainbow*. *Mosaic* 33 (3): 165–182.

Clarke, Colin. 1969. *River of Dissolution: D.H. Lawrence and English Romanticism*. London: Routledge & Kegan Paul.

DeVoto, Mark. 2004. *Debussy and the Veil of Tonality*. Hillsdale: Pendragon Press.

Draper, R.P. 1986. *D.H. Lawrence: The Critical Heritage*. London/New York: Routledge and Kegan Paul.

Elder, R. Bruce. 2008. *Harmony and Dissent: Film and Avant-garde Art Movements in the Early Twentieth Century*. Waterloo: Wilfred Laurier University Press.

Enns, Anthony. 2013. Vibratory Photography. In *Vibratory Modernism*, ed. Anthony Enns and Shelley Trower. Basingstoke: Palgrave Macmillan.

Fernihough, Anne. 2000. Introduction. In *The Rainbow*, ed. Mark Kinkead-Weekes, xiii–xxxiv. Harmondsworth: Penguin.

Frisch, Walter. 2010. Schoenberg's Lieder. In *The Cambridge Companion to Schoenberg*, ed. Jennifer Shaw and Joseph Auner, 15–29. Cambridge: Cambridge University Press.

Garratt, James. 2004. *Palestrina and the German Romantic Imagination: Historicising Nineteenth-Century Music*. Cambridge: Cambridge University.

Gray, Richard T. 2005. Metaphysical Mimesis: Nietzsche's *Geburt der Tragödie* and the Aesthetics of Literary Expressionism. In *A Companion to the Literature of German Expressionism*, ed. Neil H. Donahue, 39–65. Rochester: Camden House.

Harrison, Jane Ellen. 1948. *Ancient Art and Ritual*. London/New York/Toronto: Oxford University Press.

Harrison, Thomas. 1996. *1910: The Emancipation of Dissonance*. Berkeley: University of California Press.

Heffer, Simon. 2016. Jerusalem is an Ideal Song for England's Pleasant Land. *Telegraph*, March 4. https://www.telegraph.co.uk/music/classical-music/jerusalem-is-an-ideal-song-for-englands-pleasant-land/

Hyde, G.M. 1990. *D.H. Lawrence*. Basingstoke: Macmillan.

Johnson, Julian. 2010. Schoenberg, Modernism, and Metaphysics. In *The Cambridge Companion to Schoenberg*, ed. Jennifer Shaw and Joseph Auner, 108–119. Cambridge: Cambridge University Press.

Kandinsky, Wassily. 1977. *Concerning the Spiritual in Art*. Trans. Michael T.H. Sadler. New York: Dover Publications.

Keats, John. 1884. *Lamia*, Part 2. *The Poetical Works of John Keats*. http://www.bartleby.com/126/37.html

Kehler, Grace. 2012. Artistic Experiment and the Reevaluation of the Prima Donna in George Moore's *Evelyn Innes*. In *The Arts of the Prima Donna in the Long Nineteenth Century*, ed. Rachel Cowgill and Hilary Poriss, 147–166. Oxford: Oxford University Press.

Kinderman, William. 2005a. Introduction: The Challenge of Wagner's *Parsifal*. In *A Companion to Wagner's "Parsifal"*, ed. William Kinderman and Katherine R. Syer, 1–28. London: Boydell & Brewer.

———. 2005b. The Third-Act Prelude of Wagner's *Parsifal*: Genesis, Meaning, and Dramatic Form. *Nineteenth-Century Music* 29 (2): 161–184.

Kinkead-Weekes, Mark. 1968. The Marble and the Statue: The Exploratory Imagination of D.H. Lawrence. In *Imagined Worlds: Essays in Some English Novels and Novelists in Honour of John Butt*, ed. Maynard Mack and Ian Gregor, 371–418. London: Methuen.

———. 1992. D.H. Lawrence and the Dance. *The Journal of the Society for Dance Research* 10 (1): 59–77.

———. 1996. *D.H. Lawrence: Triumph to Exile 1912–1922*. Cambridge: Cambridge University Press.

———. 2001. D.H. Lawrence: "A Passionately Religious Man". *The Sewanee Review* 109 (3): 379–397.

Krockel, Carl. 2007. *D.H. Lawrence in Germany: The Politics of Influence*. Amsterdam: Rodopi.

Langbaum, Robert. 1985. Lawrence and Hardy. In *D.H. Lawrence and Tradition*, ed. Jeffrey Meyers, 69–90. London: Athlone Press.

Lewis, Pericles. 2010. *Religious Experience and the Modernist Novel*. Cambridge: Cambridge University Press.

Martin, Stoddard. 1982. *Wagner to "The Waste Land": A Study of the Relationship of Wagner to English Literature*. London: Macmillan.

Martin, Kirsty. 2013. *Modernism and the Rhythms of Sympathy: Vernon Lee, Virginia Woolf, D.H. Lawrence*. Oxford: Oxford University Press.

Mester, Terri A. 1997. *Movement and Modernism: Yeats, Eliot, Lawrence, Williams and Early Twentieth-Century Dance*. Fayetteville: University of Arkansas Press.

Meyers, Jeffrey. 1975. Fra Angelico and *The Rainbow*. In *Painting and the Novel*, 53–64. Manchester: Manchester University Press.

Milton, Colin. 1987. *Lawrence and Nietzsche: A Study in Influence*. Aberdeen: Aberdeen University Press.

Orledge, Robert. 1982. *Debussy and the Theatre*. Cambridge: Cambridge University Press.

Paglia, Camille. 1990. *Sexual Personae: Art and Decadence from Nefertiti to Emily Dickenson*. Vol. 1. New Haven/London: Yale University Press.

Pinion, F.B. 1978. *D.H. Lawrence Companion: Life, Thought and Works*. Basingstoke: Macmillan.

Pinkney, Tony. 1990. *D.H. Lawrence*. New York: Harvester Wheatsheaf.

Poplawski, Paul. 1993. *Promptings of Desire: Creativity and the Religious Impulse in the Works of D.H. Lawrence*. Westport/London: Greenwood Press.

Potter, Caroline. 2003. Debussy and Nature. In *The Cambridge Companion to Debussy*, ed. Simon Trezise, 137–151. Cambridge: Cambridge University Press.

Ravilious, C.P. 1973. Lawrence's "Chladni Figures". *Notes and Queries* ccxviii: 331–332.

Reid, Susan. 2013. D.H. Lawrence's Angelic Men. *D.H. Lawrence Review* 38 (1): 57–72.

———. 2018. Realism. In *D.H. Lawrence in Context*, ed. Andrew Harrison, 81–90. Cambridge: Cambridge University Press.

Ripley, George, ed. 1839. *Specimens of Foreign Standard Literature: Vol. IV Containing Conversations with Goethe in the Last Years of His Life, from the German of Eckermann*. Boston: Hilliard, Gray, and Company.

Sagar, Keith. 1980. *The Life of D.H. Lawrence: An Illustrated Biography*. London: Eyre Methuen.

Salter, Leo. 2008. Lawrence, Newton and Einstein. *Etudes Lawrenciennes* 38: 25–39.

Sherry, Vincent. 2015. *Modernism and the Reinvention of Decadence*. Cambridge: Cambridge University Press.

Simeone, Nigel. 2003. Debussy and expression. In *The Cambridge Companion to Debussy*, ed. Simon Trezise, 101–116. Cambridge: Cambridge University Press.

Sola Pinto, Vivien de. 1969. William Blake and Lawrence. In *William Blake: Essays for S. Foster Damon*, ed. Alvin H. Rosenfeld, 84–106. Providence: Brown University Press.

Steinberg, Michael P. 2004. *Listening to Reason: Culture, Subjectivity, and Nineteenth-Century Music*. Princeton: Princeton University Press.

Stevens, Hugh. 2014. From Genesis to the *Ring*: Richard Wagner and D.H. Lawrence's *The Rainbow*. *Textual Practice* 28 (4): 611–630.

Stewart, Jack F. 1980. Expressionism in *The Rainbow*. *NOVEL: A Forum on Fiction* 13 (3): 296–315.

———. 1999. *The Vital Art of D.H. Lawrence: Vision and Expression*. Carbondale/Edwardsville: Southern Illinois University Press.

Supino, J.B. 1902. *Fra Angelico*. Trans. Leader Scott. Florence: Alinari Brothers.

Surette, Leon. 1994. *The Birth of Modernism: Ezra Pound, T.S. Eliot, W.B. Yeats, and the Occult*. Montreal: McGill-Queen's University Press.

Taruskin, Richard. 2010. *Music in the Early Twentieth Century*. Oxford: Oxford University Press.

Thorpe, Adam. 2003. Pot of Gold: D.H. Lawrence's *The Rainbow*. *Guardian*, December 13. https://www.theguardian.com/books/2003/dec/13/classics. dhlawrence

Tresize, Simon. 1994. *Debussy: La mer*. Cambridge: Cambridge University Press.

———. 2003. Debussy's "rhythmicised time". In *The Cambridge Companion to Debussy*, ed. Simon Trezise, 232–255. Cambridge: Cambridge University Press.

Walsh, Stephen. 2018. *Debussy: A Painter in Sound*. London: Faber & Faber.

Wexler, Joyce. 2016. *Violence Without God: The Rhetorical Despair of Twentieth-Century Writers*. London: Bloomsbury.

Whelan, P.T. 1988. *D.H. Lawrence: Myth and Metaphysic in "The Rainbow" and "Women in Love"*. Ann Arbor/London: UMI Research Press.

Worthen, John. 2014. Lawrence and some Romantic Poets. *Journal of D.H. Lawrence Studies* 3 (3): 10–32.

Wright, T.R. 2000. *D.H. Lawrence and the Bible*. Cambridge: Cambridge University Press.

CHAPTER 5

"Beyond the Sound of Words": Harmony and Polyphony in *Women in Love*

Introduction

In *Women in Love,* the notion of "rhythmic form" (*2L* 184) that shaped *The Rainbow* is modified into what Lawrence described as "a pulsing, frictional to-and-fro" ("Foreword" *WL* 486). As a style of writing, this technique is illustrated by the "Moony" chapter, in which Birkin's stoning of the moon's reflection in a mill pond again evokes the Chladni patterns of sound waves (illustrated in Fig. 1.1). But here, the waves are depicted as "battling" and "clamouring" (*WL* 247), in "a novel which took its final shape in the midst of the period of war" ("Foreword" *WL* 485). Peter Preston aptly reads this scene as resembling "an artillery bombardment" or "a description of trench warfare" (Preston 2011b: 43–44); however, sound is particularly important in this performance of violence:

> there was a burst of sound, and a burst of brilliant light, the moon had exploded on the water, and was flying asunder in flakes of white and dangerous fire. Rapidly, like white birds, the fires all broken rose across the pond, fleeing in clamorous confusion, battling with the flock of dark waves that were forcing their way in. The furthest waves of light, fleeing out, seemed to be clamouring against the shore for escape, the waves of darkness came in heavily, running under towards the centre …
> … [Birkin] saw the moon regathering itself insidiously, saw the heart of the rose intertwining vigorously and blindly, calling back the scattered fragments, winning home the fragments, in a pulse and an effort of return.

© The Author(s) 2019
S. Reid, *D.H. Lawrence, Music and Modernism,*
Palgrave Studies in Music and Literature,
https://doi.org/10.1007/978-3-030-04999-7_5

And he was not satisfied. Like a madness, he must go on. He got large stones, and threw them, one after the other, at the white-burning centre of the moon, till there was nothing but a rocking of hollow noise, and a pond surged up, no moon any more, only a few broken flakes tangled and glittering broadcast in the darkness, without aim or meaning, a darkened confusion, like a black and white kaleidoscope tossed at random. The hollow night was rocking and crashing with noise, and from the sluice came sharp, regular flashes of sound. Flakes of light appeared here and there, glittering tormented among the shadows, far off, in strange places, among the dripping shadow of the willow on the island. Birkin stood and listened, and was satisfied. (*WL* 247–248)

In this extract, what Birkin hears is at least as important as what he sees. Explosive "burst[s] of sound" overlay a background of what Lawrence described as "continual, slightly modified repetition" ("Foreword" *WL* 486); for instance, flying/fleeing/fleeing, sound/asunder, clamorous/clamouring, dark/darkness/darkened. There are also internal rhymes such as light/white and the alliteration of flaying/flakes, fleeing/flock. This is poetic prose, like the words which "pair like lovers, and chime in the ear" (*STH* 140) that Lawrence praised in "Art and the Individual" (1908), except that now the words come in waves that "clash". There is a "clamorous confusion" of visual and aural images: "a burst of sound, and a burst of brilliant light" at the beginning of the passage is later compounded as "sharp, regular flashes of sound", where the visual associations inherent in the word "flash" reflect the "glittering" properties of the light that swiftly follows.

The metaphor of a kaleidoscope seems visual but its deployment in conjunction with "a rocking of hollow noise" is suggestive of the instrument's scientific use in making sound waves visible. In an adaptation of Ernst Chladni's experiments with a single-bowed frequency (discussed in Chaps. 1 and 4), the mathematician and physicist Jules Lissajous (1822–1880) refined the kaleidoscope to study the curves created by the combination of two perpendicular vibrations (illustrated in Figs. 5.1 and 5.2).[1] By designing an

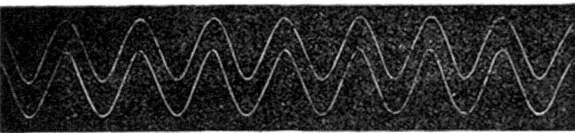

Fig. 5.1   Lissajous patterns from *Sound* (1857), by William Tyndall (Fig. 23)

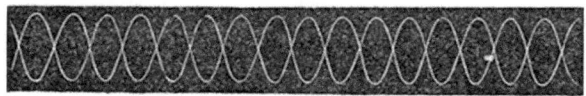

Fig. 5.2 Lissajous patterns from *Sound* (1857), by William Tyndall (Fig. 24)

instrument consisting of two little mirrors mounted on tuning forks Lissajous found that "If the tuning forks sound in a 'pure' interval, the resulting image is static and symmetric … If the interval is not 'pure', the result is a chaos of lines" (Rekveld 1998: n.p.). Birkin produces his own "chaos of lines" on the surface of the pond, yet what emerges from his subsequent dialogue with Ursula is a desire for the "static and symmetric", which he expresses as a yearning "to be together in happy stillness" (*WL* 252). In part, this "happy stillness" is defined by a cessation of the "frictional to-and-fro" (*WL* 486) of words, since as Birkin wonders to himself: "What was the good of talking, anyway? It must happen beyond the sound of words" (*WL* 250).

What happens "beyond the sound of words" is a central concern of the novel that extends beyond a thematic use of silence, which in Preston's nuanced analysis "cannot simply be defined as the absence of sound" (Preston 2011a: 64). As in music, there is a symbiotic relationship between sound and silence in this text, which corresponds with Chladni patterns where the lines form at the points of stillness on the sanded plate vibrating to the frequency of a fiddle-bow. Leo Bersani has argued persuasively that *Women in Love* is animated by "the Lawrentian contrast between agitation and stillness" (Bersani 1978: 163), but to what extent is this opposition also articulated through contrasting sound worlds denoting agitation and stillness, which are represented by models of harmony and polyphony? An initial comparison of Gerald's characterisation as a representative of Wagnerian harmony with Birkin's more ethically oriented model of polyphony suggests two opposing sound worlds within the novel, which open into parallels with the music of Debussy, Stravinsky, Bax, and Holst, as well as a continuing interest in folk song.

HARMONY AND POLYPHONY

Aligned with a mode of agitation, the "madness" that compels Birkin to "go on" stoning the pond (*WL* 247) is closely associated with the relentless momentum of the machinery that drives industry and war, and which provides the ground bass that reverberates throughout the novel "like a machine's burring, a music more maddening than the siren's" (*WL* 116). Gerald, an "Industrial Magnate" (*WL* 211), personifies this deathly momentum, embracing "repetition" in the form of harmony and setting "himself to work, to put the great industry in order":

> In his travels, and in his accompanying readings, he had come to the conclusion that the essential secret of life was harmony. He did not define to himself at all clearly what harmony was. The word pleased him, he felt he had come to his own conclusions. And he proceeded to put his philosophy into practice forcing order into the established world, translating the mystic word harmony into the practical word organisation. (*WL* 227)

It is no accident that Gerald is also the novel's most Wagnerian character; his resistance to "the fact of intrinsic difference" between self and other (*WL* 209) maps against a Wagnerian loss of boundaries in life and love, orchestrated by a sea of endless melody (as discussed in Chap. 3). He is thus a successor to Siegmund in *The Trespasser*, the doomed hero driven on to his death by the insistent beats of the "Ride of the Valkyries" (*T* 165).[2] But Gerald also represents a pure instrumentality, which in its cosmic imagery suggests a state of universal harmony and a Pythagorean view of harmonics (echoed by Boethius), in which an unheard music sounds as the planets move together:

> It was like being part of a machine. He himself happened to be a controlling, central part, the masses of men were the parts variously controlled. This was merely as it happened. As well get excited because a central hub drives a hundred outer wheels—or because the whole universe wheels round the sun. After all, it would be mere silliness to say that the moon and the earth and Saturn and Jupiter and Venus have just as much right to be the centre of the universe, each of them separately, as the sun. (*WL* 227)

Countering Gerald's concept of harmony, however, are the dissenting voices of Birkin and Ursula, both of whom aspire to autonomy rather than automation. The rhythmic "pulsing to-and-fro" between different voices in the novel points to "polyphonic" qualities, which have been widely recognised following David Lodge's influential Bakhtinian reading (Lodge 1985; see also Fleishman 1985, 1990; Leone 2010).[3] But what such accounts have elided is the musical origin of the metaphor of polyphony, which Bakhtin warned "should not be forgotten" (Bakhtin 1984: 22). In music, polyphony denotes two or more simultaneous lines of independent melody, providing a metaphor which, as Stephen Benson observes, has become a "founding element of the ever more overtly ethically-oriented field of contemporary literary studies" in terms of "facing up to alterity and the constructive otherness and heterogeneity of subjectivity" (Benson 2003: 295). In music, Benson argues, these ethical dimensions are embedded within "the nature of individual parts and the relation of part to whole" (Benson 2003: 300). Importantly, polyphony introduces a spatial element of distance between parts in music, which, in theory at least, is non-hierarchical since no single part predominates.

As a structuring device, then, musical polyphony offered Lawrence a way of further spatialising his text, as a development in musical form from the architectural devices of arches in churches and in nature suggestive of "frozen music" in *The Rainbow* (1915).[4] In *Women in Love*, the ethical relationship of self and other is reconceived in more expansively spatial terms in Birkin's metaphor of star equilibrium: "a strange conjunction ... a pure balance of two single beings:—as the stars balance each other" (*WL* 148). The word "conjunction", in its meaning of "the action or an instance of two or more events or things occurring at the same point in time or space" (*OED*), thus extends the novel's polyphonic qualities. The balancing of the stars also evokes ancient Greek ideas about the geometry and related music of the spheres, but in a very different way than Gerald's conception of parts subsumed within a harmonious whole.

Thomas Mann later explored remarkably similar expressions of ethical and stellar relationship as Lawrence's Birkin; for instance, in *Doctor Faustus: The Life of the German Composer Adrian Leverkühn as Told by a Friend* (1947), when Leverkühn pronounces that "The polyphonic dignity of every chord-forming note would be guaranteed by the constellation" (qtd. Benson 2003: 305). Mann had the benefit of direct experience of Schoenberg's music, as well as dialogue with Adorno, who argued that Schoenberg's 12-tone technique reconciled harmony and polyphony and revealed "polyphony as the essence of harmony itself" (Adorno 2006: 48). At the very least, *Women in Love* perceives a need to resolve a rift between harmony and polyphony, and the difficulty of this task is signalled, as Daniel Melnick points out, through the novel's own "rifts and seams ... the awkward and distorting intensities" (Melnick 1994: 104). To some degree, Lawrence also anticipates Adorno's critique of "popular culture", created for "the kind of listener destined for industrial mass culture" (Adorno 2006: 140).[5] Adorno singled out Stravinsky as "the master percussionist" of this culture, "a Wagner who has come fully into his own, who has surrendered to the repetition compulsion" (Adorno 2006: 140).

As Neil Sinyard reflects, Stravinsky's *The Rite of Spring* (1913) was a cultural phenomenon that "pulsated with the pressure of modern experience and was quickly acknowledged not as an affront to modernity but as the epitome of it" (Sinyard 2003: 408). Lawrence, as I argue below, uses similar rhythms but as a critique of the modernity they represent.

The next section of my discussion focuses on the contrasting views of harmony and polyphony in two chapters of *Women in Love*: firstly, "Coal-Dust", which evokes something of the machine-like rhythms of Stravinsky's music, and then "Excurse", which creates an atmosphere of stillness reminiscent of Debussy. Since both composers were in dialogue with Wagner, albeit in different ways, this comparison then leads into a closer examination of Lawrence's ongoing resistance to Wagnerism. A striking contrast is offered by Arnold Bax's tone poem *Tintagel* (composed 1917–1919), conceived in Cornwall as a belated outpouring of Wagnerism and romanticism amidst the noise and darkness of the First World War. Most of *Women in Love* was written in retreat from the world in Cornwall, but here Lawrence's new friendships with the composers Philip Heseltine and Cecil Gray reinvigorated his interest in folk songs. At certain points in *Women in Love*, the singing of folk songs challenges the predominant ground bass of mechanical noise and provides another counter to notions of Wagnerian limitlessness. *Women in Love* thus charts a negotiation between the local and the universal which also concerned contemporary composers, from Stravinsky's use of Russian folk tunes in *The Rite of Spring* to Gustav Holst's wartime composition of *The Planets Suite* (1918). Holst's depiction of Mars and Neptune as bringers (respectively) of war and peace has uncanny parallels with the two modes of agitation and stillness in *Women in Love* and shares its radically cosmic turn, as I will explore in my closing discussion.

SOUNDS OF MODERNITY: DEBUSSY AND STRAVINSKY

The symbiotic states of mechanical motion and inertia discussed in the *Study of Thomas Hardy* (*STH* 54–55) became central to *Women in Love* in ways that relate closely to the musical developments of his time.[6] As Paul Rosenfeld observed in his 1920 essay on the music of Stravinsky:

> The elegance of Debussy, the golden sensuality, the quiet classic touch, are flown. Instead, there come to be great, weighty, metallic masses, molten piles and sheets of steel and iron, shining adamantine bulks ... Above all,

there is rhythm, rhythm rectangular and sheer and emphatic, rhythm that lunges and beats and reiterates and dances with all the steely perfect tirelessness of the machine ...

And yet, the two styles, Debussy's and Strawinsky's [sic], are related. Indeed, they are complementary ... But the chief difference, the difference that made "Le Sacre du printemps" almost antithetical to "Pelléas et Mélisande", is essentially the divergence between two cardinal manners of apprehending life. (Rosenfeld 1920: 192–194)

Rosenfeld's characterisation of the "golden sensuality" of Debussy's music strikes an immediate parallel with the "golden light" that Birkin perceives in Ursula in the "Moony" chapter (*WL* 249), while the "quiet" qualities which are Debussyan hallmarks (as noted in previous chapters) resonate with the silence and stillness of "Excurse" in ways that I will discuss below. As in Rosenfeld's analysis, this quieter soundscape in Lawrence's novel is relational to another which parallels Stravinsky's "steely perfect tirelessness of the machine" and threatens to predominate in an increasingly mechanised world.

Women in Love refers directly to the "Russian Ballet of Pavlova and Nijinsky" (*WL* 91), which played a large part in launching Stravinsky's career. The novel's opening pages mock the formalities of the marriage rite,[7] in a scene in which a bridegroom pursues his bride with Nijinsky-like "leaps" powered by "supple haunches" (*WL* 19).[8] Nijinsky was both the principal dancer in Debussy's ballet *Prélude á l'après-midi d'un faune* (implied by this leaping pursuit of a bride/nymph) and the choreographer of Stravinsky's *The Rite of Spring*. The two composers were linked through dance, with Melnick (after Adorno) perceiving a certain continuity whereby Stravinsky's "ballet scores transform Debussy's fluid strategy and harmony into a new means to shock bourgeois listeners of 1913 into reaction, rather than self-reflection" (Melnick 1994: 81).[9] Lawrence's polyphonic novel engages with the modes of both composers.

While he was writing *Women in Love*, Lawrence corresponded with the Imagist poet Amy Lowell about her 1916 poem, named after and modelled on "Stravinsky's Three Pieces 'Grotesques', for String Quartet" (*3L* 31). As Regina Schober observes, Lowell's poem "does not only imitate the sounds and rhythms, but also tries to capture the music by means of vibrant descriptions" (Schober 2008: 163)—a technique which also applies to passages such as "Coal-Dust" in *Women in Love*. After hearing *The Rite of Spring* in London 1914, Lowell "accepted it instantly as a masterpiece, and eventually came to consider Stravinsky as the greatest living composer" (Damon 1935: 229). Lawrence was more critical, influenced perhaps by the ambivalence towards Stravinsky of his friend Heseltine, whose favourite composers, when he lived briefly with the Lawrences in Porthcothan, were "Delius, Goossens, Arnold Bax, and some few others" (*2L* 548).[10] In his letter to Lowell, Lawrence dismisses Stravinsky's music along with the *"mere noises"* of "Italian futurismo poems" (*3L* 31).[11]

Periodically, however, mechanical noises erupt into the foreground of *Women in Love* as a virtuosic performance to rival the Futurist compositions of Luigi Russolo (author of *The Art of Noises*, 1913), or *The Rite of Spring*. In the chapter "Coal-Dust", a "locomotive, as if wanting to see what could be done, put on the brakes, and back came the trucks rebounding on the iron buffers, striking like horrible cymbals, clashing nearer and nearer in frightful strident concussions" (*WL* 111). To the accompaniment of this "mad clamour", and in front of a small audience, Gerald compels his mare to enact a kind of frenzied dance, so that "she spun round and round, on two legs, as if she were in the centre of some whirlwind" (*WL* 111). This frenzied circle dance at the level crossing resonates with the climax of Nijinsky's choreography in *The Rite of Spring* (1913); the "Sacrificial Dance" in which the "Chosen One" dances herself to death amidst the bewildering noise and cross-rhythms of Stravinsky's music.[12]

With the benefit of hindsight, we can hear how *The Rite of Spring* prefigured the human sacrifice of the First World War and its discordant soundscape of machine warfare (see, for example, Eksteins 1990). According to Rosenfeld, Stravinsky's radical score "pounds with the rhythm of engines, whirls and spirals like screws and fly-wheels, grinds and shrieks like laboring metal" (Rosenfeld 1920: 202), which resonates with Cecil Barber's observation in his article "Battle Music" (1918) of how even the noisiest symphonies "pale like the stars before the mildest strafe on the Western Front" (qtd. Epstein 2014: xvi). Lawrence had experienced a preview of this "battle music" during his pre-war visit to Germany in 1913, when he witnessed "the sound of guns thudd[ing] continuously" and "the intolerable crackling and bursting of rifles" (*TI* 82–83). His article "With the Guns", published soon after the outbreak of the war in August 1914, presciently stated that he "could see what war would be like—an affair entirely of machines, with men attached to the machines as the subordinate part thereof, as the butt is the part of a rifle" (*TI* 81).

The machinery of war is a logical extension of a mechanised culture, which accordingly produces mechanistic art as epitomised in *Women in Love* by Loerke's industrial sculpture:

> It was a representation of a fair, with peasants and artizans [sic] in an orgy of enjoyment, drunk and absurd in their modern dress, whirling ridiculously in roundabouts, gaping at shows, kissing and staggering and rolling in knots, swinging in swing-boats and firing down shooting galleries, a frenzy of chaotic motion. (*WL* 423)

Like Mark Gertler's nightmarish painting *Merry-Go-Round* (1916), Loerke's frieze mirrors a culture condemned to go round and round like squirrels in a cage (to paraphrase Birkin, *WL* 251), accompanied by the inevitable mechanical music of the fairground, evoked by Stravinsky in another pre-war work *Petrushka* (1911).[13] Such art is mimetic and, although seemingly avant-garde, did not offer contemporary writers a model for freeing themselves from the constraints of mimesis in which realism was rooted. As Leigh Wilson suggests, "pure sound"—akin to "absolute music" with no programme or attributable meaning—offered one such route to freedom (Wilson 2013: 78).

Ursula seeks absolution "from the rhythm of life, [to] fix myself and remain static ... better to die than live mechanically a life that is a repetition of repetitions" (*WL* 192). The achievement of such a state is demonstrated by a different approach to sound in "Excurse":

> As they [Ursula and Birkin] descended, they heard the Minster bells playing a hymn, when the hour had struck six.
>
> "Glory to thee my God this night
> For all the blessings of the light— —"
>
> So, to Ursula's ear, the tune fell out, drop by drop, from the unseen sky on to the dusky town. It was like dim, bygone centuries sounding. It was all so far off ... Above, she could see the first stars. What was it all? This was no actual world, it was the dream-world of one's childhood—a great circumscribed reminiscence. The world had become unreal. She herself was a strange, transcendent reality. (*WL* 312)

This scene privileges "Ursula's ear" in a way that engages with scientific investigations of sound as a quantifiable and measurable substance (as in Chladni's experiments, for example, but see also Wilson 2013: 78–79). The materiality of sound is reinforced by the description of a tune falling out of the sky "drop by drop"—like the raindrops evoked in Debussy's "Jardin sous la pluie" (1903), a piece for solo piano that Lawrence recommended to his fiancée Louie Burrows in October 1911 (*1L* 308–309). More generally, the passage resembles a Debussyan sound world that draws on "the old church modes" and convent "bells" and a "potency of pure sound" (as described in *Rhythm* magazine by Rollo H. Myers [1911: 31]),[14] reminiscent of the "unreal" soundscapes of *Pelléas et Mélisande* and "La cathédrale engloutie" (The Submerged Cathedral). In a similar way to Debussy's music, Lawrence's prose evokes a "pure sound" to create a world that is not purely mimetic, so that "The world had become unreal" (*WL* 312). Time has dissolved into space in this passage and Ursula feels that she has become part of "a strange, transcendent reality", which prepares her for the harmonious relationship suggested by Birkin's star equilibrium: indeed, "she could see the first stars" (*WL* 312).

In the earlier "Moony" episode, Birkin's stoning of the moon's reflection produces wave patterns on the surface of the water that are both visible and audible, but "Excurse" culminates with the invisible and inaudible:

> [Ursula and Birkin] sat in stillness and mindless silence. There were faint sounds from the wood, but no disturbance, no possible disturbance, the world was under a strange ban, a new mystery had supervened.
>
> They threw off their clothes, and he gathered her to him, and found her, found the pure lambent reality of her forever invisible flesh. Quenched, inhuman, his fingers upon her unrevealed nudity were the fingers of silence upon silence, the body of mysterious night upon the body of mysterious night, the night masculine and feminine, never to be seen with the eye, or known with the mind, only known as a palpable revelation of living otherness. (*WL* 320)

The seemingly impenetrable mysticism of "Excurse" has long puzzled critics, although John Worthen (1999: 8) suggests a theosophical influence, which also has acoustic implications. In *The Secret Doctrine* (which Lawrence read before revising *Women in Love*, *3L* 299), Madame Blavatsky warns against the "potency" of the "spoken word": "Because sound and rhythm are closely related to the Four elements of the Ancients; and because such or another vibration in the air is sure to awaken corresponding powers, union with which produces good or bad results, as the case may be" (qtd. Wilson 2013: 82). This suggests another possible model for the transformative vibrations experienced by Ursula and Birkin versus the "waves of darkness" (*WL* 247) that permeate the industrialised, war-torn world. Indeed, the Chladni experiments that influenced Lawrence's perceptions of rhythm were also a shared influence with theosophers (Wilson 2013: 85), although in other respects their thinking clashed.[15] For Lawrence, sound offered the potential to reconcile the forces of dark and light, materiality and spirituality, whereas for theosophers the material world must be transcended. Thus, while for some theosophers, Wagner's *Parsifal* represented a model for the fight against "dark magicians" (qtd. Sessa 1979: 131), Lawrence's view (as discussed in Chap. 4) was closer to that of Nietzsche, who regarded Wagner as "this old magician, mightiest of Klingsors; how he wages war against us with his art" (Nietzsche 1911: 40).[16]

SICK TRISTANS: WAGNER AND THE FIRST WORLD WAR

Increasingly, Lawrence perceived Wagnerism as a symptom of a culture in love with death. Several critics have noted the Wagnerian elements of *Women in Love*, although Joyce Carol Oates draws particular attention to how the novel's parallels with Wagner are "despairing, floridly tragic and rather mad" (Oates 1978: 568) and therefore align with an old order that the novel condemns to destruction.[17] Gerald combines characteristics of three races depicted in the *Ring* cycle: he is at once a "Nibelung" (*WL* 47), a Siegfried-like human hero who meets his downfall through characters with Wagnerian names (Gudrun/Gutrun and Loerke/Loki), and godlike, "God of the Machine, Deus ex Machina" (*WL* 228). But he is also a version of Tristan: his "fatal halfness" (*WL* 207) drives Gerald to complete himself through Gudrun, in a doomed romance in which he completes himself only in death, like Wagner's tragic hero.

When Lawrence retreated from wartime London to Cornwall at the end of 1915, he heard the call of Tristan, writing that "It is not England. It is bare and dark and elemental, Tristan's land ... It is old, Celtic, pre-christian—Tristan and his boat, and his horn" (*2L* 503).[18] This is a sound he mimics in *Women in Love* when Gerald "blew a shattering blast", albeit on a conch shell rather than a horn, but with similar effect: "It was a strange, rousing noise, that made the heart beat. The summons was almost magical. Everybody came running, as if at a signal" (*WL* 26). Lawrence was not thinking, he emphasised, of "the ridiculous Malory, with his Grails and his chivalries" (*2L* 495), so we may infer that it is Wagner's opera *Tristan und Isolde* that was on his mind, as it had been when he wrote *The Trespasser*.

The composer and poet Arnold Bax also retreated to Cornwall for respite from the war (like Lawrence, he was declared medically unfit for military service). Soon after the war began, Bax wrote from Zennor to his lover and muse, the pianist Harriet Cohen: "I am often thinking of you these days—a thought that is really a star in the presence [sic] darkness of light—with our careers smashed up and the awful restlessness which prevents one's concentration on any kind of work" (qtd. Fry 2008: 31). There are uncanny resonances here with the restless wanderings of characters in *Women in Love* (not least Birkin) and with its cosmic imagery of darkness and light, although Bax (unlike Lawrence) casts himself as something of a star-crossed lover.[19] Cohen was also despondent about the war and her separation from Bax, but struck up a brief friendship with Lawrence in 1915 and they shared some lighter-hearted moments together (Fry 2008: 40). Bax warned her that Lawrence would "put [her] in a book" and she would later claim that he named the heroine of *Kangaroo* (1923) after her.[20] Cohen was one of many mutual acquaintances, and although there is no evidence that Lawrence and Bax ever met, they knew of each other's work and shared similar influences (Richards 2015: 91–92), notably Wagner.[21]

In 1917, together with Cohen at the height of their affair, Bax visited Tintagel, which evoked "memories of the historical and legendary association of the place, especially those connected with King Arthur, King Mark, and Tristram and Iseult" (Webber 2007: n.p.). Bax's identification is inevitably with Wagner's *Tristan und Isolde*, given his own entanglement in an adulterous love triangle and his long-standing musical passion for the German master: "For a dozen years of my youth I wallowed in Wagner's music to the almost total exclusion ... [of] any other" (Bax 1943: 22). He was immediately inspired to write the poem "Tintagel Castle", and over the following two years the orchestral tone poem, *Tintagel*. The text of the poem testifies to a phase in the relationship between Bax and Cohen when the lovers found it unbearable to be apart (Fry 2008: 61–62). Bax traces forward from the legend of Tristram and Iseult a centuries-long history of despairing lovers—"English, Celt or Norman, / Love hurt them still the same"—culminating in his own consuming passion for Harriet:

> Strain closer yet, my lovely,
> Till all your breasts aglow,
> Nor think how new sad ages
> Will never care to know

If your white body's beauty
Were thrall to Love or Duty,
Or how I burned and hungered
Long centuries ago.

The mood and burning imagery of Bax's poem is closer to Lawrence's earlier novel *The Trespasser*—in which Helena's white skin is symbolically burned (*T* 43) during her passionate encounter with the doomed musician Siegmund—although the imperative to "Strain closer" bears some resemblance to Gerald's desire to "pour" himself into Gudrun to become "whole again", in the chapter ominously titled "Death and Love" (another play on Wagnerian *Liebestod*).

Bax acknowledged only a "brief reference" in his *Tintagel* to Wagner's *Tristan und Isolde*, but his first biographer Colin Scott-Sutherland perceived that "the languid drooping 'sick Tristan' motif... comes increasingly to dominate the *Tintagel* development section" (qtd. Foreman 1983: 151) (Fig. 5.3). Christopher Webber concurs that "in truth, once Sick Tristan is with us, about five minutes into the piece, his debilitating emotional influence is felt until the very last page" (Webber 2007: n.p.). The "sick Tristan" leitmotif in Wagner's opera relates specifically to Tristan's physical wounds: it is first heard in Act I when Isolde recalls tending Tristan when he "Arrived on Ireland's shore ... Wounded and nearly dead" (Millington 2006: 52), and the motif returns in Act III as Tristan, now wounded on Cornwall's shore, learns that Isolde is on her way to tend him again. Webber thus conflates physical and emotional wounds in his claim for the motif's "debilitating emotional influence" on Bax's composition. For Webber, Bax's quotation of this motif perfectly expresses a conflict between "self-gratification and self-sacrifice" that is played out against the backdrop of a turbulent seascape that further "conveys a sense of the transient tragedy of the emotions being subsumed by the larger, eternal drama of

Fig. 5.3 "Sick Tristan" motif from Wagner's *Tristan und Isolde*. (Courtesy of arnoldbax.com)

the wind and the waves" (Webber 2007: n.p.). In the context of the First World War, however, we might read Bax's intense focus on the "sick Tristan" motif as symptomatic not only of his own inner conflict about his emotional relationships, but also of the literal wounds and deaths sustained on the battlefields of Europe. Bax was resistant to reading such meanings into his works published after the war, and yet there can be no doubt that the war and events in Ireland affected him deeply. At the beginning of the war, he wrote of "plunging into a narcotic ocean of creative work" and the most enduring product of this was his tumultuous seascape *Tintagel* (qtd. Foreman 1983: 123).

Lawrence, however, specified in his Foreword to *Women in Love* that "it is a novel which took its final shape in the midst of the period of war, though it does not concern the war itself. I should wish the time to remain unfixed, so that the bitterness of the war may be taken for granted in the characters" (*WL* 485). Conceived during its writing as a "Dies Irae" (*2L* 669)—the part of the Roman Catholic requiem mass that deals with the "Day of Wrath"—*Women in Love* has been interpreted as Lawrence's reckoning with the fall of western civilisation (e.g. Worthen 1999: 24). This is a theme that re-echoes in Lawrence's late poem titled "Dies Irae" (published in *Pansies*, 1929) as "a consummation devoutly to be wished / in this world of mechanical self-assertion" (*Poems* 443). In *Women in Love*, Gerald is representative of "mechanical self-assertion" and if we concur with Sarah Cole's insightful reading of his death "in several senses, as a kind of transmuted war death" (Cole 2003: 234), then the novel is also a requiem for his war death. I would argue further that the universal death wish being enacted on the Western Front, implicit in the "bitterness" of Lawrence's war novel, is enacted by Lawrence's own "sick Tristan" in the person of Gerald.

Gerald's death is in part a love-death, resulting from an erotic triangle with Gudrun and Loerke (both Wagnerian names, albeit derived from the *Ring*), but, like Wagner's Tristan, Gerald is at least as much in love with death as he is with his beloved, a problem which the war convinces Lawrence is endemic within western culture, with Wagner as a leading exponent. Gerald has been marked by death as a child, having accidentally killed his brother and, ultimately, he abandons himself to a frozen death in the snow, fulfilling Birkin's opening prediction that "a murderee is a man who is murderable. And a man who is murderable is a man who in a pro-found if hidden lust desires to be murdered" (*WL* 33). Gerald's death, then, is much more fully contextualised than the suicide of his forerunner

Siegmund in *The Trespasser*, as being the product of a society in love with death. And as John Worthen points out, this message is even more overt in the 1916 version that publishers unanimously decided "could not" be published during the war (*FWL* xxxvii). In *The First Women in Love*:

> Birkin is haunted by the tragedy of Gerald because "It was not the death he could not bear, but the nothingness of the life and death put together" (*FWL* 443). The wartime novel found not just the deaths in war unbearable, but "the nothingness of the life and death put together": its summing-up of the civilization which led to such a war. (Worthen 1999: 24)

In this light, Lawrence's engagement with Wagner in *Women in Love* is also an indictment of—and something like a requiem to Wagner—a turn away from the limitlessness of Wagner that threatens to dissolve selfhood and towards the miniaturism of song reinforced by his friendships with Heseltine and Gray.

Bax, on the other hand, would remain throughout his life a self-confessed "brazen romantic" (Bax 1943: 111) and Wagnerite, despite the burgeoning of musical modernism. After the war he was known for a while as Britain's leading symphonist, but his work for large-scale orchestra seemed closer to nineteenth than to twentieth-century tastes and thus outdated compared to his contemporaries, Holst and Ralph Vaughan Williams.[22] Bax's tone poem *Tintagel* is his sole work to maintain a presence in the concert repertoire. Lawrence, however, would embrace smaller parts within increasingly fragmentary wholes, heralded by a return to the folk song in *Women in Love*.

Sing-Songs in Cornwall: From Wagner to Warlock

Philip Heseltine, who also composed under the pseudonym of Peter Warlock, is now usually remembered for his "exclusively miniaturist and lyrical" talent, mostly his songs for voice and piano (Gray 1938: 23). His close friend, and first biographer, Cecil Gray attests that "he wrote no works on a heroic scale, and very little music for the larger instrumental or vocal combinations", but was "quite simply, the best song-writer this country has produced since the death of John Dowland some three centuries ago" (Gray 1938: 23–25). His first song publications were in 1919, but he was writing songs during his two-month stay with the Lawrences in Cornwall in 1916 as his correspondence with Delius reveals (Gray

1938: 110).[23] Two of his best-loved pieces are "Kan Kernow" (A Cornish Carol) and "Kan Nadelik" (A Cornish Christmas Carol), settings of texts in Cornish by Henry Jenner, whose *Handbook of the Cornish Language* published in 1904 launched a revival of the dead language that Heseltine undertook to learn (Gray 1938: 162).[24] Heseltine explained that "The music of these carols is inseparably associated with the actual Cornish words" (Gray 1938: 170). In a similar way, the strange sounds of the Gaelic language appealed to Lawrence in Marjory Kennedy-Fraser's *Songs of the Hebrides*, loaned to him by Gray in Cornwall. Catherine Carswell recalls how he howled "The Seal Woman's Song" "in what he ingenuously supposed to be the Gaelic, at the same time endeavouring to imitate the noise made by a seal!" (quoted *3L* 164 n.6).

Through Heseltine, we can begin to trace a confluence of musical connections that though small would become important to Lawrence's wartime thinking about the arts and the role of the artist; central themes of *Women in Love*, in which Birkin proclaims that "every true artist is the salvation of every other ... only artists produce for each other the world that is fit to live in" (*WL* 208). Such was the basis for Lawrence's ideal community of Rananim, conceived at a house party during the first Christmas of the war and for which various possible locations were mooted. In November 1915, Heseltine suggested an exodus to the composer Delius's abandoned orange plantation in Florida, but instead, on 1 January 1916, he joined Lawrence on his arrival in Porthcothan, Cornwall, where they drew up plans for a private publishing venture "The Rainbow Books and Music" (*2L* 542).

Although their plans foundered, for a while Lawrence believed that Heseltine "is one of the men who will count, in the future" (*2L* 442). As Gray records, "There is abundant evidence in Lawrence's correspondence at this time ... to show that he regarded Philip as his chosen disciple, together with Middleton Murry and Katherine Mansfield" (Gray 1938: 116). Through Heseltine, Lawrence met Gray, another composer and musical critic, and both left deeper marks on Lawrence's work than the brief sketches of Heseltine as the composer Julius Halliday in *Women in Love* or of Gray as Cyril Scott in *Aaron's Rod* (1922).[25] Indeed, Halliday plays a decisive, if small, role in the chapter titled "Fetish", by denouncing a predominantly visual culture and thus alerting the reader to the importance of sound in *Women in Love*: "I'm sure life is all wrong because it has become much too visual—we can neither hear nor feel nor understand, we can only see" (*WL* 78).[26]

The influence of Heseltine and Gray was all the greater because Lawrence was otherwise largely starved of the company of artists and particularly of music during his time in Cornwall (from January 1916 to October 1917). The wide-ranging references to music that fill his early letters are conspicuously absent from his letters from Zennor, where the Lawrences lived without a piano from April 1916 until August 1917, when they finally acquired an old one with a "red silk front—five guineas—nice old musty twang with it" (*3L* 153). The arrival of the piano coincided with Gray's move to nearby Bosigran and his loan to Lawrence of *Songs of the Hebrides*, which included songs like "Kishmul's Galley" that would remain a firm favourite (*5L* 570).

A particularly riotous sing-song—of songs from Frieda's native land of Germany—drew an angry visit from the coastal watch, as Lawrence describes in "The Nightmare" chapter of *Kangaroo* and which Gray recalls as follows in his memoir *Musical Chairs*:

> The Lawrences were spending the night at my house, and after supper, when it was already dark, we were sitting around the fire amusing ourselves by singing German folk-songs (it must have been a horrible noise) when suddenly there came a peremptory hammering at that the front door ... in marched half a dozen or so men with loaded rifles, who proceeded to search the house ... Finding nothing incriminating on the premises, the intruders withdrew, with operatic gestures like a Verdi chorus, and blood-curdling threats. (Gray 1948: 127)

Gray's mocking reference to Verdi finds an echo in Lawrence's feelings of disgust about *Aïda* expressed in *Aaron's Rod* (discussed in Chap. 6), although opera may have been another bond between the two men. During the war, Gray was engaged in writing two operas: *Deirdre*, based on the Irish legend that was "probably the progenitor of the Tristan story" (Parlett 1997: n.p.), and *The Temptation of St Anthony* (after Flaubert).[27] In Lawrence's fictionalised version of the events described above, Gray (renamed Sharpe, perhaps after another Cecil, the folk-song collector Cecil J. Sharp discussed in Chap. 2) is less insouciant than Richard Lovatt Somers (based on Lawrence): "Then Somers sang to himself, in an irritating way, one German song after another, not in a songful, but in a defiant way. / *'Ännchen von Tharau'*—*'Schatz mein Schatz, reite nicht so weit won mir.'*—*'Zu Strasbourg auf der Schanz, da fing mein Trauern an*—' This went on until Sharpe asked him to stop" (*K* 233).

In the final months of the war, Lawrence turned more fully to the solace of song, writing to Gray nostalgically in January 1918 about Cornwall (following his expulsion under the Defence of the Realm Act in October 1917) and confiding: "I'm not writing anything – only sit learning songs, which I find a great amusement. I can read well enough to learn a song nicely in about a quarter of an hour – so I have already got off twenty or thirty. I don't know why it amuses me so much more than reading or writing" (*3L* 197). I will consider this turn to song more fully in Chap. 6, but already there are clues in *Women in Love*, as regards the self-sufficiency of Ursula's solo singing as opposed to Gerald's Wagnerian limitlessness. Towards the end of the novel, Ursula sings an old Scottish song "Annie Laurie", included in *The National Song Book* (Lawrence's college textbook [Chambers 1980: 81]). There is, perhaps, a nationalistic aspect to Ursula's performance of this old British song to an audience of Germans but, balancing against this, there are also instances of German songs; for instance, in "Water-Party", Ursula (like Somers in *Kangaroo*) sings "Ännchen von Tharau". In context, her singing is an expression of self-sufficiency that contrasts with Gudrun's need for connection[28]:

> Ursula seemed so peaceful and sufficient unto herself, sitting there unconsciously crooning her song, strong and unquestioned at the centre of her own universe. And Gudrun felt herself outside. Always this desolating, agonised feeling that she was outside of life, an onlooker, whilst Ursula was a partaker, caused Gudrun to suffer from a sense of her own negation, and made her, that she must always demand the other to be aware of her, to be in connection with her. (*WL* 165)

By the end of the novel, this difference between the sisters is even more marked. Ursula's performance of "Annie Laurie" brings her a perfect flowering of self and a demonstration of her "golden" quality (coveted by Birkin in "Moony"): "She was dilated and brilliant, like a flower in the morning sun. She felt Birkin looking at her, as if he were jealous of her, and her breasts thrilled, her veins were all golden. She was as happy as the sun that had just opened above clouds. And everybody seemed so admiring and radiant, it was perfect" (*WL* 407). Immediately, however, the text reminds us of the world outside the Alpine hut—"it was so terribly cold … intense, murderous coldness" (*WL* 407)—and so an alternative stage is set for the contrasting tragedy of Gerald's self-abandonment amidst the icy wastes. A few pages later, Gudrun hears a "manly, reckless, mocking voice" singing

"Die Müllerin" (*WL* 419), an old soldier's song about a rebellious miller's wife; a prelude to her final deathly struggle with Gerald.[29] Ursula's self-sufficiency, on the other hand, opens into a contrasting world of sunshine and flowers, in which she is a self-contained individual in tune with the cosmos, as she moves closer to Birkin's notion of star equilibrium.

"War in Heaven": Lawrence and Holst

As a love death, or even as a war death, there is nothing heroic about Gerald's end: for Gudrun, "this was a barren tragedy, barren, barren" (*WL* 476). Such feelings of futility are echoed by war poets, particularly Wilfred Owen, and in combatant war novels, such as Richard Aldington's anti-heroic *Death of a Hero* (1929). But Holst's *Mars the Bringer of War*, the first movement of *The Planets* (1918), also insists on "the reality of warfare rather than glorify[ing] deeds of heroism", as Michael Short asserts (Short 1990: 123). A stark contrast with Elgar's rousing *The Spirit of England* (composed 1915–1917), *Mars* also breaks decisively with the traditions of battle music exemplified in Strauss's tone poem *Ein Heldenleben* (*A Hero's Life*): instead it is "played at a quick tempo, faster than a normal march, to give an enhanced impression of inhuman mechanical forces, lurching forward relentlessly and unstoppable; an uncanny premonition of the mechanized warfare of the later twentieth century" (Short 1990: 123). When *Mars* was premiered in the final weeks of the war, it was described by a contemporary as "the most ferocious piece of music in existence" (qtd. Short 1990: 124).

Like Stravinsky's *The Rite of Spring*, Holst's *Mars* was composed shortly before the First World War and was similarly prescient of a coming conflagration that would strike observers like Lawrence as resembling "a war in heaven" (*2L* 390). Stravinsky had been a major influence on Holst's decision to embark on a large-scale orchestral work, following two seasons of the Ballets Russes in London in 1913. "For Holst", Short argues, "Stravinsky's music opened up a new world of sound, particularly the rhythms of *The Rite of Spring* and the orchestral colour of *The Firebird* and *Petrushka*" (Short 1990: 115). Indeed, *The Planets* has been described as the "English *Sacre du Printemps*", although at its premiere in 1918, Ernest Newman felt that Holst's *Suite* made "the latest Stravinsky 'seem comically infantile'" (qtd. Head 1993: 22). And Short observes that "it might just as well have been called the English *Five Pieces for Orchestra*: for there is as much evidence of Schoenberg as there is of Stravinsky in the music"

(Short 1990: 120–121). Indeed, the provisional title for *The Planets* was *Seven Pieces for Large Orchestra*, in homage to Schoenberg's work that Holst heard in January 1914. Schoenberg's experiments in chromaticism revolutionised traditional harmonic structures by redefining the relationship between notes: this not only developed the spatial dimension of music, as discussed in Chap. 4 but had ethical implications since the notes in the 12-tone row were equally weighted. Holst also gave equal weighting to the movements in his *Suite*, which he perceived as parts within a whole. Accordingly, his daughter, Imogen Holst, relates that he was very unhappy when the pieces were separated, as frequently they were (Short 1990: 120).

In the autumn of 1914, amidst continuing concern about German atrocities in Belgium, reports of casualties on the Western Front and growing uncertainty in Britain, Holst began work on *Venus, the Bringer of Peace*, which Short describes as "one of the most sublime evocations of peace in music" (Short 1990: 126). A much slower tempo and thinner texture than *Mars*, with orchestration for harps, flutes, triangle, shimmering strings, and solo violin, create an ethereal soundscape for *Venus*. The contrast between *Mars* and *Venus* is strikingly similar to the two modes of agitation and stillness in Lawrence's *Women in Love*. The opening bars of *Venus* are identical to the beginning of an earlier song setting by Holst "A Vigil of Pentecost", reflecting a contemporary trend to weave songs into larger compositions, which Lawrence imitates in his novel. Conversely, a section of *Jupiter* was subsequently adapted as a hymn setting of "I vow to thee my country", although the "heavens" which Holst depicted in *The Planets* are more influenced by mystical sources than conventionally Christian ones. Like Lawrence, Holst was interested in theosophy, however both men developed their own unique mystical beliefs.[30] Holst was also a very literary composer, who shared some of Lawrence's great influences including Thomas Hardy: Holst's tone poem *Egdon Heath: A Homage to Thomas Hardy* (1927) is among his finest works. It is intriguing that these two artists shared similar sources in creating the earliest works of British modernism and that both took a radically spatial turn in their wartime compositions.

As Short writes, "Holst's aim was to depict in music the mystery and wonder of outer space", culminating in *Neptune*, the final movement of *The Planets*.

Neptune then being the furthest known planet of the solar system [Pluto was only discovered in 1930]. He conveyed its remoteness by keeping the dynamics *pp* throughout, ending in total silence; a silence which is as much a part of the music as the preceding notes. This transcendental evocation of the vastness of space is an evocative example of the power which music has to express concepts beyond the comprehension of the rational mind. (Short 1990: 131)

This description evokes the "transcendent reality" of the "Excurse" episode in *Women in Love*, discussed earlier in this chapter, in which Ursula and Birkin arrive at a consummation of "star equilibrium" in "a living body of darkness and silence and subtlety, the mystic body of reality" (*WL* 312, 320). Significantly, Holst ends *Neptune* (and the *Suite*) with an unseen chorus of female voices singing wordlessly and fading into silence after the orchestra ceases to play. Imogen Holst, describes the first performance as "unforgettable, with its hidden chorus of women's voices growing fainter and fainter ... until the imagination knew no difference between sound and silence" (Holst 2008: 53). This innovative fade-out suggests the immateriality of sound and so takes a very different line from the "great, weighty, metallic" music of Stravinsky described at the beginning of this chapter (Rosenfeld 1920: 192). Holst's music speaks instead to a return to the idea of "absolute music", without programme or meaning, fading into an inaudible Pythagorean music of the spheres.

After *The Planets*, and after the war, "Holst's compositional style took a decided turn towards austerity and modernity", as Christopher M. Scheer notes of his *First Choral Symphony* (1925); "a four-movement choral work based on texts of John Keats" (Scheer 2016: 116). In a similar way to *Women in Love*, Holst's setting of "Ode on a Grecian Urn" is characterised by "musical momentum and stasis": Scheer describes it as "a meditation on his own experience of war", in which "The image of youth forever frozen on the side of the urn, happy, in love, free from the passions and strife of human existence, call to mind 'the fallen' of the First World War" (Scheer 2016: 118–120). For Lawrence, however, "passions and strife" remained a necessary condition in the "frictional to-and-fro" of both art and life that he continued to explore in his modernist works of the 1920s. He was increasingly critical not only of Wagnerian harmonies but of large-scale productions, preferring the simplicity and self-containment of solo song. His ethical and musical interests in the spatial relationships between part and whole registered in *Women in Love* become more marked in his sequences of war poems, "All of Us" (1916) and *Bay* (1920), and his novel about an itinerant flute player, *Aaron's Rod* (1922).

Recommended Listening

Bax	*Tintagel*
Debussy	"Jardin sous la pluie"
Herder	"Ännchen von Tharau"
Holst	*The Planets Suite*
Kennedy-Fraser	"The Seal woman's song" from *Songs of the Hebrides*
Stravinsky	*The Rite of Spring*; *Three Pieces for String Quartet.*
Wagner	*Tristan und Isolde* (particularly Act III)
Warlock	"Kan Kernow" (A Cornish Carol); "Kan Nadelik" (A Cornish Christmas Carol)

Notes

1. Lissajous patterns are discussed, for example, in John Tyndall's study of *Sound* (1857). Tyndall (1820–1893) was a prominent physicist who published popular books, based on his public lectures. Jeff Wallace provides some context of his influence, within a broader study of Lawrence's engagement with science (Wallace 2005: 68–69, 92–93).
2. In the second opera in Wagner's *Ring* tetralogy, *Die Walküre* (first performed in 1870), the Valkyries are horsewomen who bear slain heroes to Valhalla.
3. The term "polyphonic novel" appears in the heading of the first chapter in Bakhtin 1984.
4. This well-known metaphor derives from Goethe.
5. For a discussion of parallels with Adorno and Schoenberg in Lawrence's novella *St. Mawr*, see Moss 2015.
6. In my view, the best discussion of motion and inertia in Lawrence's work remains "Lawrentian Stillness" in Bersani 1978: 156–85. In his psychoanalytical reading, Bersani notes how Lawrentian stillness maps against "a profound tendency in Lawrence to get rid of sex altogether" (Bersani 1978: 169), which problematises the relationship that Birkin seeks with Ursula.
7. For a discussion of the theme of "rites" in *Women in Love*, see Joyce Carol Oates: "*Women in Love* is a strangely ceremonial, even ritualistic work. In very simple terms it celebrates love and marriage as the only possible salvation for twentieth-century man and dramatizes the fate of those who resist the abandonment of the ego demanded by love: a sacrificial rite, an ancient necessity" (Oates 1978: 561).
8. Nijinsky introduced a new athleticism into ballet, which also drew attention to the male body, as discussed in Jones 2013: 8. In a section of her book titled "*The Rite of Spring* and D.H. Lawrence", Jones mainly discusses "The Woman Who Rode Away" (109–117). For discussion of the

"Russian Ballet" scene in the "Breadalby" chapter of *Women in Love* (and other dance scenes in the novel), see Zimring 2013: 69–71. There is also a reference to the "Russian ballet" in Lawrence's essay "The Hopi Snake Dance" (*MM* 80).

9. Debussy's ballet *Jeux* (1913) was premiered one month before *Le Sacre du Printemps* and has been overshadowed by it, but his depiction of a tennis match between Bloomsbury artists might suggest another model for what Lawrence calls "frictional to-and-fro" (*WL* 486).

10. Heseltine "saw little merit in the early Stravinsky works (though he would later revise his opinion somewhat)" (Smith 1997: 14). Intriguingly, however, Heseltine may have been involved in making the first recordings of *The Rite*: http://www.arkivmusic.com/classical/album.jsp?album_id=544061

11. For a discussion of the complexities of Lawrence's relationship with Futurism as it pertains to this novel, see Harrison 2003: 126–75.

12. There are many critical interpretations of this much-discussed scene: my intention here is not to elide other readings but to draw attention to neglected acoustic aspects of the novel. Most relevant to my analysis here is Terri Mester's reading of Gudrun's dance in front of the cattle in "Water-Party", in which her "atavistic, convulsive movement reminiscent of Nijinsky's Dalcroze-inspired choreography for the dehumanized masses in *Le Sacre du printemps*" becomes "a 'constitutive symbol' of an earlier scene in which Gudrun observed Gerald violently compel his horse at a railway crossing" (Mester 1997: 113–114).

13. For a brief consideration of the congruity between Gertler's painting and Lawrence's project in *Women in Love*, see Kinkead-Weekes 1996: 343.

14. Lawrence met Katherine Mansfield and John Middleton Murry, co-editors of *Rhythm*, following an invitation from Mansfield to contribute to the journal in January 1913 (*1L* 507).

15. Thomas Gibbons (1988) suggests that Lawrence discovered Chladni patterns through the theosophical book *Thought-Forms* (1901), by Annie Besant and C.W. Leadbetter.

16. The quotation is from *Lohengrin and Parsifal* (1904) by Alice Leighton Cleather and Basil Crump. Another theosophist, William Ashton Ellis, was the founding editor of *The Meister*, the quarterly journal of the London Wagner Society (Furness 1982: 90).

17. See also DiGaetani 1978; Martin 1982.

18. In this letter to Catherine Carswell, Lawrence also writes about rhythm and movement in her poetry and the free verse of Edgar Lee Masters's *Spoon River Anthology*, which he commends as "good, but too static" (*2L* 503).

19. Despite their mutual despondency and distress about the war, both produced some of their best work during this period. Bax's *Tintagel* remains his most played piece and Lawrence's two major novels, *The Rainbow* and *Women in Love*, were substantially written during the war. This was a

surprisingly prolific period for his writing and the development of his thinking: his philosophical essays *The Crown* were serialised in *Signature* (1915),
four volumes of poetry *Look! We Have Come Through* (1917), *Amores*
(1916), *New Poems* (1918), *Bay* (1920), his first travel book *Twilight in
Italy* (1916), his first (unpublished) attempt at literary criticism/philosophy
Study of Thomas Hardy and the beginnings of a second, *Studies in Classic
American Literature*, and several short stories, some of which were later
revised for inclusion in his second collection *England, My England* (1922).

20. William May suggests that Lawrence features Cohen in his poem "Piano"
    (1918), written "after their brief meeting" (May 2013: 51), although this
    seems unlikely given its origins in a draft written several years earlier in
    1906–1908.

21. Bax also knew Heseltine, Gray, and Maitland Radford, the son of Dolly
    Radford and a doctor, who attended to Lawrence in Porthcothan in
    February 1916 (*2L* 530).

22. It is interesting to consider whether Bax's Wagnerian background was a
    limiting factor in his success, in terms of what Lewis Foreman describes as
    a continuance in British institutions of "the very real musical conflict that
    had been fought on the Continent twenty years before between the parti-
    sans of Wagner" (Foreman 1983: 11). At the Royal College of Music,
    which Holst and Vaughan Williams attended, "composition was taught
    under the gimlet eye of Stanford, reflecting the Brahmsian approach",
    while the Royal Academy of Music, attended by Bax, "tended to be freer
    and more Wagner-orientated".

23. Delius wrote to Heseltine in January 1916: "Your song The Curlew is
    lovely and gave me the greatest pleasure … there is real emotion in your
    song—the most essential quality for a composer". As Gray notes this set-
    ting was destroyed and has "no connection with the later song-cycle of the
    same name … although the germ of the music may have been the same"
    (Gray 1938: 110–111).

24. Jenner's wife Katharine Jenner wrote the book titled *Christian Symbolism*
    (1910) that Lawrence read in the early months of the war and which
    helped him to "understand the Celtic Symbolism in its entirety" (*2L* 250).
    This interest in Celticism was another link with Bax, Gray, and Heseltine.

25. Cyril Scott is the name of another composer (1879–1970), also a poet,
    philosopher, and enthusiast of the occult.

26. Their relationship was increasingly strained, although Heseltine visited
    again in August 1916, made efforts in December 1917 to get *Women in
    Love* published and in January 1918 sent Lawrence a copy of the *Book of
    Kells* (*3L* 196). The final rupture came in 1921 when Heseltine demanded
    changes to allegedly libellous details in the final version of *Women in Love*
    (primarily relating to his relationship with a woman called the "Puma"
    thinly veiled as the "Pussum").

27. The *Deirdre* legend had been taken up in the Celtic revival by W.B. Yeats (1907) and J.M. Synge (1910) and was a shared interest with Bax. Gray's operas would only be finished many years later.
28. Terri Mester observes that Gudrun's dance dramatises her "jealousy over Ursula's self-sufficiency and her own feelings of jealousy" (Mester 1997: 114).
29. "Die Müllerin" is probably drawn from Frieda's repertoire of soldiers' songs (see *WL* 577 n.419: 38).
30. The evocation of *Uranus* as "a Magician" may point to theosophical sources, which Raymond Head has argued play a significant role in *The Planets*: he emphasises the influence of Alan Leo's book *The Art of Synthesis* (1912) and of Holst's association with George R.S. Mead, former secretary to Blavatsky and active theosophist until 1907 (Head 1993: 17–19).

REFERENCES

Adorno, T.W. 2006. *Philosophy of New Music*. Trans. Robert Hullot-Kentor. Minneapolis/London: University of Minnesota Press.

Bakthin, Mikhail. 1984. *Problems of Dostoevsky's Poetics*. Minneapolis: University of Minnesota Press.

Bax, Arnold. 1943. *Farewell, My Youth*. London: Longman's, Green and Co.

Benson, Stephen. 2003. Polyphony and Music in Bakhtin and Kundera. *Narrative* 11 (3): 292–311.

Bersani, Leo. 1978. Lawrentian Stillness. In *A Future for Astyanax: Character and Desire in Literature*, 156–185. London: Marion Boyars.

Chambers, Jessie [E.T.]. 1980. *D.H. Lawrence: A Personal Record by E.T.* Cambridge: Cambridge University Press.

Cole, Sarah. 2003. *Modernism, Male Friendship and the First World War*. Cambridge: Cambridge University Press.

Damon, Samuel Foster. 1935. *Amy Lowell: A Chronicle*. Boston: Houghton.

DiGaetani, John Louis. 1978. Chapter 2: Situational Myths: Richard Wagner and D.H. Lawrence. In *Richard Wagner and the Modern British Novel*, 58–89. London: Associated University Presses.

Eksteins, Modris. 1990. *Rites of Spring: The Great War and the Birth of the Modern Age*. London: Black Swan.

Epstein, Josh. 2014. *Sublime Noise: Musical Culture and the Modernist Writer*. Baltimore: Johns Hopkins University Press.

Fleishman, Avrom. 1985. "He Do the Polis in Different Voices": Lawrence's Later Style. In *D.H. Lawrence: A Centenary Consideration*, ed. Peter Balbert and Philip L. Marcus, 162–179. Ithaca: Cornell University Press.

———. 1990. Lawrence and Bakhtin: Where Pluralism Ends and Dialogism Begins. In *Rethinking Lawrence*, ed. Keith Brown, 109–119. Milton Keynes: Open University Press.

Foreman, Lewis. 1983. *Bax: A Composer and His Times*. London/Berkeley: Scolar Press.

———. 2018. Arnold Bax. *Oxford National Dictionary of Biography Online*. https://doi.org/10.1093/ref:odnb/30645

Fry, Helen. 2008. *Music & Men: The Life and Loves of Harriet Cohen*. Stroud: The History Press.

Furness, Raymond. 1982. *Wagner and Literature*. Manchester: Manchester University Press.

Gibbons, Thomas. 1988. "Allotropic States" and "Fiddle-Bow": D.H. Lawrence's Occult Sources. *Notes and Queries* 35 (3): 338–341.

Gray, Cecil. 1938. *Peter Warlock: A Memoir of Philip Heseltine*. London/Toronto: Jonathan Cape.

———. 1948. *Musical Chairs or Between Two Stools: Life and Memoirs*. London: Home & Van Thal.

Harrison, Andrew. 2003. *D.H. Lawrence and Italian Futurism: A Study of Influence*. Amsterdam/New York: Rodopi.

Head, Raymond. 1993. Holst—Astrology and Modernism in *The Planets. Tempo* 187: 15–22.

Holst, Imogen. 2008. *Gustav Holst: A Biography*. London: Faber.

Jones, Susan. 2013. *The Rite of Spring* and D.H. Lawrence. In *Literature, Modernism and Dance*, 109–117. Oxford: Oxford University Press.

Kinkead-Weekes, Mark. 1996. *D.H. Lawrence: Triumph to Exile 1912–1922*. Cambridge: Cambridge University Press.

Leone, Matthew. 2010. *Shapes of Openness: Bakhtin, Lawrence, Laughter*. Newcastle-upon-Tyne: Cambridge Scholars.

Lodge, David. 1985. Lawrence, Dostoevsky, Bakhtin: D.H. Lawrence and Dialogic Fiction. *Renaissance and Modern Studies* 29 (1): 16–32.

Martin, Stoddard. 1982. Chapter 9: Lawrence. In *Wagner to "The Waste Land": Swinburne, Wilde, Symons, Shaw, Moore, Yeats, Joyce, Lawrence, Eliot*, 168–193. London: Macmillan.

May, William. 2013. Modernism's Handmaid: Dexterity and the Female Pianist. *Modernist Cultures* 8 (1): 42–60.

Melnick, Daniel C. 1994. *Fullness of Dissonance: Modern Fiction and the Aesthetics of Music*. London/Toronto: Associated University Presses.

Mester, Terri A. 1997. *Movement and Modernism: Yeats, Eliot, Lawrence, Williams and Early Twentieth-Century Dance*. Fayetteville: University of Arkansas Press.

Meyers, Rollo H. 1911. The Art of Claude Debussy. *Rhythm* 2: 29–34.

Millington, Barry. 2006. *The New Grove Guide to Wagner and His Operas*. Oxford: Oxford University Press.

Moss, Gemma. 2015. A "Beginning Rather than an End": Popular Culture and Modernity in D.H. Lawrence's *St. Mawr. Journal of D.H. Lawrence Studies* 4 (1): 119–139.

Nietzsche, Friedrich. 1911. *The Case of Wagner*. Trans. Anthony M. Ludovici. Edinburgh/London: T.N. Foulis. Project Gutenberg. http://www.gutenberg. org/files/25012/25012-pdf.pdf

Oates, Joyce Carol. 1978. Lawrence's *Götterdämmerung*: The Apocalyptic Vision of *Women in Love*. *Critical Inquiry* 4 (3): 559–578.

Parlett, Graham. 1997. The Unwritten Operas of Arnold Bax. http://arnoldbax. com/the-unwritten-operas-of-arnold-bax-by-graham-parlett

Preston, Peter. 2011a. "Beyond the Sound of Words": Speech and Silence in *Women in Love*. In *Working with Lawrence: Texts, Places, Contexts*, 58–71. Nottingham: Communications Press.

———. 2011b. "A Wave of Disruptive Force": Violence in *Women in Love*. In *Working with Lawrence: Texts, Places, Contexts*, 37–57. Nottingham: Communications Press.

Rekveld, Joost. 1998. Symmetry and Harmonics. http://www.joostrekveld. net/?p=252

Richards, Fiona. 2015. The Goat-God in England: A Musical Context for Lawrence's Fascination with Pan. *D.H. Lawrence Review* 40 (1): 90–106.

Rosenfeld, Paul. 1920. *Musical Portraits: Interpretations of Twenty Modern Composers*. New York: Harcourt, Brace and Howe.

Scheer, Christopher M. 2016. "A Direct and Intimate Realization": Holst and Formalism in the 1920s. In *British Music and Modernism, 1895–1960*, ed. Matthew Riley, 109–124. Abingdon/New York: Ashgate.

Schober, Regina. 2008. Amy Lowell's Peasant Dance: Transcribing Primitivism in 'Stravinsky's Three Pieces, Grotesques, for String Quartet. *Amerikastudien/ American Studies*: 153–170.

Sessa, Anne Dzamba. 1979. *Richard Wagner and the English*. London: Associated University Presses.

Short, Michael. 1990. *Gustav Holst: The Man and His Music*. Oxford: Oxford University Press.

Sinyard, Neil. 2003. Stravinsky, Igor: *The Rite of Spring*. In *Encyclopedia of Literary Modernism*, ed. Paul Poplawski, 406–408. Westport: Greenwood Press.

Smith, Barry, ed. 1997. *The Occasional Writings of Philip Heseltine (Peter Warlock)*. London: Thames Publishing.

Wallace, Jeff. 2005. *D.H. Lawrence, Science and the Posthuman*. Basingstoke: Palgrave Macmillan.

Webber, Christopher. 2007. *Tintagel* on Record: A Survey. http://arnoldbax. com/tintagel-on-record-a-survey-by-christopher-webber

Wilson, Leigh. 2013. *Modernism and Magic: Experiments with Spiritualism, Theosophy and the Occult*. Edinburgh: Edinburgh University Press.

Worthen, John. 1999. The First *Women in Love*. *D.H. Lawrence Review* 28 (1–2): 5–28.

Zimring, Rishona. 2013. *Social Dance and the Modernist Imagination in Interwar Britain*. Farnham: Ashgate.

CHAPTER 6

Music, Noise, and the First World War: "All of Us", *Bay* and *Aaron's Rod*

INTRODUCTION

In July 1919, D.H. Lawrence wrote to Edward Marsh that "London made me so sick, physically, not metaphorically that I couldn't go out today. I should have liked so much to hear some Scarlatti also. / This place is so noisy" (*3L* 370). Lawrence frequently complained of the adverse effects of London on his physical health, but by 1919 he displayed an uncanny empathy for what was later understood as the shell-shocked combatant's "hypersensitivity to noise" (Jones et al. 2007: 1641).[1] He had witnessed the war trauma of friends serving on the Western Front, including Robert Nichols, whom he first met in 1915 in Lord Knutsford's Hospital for Officers suffering from "nerves ... shattered at the war" (*2L* 445). But Lawrence had also endured the horror of Zeppelin raids over London as recorded in letters (*2L* 389–390) and in his poems "Zeppelin nights" and "Bombardment".[2] The extent to which music could continue to offer consolation in a shatteringly "noisy" world is challenged by Lawrence's letter to Marsh and explored in his works written during and after the war.

Originating in wartime London, Lawrence's hypersensitivity to explosive and mechanical noises persisted throughout the final decade of his life, accompanying him on his departure from Europe in 1922 to Ceylon—where the "birds and creatures ... hammer and clang and rattle and cackle and explode all the livelong day, and run like little machines all the livelong night" (*4L* 225)—and to San Francisco: "Terrible the noise of *iron* all the

© The Author(s) 2019
S. Reid, *D.H. Lawrence, Music and Modernism*,
Palgrave Studies in Music and Literature,
https://doi.org/10.1007/978-3-030-04999-7_6

while, breaks my head: and the black, glossy streets with steel rails in ribbons like the path of death itself" (*4L* 290). Unable to unhear the sounds associated with war, for Lawrence they became conflated with the sounds of ever-encroaching industrialisation, affecting his responses to music and influencing a shift away from large-scale, unified forms during the war and its aftermath. This is a trajectory, already suggested in the use of folk songs as a counter to Wagnerism in *Women in Love*, which this chapter traces through his "little" books of war poems (*3L* 233), "All of Us" (1916–1918) and *Bay* (1920), into his episodic modernist novel *Aaron's Rod* (1922).

At the beginning of *Aaron's Rod*, we are told that "the War was over, and there was a sense of relief that was almost a new menace. A man felt the violence of the nightmare released now into the general air" (*AR* 5). The opening chapters take place in darkness, intensifying the resonances with the violent "waves of darkness" so vividly evoked in the "Moony" chapter of *Women in Love* (*WL* 247) and which reverberate throughout that novel. To some extent Aaron continues the picaresque wanderings of Birkin (Vine 1995: xvi–xvii), but his flight from his Midlands home, and then from England, is specifically enacted through music. Aaron's flute-playing supports his travels but also registers a phased withdrawal from the "nasty" spectacle of the Covent Garden opera (*AR* 46) and the "big, deep music" of the "great masters, Bach, Beethoven" (*AR* 167–168) in favour of the music of Scarlatti that Lawrence singled out in his letter to Marsh, and also Corelli and Pergolesi: "frail, sensitive, abstract music, with not much feeling in it, but a certain limpidity and purity" (*AR* 210).

In the world of *Aaron's Rod*—as in Lawrence's experiences of London during and after the war—there is little respite from violence and disintegration. The opening chapter describes the careless "smash[ing]" of a Christmas bauble as a metaphor for a shattered world—"[Aaron] felt the curious soft explosion of its breaking still in his ears", followed swiftly by "the vocal violence" of carol-singers outside (*AR* 11)—and ultimately Aaron's flute is "Smashed" to pieces by an anarchist bomb in "noisy Florence" (*AR* 284, 247). However, this is a fate that Lawrence felt the contemporary novel ought to share. His essay, "The Future of the Novel" (1923)—retitled by the publisher as "Surgery for the Novel—Or a Bomb"—recommended radical treatment: "Supposing a bomb were put under this whole scheme of things, what would we be after? What feelings do we want to carry through, into the next epoch? What feelings will carry us through?" (*STH* 154). His series of essays about the novel in the 1920s diagnoses the problem in musical terms: "all our civilisation consists in harping on one string. Or at most, on two or three strings. Harp, harp, harp, twingle-twingle-twang! That's our civilisation, always on one note" or "Like a pianoforte with half the notes mute" (*STH* 201, 198). The problem is conceived as a matter of harmony, as illustrated by the Marchesa in *Aaron's Rod*: "What I can't stand is chords, you know: harmonies. A number of sounds all sounding together. It just makes me ill. It makes me feel so sick" (*AR* 225). Instead of conformity what is required, in this novel and his essays on *the* novel, is difference: an ethical relationship of part to whole, similar to the polyphonic qualities discussed in *Women in Love*, except that the "frictional to-and-fro" has been superseded by a more fluid conception that "All things flow and change, and even change is not absolute. The whole is a strange assembly of apparently incongruous parts, slipping past one another" (*STH* 196).[3]

The ability of music to evoke feelings and memories is an important theme in *Aaron's Rod*, as it was in Siegfried Sassoon's poem "Dead Musicians" (1918), which also pronounced the "Great names" obsolete ("Beethoven, Bach, Mozart"), since their "fugues and symphonies have brought / No memory of my friends who died" (qtd. Kennedy and Tate 2011: 2). *Aaron's Rod* explores how the association of music and memory has been complicated by the war; there are veterans in almost every chapter who tell of shattering events they are unable to forget, while Aaron's wealthy hostess Lady Franks trivialises notions of memory and loss by recounting how Beethoven makes her feel that she "will always find the things [she] ha[s] lost", such as her cloak (*AR* 169). Conversely, the Marchesa he meets in Florence, who has lost her ability to sing because of the war, says that orchestral music makes her "blind with hate" and "want to throw bombs" (*AR* 225): she recovers her voice by singing a "little" French song, "Derrière chez mon père" (*AR* 255–256), which is the antithesis of "the great Masters" (*AR* 167–168).[4]

A more general shift away from large-scale musical forms was asserted by Paul Rosenfeld in *Musical Portraits* (1920), in his claim that:

Of late a great adventure has befallen us ... We who were born and grew under the sign of Wagner have witnessed the twilight of the God ...

He has been displaced. A new music has come into being, and drawn near ... A song of Moussorgsky's or Ravel's, a few measures of Pelléas [et Mélisande] or Le Sacre du Printemps, a single fine moment in a sonata of Scriabine's or a quartet or a suite of Bloch's, give us a joy, an illumination, a satisfaction that little of the older music can equal. (Qtd. Deems Taylor 1920: 313)

This passage was quoted in a review in the same number of the *Dial* (September 1920) as Lawrence's short story "Adolf", so it is possible that he read it, although his sympathies were already shifting towards songs and away from opera, as my previous chapter suggested and as I will explore further in the next section of this chapter. Although Scriabin, Mussorgsky, and Debussy are favourably presented in *Aaron's Rod*, its main protagonist also turns to "older music" that uses smaller forms and structures. In this way, the seemingly modernist tendency towards fragmentation in *Aaron's Rod* also reaches back through Romanticism, although not in the sense of Wagner's utopian project of the *Gesamtkunstwerk* (Total Artwork): indeed, the notion of a unified whole is blown to pieces like Aaron's flute. Instead, Lawrence looks back to older traditions of song, which the Romantics had conceived as fragments. Beate Perrey, for example, describes a Romantic conception of musical form which "rejects the cardinal neo-Classical ideal of a whole, and advances instead an *aesthetics of fragmentation*" (qtd. Ferris 2010: 389). This provides a context for re-reading the "fragmented, wartime relationships, which occur in bits of time with almost no hint of progression" that Holly Laird perceives in *Bay* and "All of Us" (Laird 1988: 107), a description that also applies to *Aaron's Rod*. Musically, Perrey's argument extends to German *Lieder* by Schumann and Schubert and thus suggests thematic and structural parallels between *Aaron's Rod* and the picaresque wanderings of Schubert's *Winterreise*, which I will explore at the end of this chapter.

Firstly, however, I will consider more closely how Lawrence's wartime experiences in London exacerbated a shift away from the large-scale works of Handel and Wagner towards the simplicity of song, by way of a comparison with the pre-war swansongs to imperial London and unified aesthetic forms in H.G. Wells's *Tono-Bungay* (1909) and Ralph Vaughan Williams's *A London Symphony* (1914). The imperial aspects of the War provide the context for an exploration of Lawrence's outburst of "disgust" at the "sham Egypt" depicted in a performance of *Aïda* (*AR* 46), and how this is counterpointed by "All of Us", his "tiny book" of war poems (*3L* 51) based on the songs of the Egyptian fellaheen (labourers). Analysis of his other "little book" of war poems (*3L* 233), *Bay*, suggests thematic and structural interests in song and silence that on the one hand resonate with Debussy's muted response to war and, on the other, with the loose-knit structure and themes of Schubert's *Winterreise*, including the idea of "wintering" that helped to shape *Aaron's Rod* (*3L* 197).

"Noisy" London: Handel, Wagner, Vaughan Williams

Lawrence's response to wartime London was inextricably linked with the city's function as the command centre of the imperial war machine: "London—mid-war London, nothing but war, war. Lovely sunny weather, and bombs at midday in the Strand" (*K* 230). Significantly, Lawrence's letter about "noisy" London (*3L* 370), discussed above, is addressed to Marsh, who served as a Private Secretary for the wartime and post-war governments. It is significant, too, that Lawrence wrote this letter at 13 Guilford Street (London WC1) around the corner from Mecklenburgh Square (where he had begun writing *Aaron's Rod* in the autumn of 1917), and that both addresses are close to Coram's Fields, the site of the Foundling Hospital, where Handel had conducted annual performances of his *Messiah*.[5] This juxtaposition of Scarlatti—whose music he "should have liked so much to hear" (*3L* 370)—and Handel—whom he omits to mention—suggests an opposition between grand musical productions and simpler pieces that retain some ability to console on an individual basis rather than for a collective audience.

As early as 1908, in his first essay "Art and the Individual", Lawrence criticised the "drum thumping and artifice and extravagance" of the March in Handel's *Saul* (*STH* 141), and as the war loomed in 1914 he associated the music of the German-born composer with militarism in his short story "The Prussian Officer" (1914), originally titled "Honour and Arms" in reference to an aria from Handel's *Samson* (qtd. Cushman 1978: 209):

> Honour and arms scorn such a foe,
> Though I could end thee at a blow,
> Poor victory, to conquer thee,
> Or glory in thy overthrow!
> Vanquish a slave that is half slain!
> So mean a triumph I disdain.

Lawrence was not a pacifist, but the military triumphalism of such language, reinforced by Handel's rousing music, would have seemed repellent in light of the mass casualties of the First World War.[6] Instead, in his letter to Marsh in 1919, Lawrence yearns for Handel's near contemporary, Scarlatti, the Italian composer who had pleasant associations with his early years in London, when the singer Grace Crawford sang him an aria from

Scarlatti's opera *Il Pompeo* (Lovat Fraser 1970: 135),[7] and whose *Cantata Pastorale* shared the same origins as the traditional "Pastorella" sung to him by 16 Italian peasants on Christmas Eve of 1913 (*2L* 133)[8]—the last before the outbreak of the First World War. In *Aaron's Rod*, the titular protagonist will similarly turn to the Baroque music of Italy rather than to Handel, whose appeal to the massive choirs who sung his oratorios at venues such as Crystal Palace was decidedly at odds with this novel's revulsion against the "masses": "all that mass-consciousness, all that mass-activity—it's the most horrible nightmare" (*AR* 119).[9] Lawrence's quieter treatment of the biblical story of Aaron contrasts starkly with Handel's oratorio *Israel in Egypt*, in which large choruses predominate.

Increasingly, Lawrence conflated the cultural life of London with warmongering values that he rejected, until the noisiness of its streets became indistinguishable from many of the musical performances that he used to enjoy there. Cynthia Asquith noted that, in 1917, going to the opera was "The one thing which seemed able temporarily to take [Lawrence's] mind off the war" (Nehls 1957: 441) and, as late as April 1919, he was writing to S.S. Koteliansky that "I should like to go with you to the opera, en garçon, in the cheapest seats" (*3L* 354). But an anti-operatic stance emerges starkly from the London chapters of *Aaron's Rod*, in which the eponymous flautist plays for a season in the orchestra for the opera in Covent Garden. On his way to perform, Aaron Sisson falls ill in Covent Garden, where he is found and nursed back to health by his friend Rawdon Lilly, although: "The din in the market was terrific ... and Aaron suffered bitterly" (*AR* 93). Aaron, who has been seeking to detach himself from relationships, attributes his sickness to his affair with Josephine Ford—"I felt, the minute I was loving her, I'd done myself" (*AR* 89)—but it is significant that their liaison follows a performance of *Aïda*, an opera associated with nationalism and militarism which features in the chapter "At the Opera" as a disgusting spectacle that I discuss in the next section of this chapter.

Aaron's Rod marks a retreat from the noisy grand productions of Verdi and Wagner to the sensitivity of solo song. The Marchesa regains her voice by undergoing an awakening that reverses the process of "the fire-music putting Brunnhild [sic] to sleep" at the end of *Die Walküre*, the second part of Wagner's *Ring* cycle (*AR* 253–254).[10] The Marchesa's initial response to Aaron's flute is that "Perhaps it was more like waking to a sweet, morning-awakening, after a night of tormented, painful tense sleep" (*AR* 254). Then she is fully revived through the simplicity of an old

French song: "She sang free, with the flute gliding along with her. And oh, how beautiful it was for her! How beautiful it was to sing the little song in the sweetness of her *own* spirit ... The song ended, she stood with a dazed, happy face, like one just coming awake" (*AR* 256, my emphasis). Her husband stands by looking "strange and withered and gnome-like", reminiscent of the Nibelung Alberich, who forged the ring that precipitates the drama of Wagner's opera cycle.

Accordingly, while Paul Baker discerns a return to literary Wagnerism in *Aaron's Rod*, he rightly recognises Lawrence's ironic treatment since "the anti-heroic Aaron Sisson and the phlegmatic Marchesa are really the antithesis of the Wagnerian demi-gods" (Baker 1983: 84, 86). Nonetheless, Baker detects a "few passages of Wagnerian intensity", which demonstrate "Lawrence's mature control of Wagnerian cadence" (Baker 1983: 89). For example:

> [The Marchesa] was absolutely gone, like a priestess utterly involved in her terrible rites. And [Aaron] was part of the ritual only, God and victim in one. God and victim! All the time, God and victim. When his aloof soul realised, amid the welter of incantation, how he was being used,—not as himself but as something quite different—God and victim—then he dilated with intense surprise, and his remote soul stood up tall and knew itself *alone*. (*AR* 273, my emphasis)

Baker's analysis discerns that "The incantatory rhythm" is Wagnerian in its function of underlining the "destructiveness" of this love affair (Baker 1983: 89), but it would also be appropriate to describe the passage as anti-Wagnerian. The magical associations of "the welter of incantation" (quoted above) resonate with the wizardry attributed to Wagner (e.g. by Nietzsche in *The Case of Wagner*), but Aaron resists being subsumed by this music like a Wagnerian hero. Instead his soul stands "remote" and "alone", just as, in the preceding chapter, song reconnected the Marchesa with "the sweetness of her own spirit" (*AR* 256). In this respect, the shared root of "incantation" with "cantata"—from the Latin root "cantare" meaning "to sing"—reinforces the novel's positive associations with the cantatas of Scarlatti, Corelli, and Pergolesi.

For Lawrence, the ideal of Wagnerian synthesis was shattered by the war, but this concept had already been called into question by pre-war works which sought to reaffirm a unified model of the artwork even as they heralded the end of an era. The narrator of *Tono-Bungay*, Wells's condition of England novel, travels down the Thames in a destroyer pre-figuring the war, in a journey described as movements "in the London symphony": "Light after light goes down. England and the Kingdom, Britain and the Empire, the old prides and the old devotions, glide abeam, astern, sink down upon the horizon, pass—pass. The river passes—London passes, England passes" (qtd. Kennedy 2002: 140). This passage inspired Ralph Vaughan Williams to compose *A London Symphony* (Arblaster 1987: 21–25), premiered in 1914.[11] Vaughan Williams's second symphony cre-ates a beautiful and integrated soundscape from what he called "the noise and scurry" of pre-war London (qtd. Kennedy 2002: 137), including church bells, rain in Bloomsbury, street cries, night scenes, and the ebbing of the river Thames. But in hindsight, we can perceive a powerful elegy for a London that was about to be extinguished by war: there are apprehen-sions of darkness, decay, and impending doom throughout, particularly in its uncut 1914 version.

Both these works also suggest a powerful elegy for the large-scale uni-fied forms inherited from the nineteenth century: the realist novel and the symphony. Wells championed the inclusiveness of the novel form as against the formal strictures of Henry James and the Bloomsbury group and, accordingly, the narrator of *Tono-Bungay* insists that "I suppose what I'm really trying to render is nothing more nor less than Life—as one man has found it".[12] The broad sweep of *A London Symphony* mirrors this ambi-tion, even as its Epilogue fades out into silence. When Lawrence read *Tono-Bungay* (serialised in the first four issues of the *English Review* from December 1908—March 1909), he declared it "the best novel Wells has written—it is the best novel I have read for—oh, how long? But it makes me so sad. If you knew what a weight of sadness Wells pours into your heart as you read him—Oh, Mon Dieu! He is a terrible pessimist" (*1L* 119). Two poems that Lawrence drafted in 1909 (published during the war in his 1918 collection *New Poems*) respond to Wells's social criticism of London: "Embankment at Night, Before the War: Charity" and "Embankment at Night, Before the War: Outcasts" (*Poems* 104–107) contrast the mixed fortunes of those who dwell in "the singing mansions" beside the Thames with "this human blight" sleeping beneath the bridges (*Poems* 106). Like Vaughan Williams's music, Lawrence's poems also evoke a Wellsian ebbing of "The river's invisible tide" (*Poems* 107), a sense of receding or emptying out that is also emphasised in metaphors of stasis and silence. Although he had called Wells "a terrible pessimist", after the war Lawrence seems less optimistic about the unity of large-scale forms than either Wells or Vaughan Williams.[13] In the early 1920s, Lawrence turned instead to the fragment or the part. His essay "The Future of the Novel" describes the Gospels of Matthew, Mark, Luke, and John as "little early novels" and adds that "Plato's Dialogues, too, are queer little novels" (*STH* 154). By the time Lawrence wrote this in 1923, he had already experimented with two novels of his own that were composed from, or perhaps decomposed into, fragments or bits—namely the episodic *Aaron's Rod* and *Kangaroo* (1923), with its flashback "The Nightmare" chapter and another simply titled "Bits", recalling his provisional title for "All of Us".

From *Aïda* to *Lieder*: *Aaron's Rod* and "All of Us"

Aaron's Rod was conceived in London shortly after Lawrence's visits to the opera in November 1917 (*3L* 216), when he attended Puccini's *Madama Butterfly* and Mussorgsky's *Khovanshchina* (*3L* 179), Mozart's *The Abduction from the Seraglio* and, significantly for his novel about a flute player, *The Magic Flute* (*3L* 182, 181).[14] But it is Verdi's *Aïda* which features prominently in the early chapter "At the Opera".[15] Lawrence attended a performance on 13 November 1917, hosted by Cynthia Asquith (1968: 365) and accompanied by Nichols (no longer on active service, but "looking unbelievably strained and taut") and Augustus John, who recorded the extremity of Lawrence's reaction: "On leaving ... D.H.L. announced that he would like to howl like a dog" (Nehls 1957: 440–441). In Lawrence's fictional rendition, Aaron plays his flute in the orchestra, while his new friends in the audience are disgusted by the performance, especially Josephine: "The artist in her forgot everything, she was filled with disgust. The sham Egypt of *Aida* [sic] hid from her nothing of its shame. The singers were all colour-washed, deliberately colour-washed to a bright orange tint" (*AR* 46). The word "disgust" is used three times in this page-long description, culminating in "floods of burning disgust, a longing to destroy it all" (*AR* 47). Josephine then turns her attention to the audience, who unanimously "loved it":

> They cheered with mad enthusiasm. Josephine looked down on the choppy sea of applause, white gloves clapping, heads shaking. The noise was strange and rattling. What a curious multiple object a theatre-audience was! It seemed to have a million heads, a million hands, and one monstrous, unnatural consciousness. The singers appeared before the curtain—the applause rose up like clouds of dust. (*AR* 47)

The dust metaphor evokes both the sandy Egyptian landscape which is the setting for *Aïda* and the idea of a dead civilisation with a culture of death, associated with ancient Egypt but also with the post-war world depicted in *Aaron's Rod*. "The sham Egypt" described by Lawrence (*AR* 46) foreshadows the cultural imperialism that Edward Said would later attribute to *Aïda*. Verdi's opera was commissioned by the Khedive of Egypt as a special opera for Cairo (where it premiered in 1871) but operates entirely within European cultural codes, "one of which is to confirm the Orient as an essentially exotic, distant, and antique place in which Europeans can mount certain shows of force" (Said 1994: 134). Egypt was in fact a battleground during the First World War, which caused much suffering for the civilian population as well as Egyptian troops.

Said emphasises the "splendid noisiness" of Verdi's operas, as remarked, for instance, by the historian Paul Robinson, who links their musical stridency with their political intent:

> they were almost all intended as political operas, replete with rhetorical stridency, martial music, and unbuttoned emotions … "Drop the needle at random on a recording of a Verdi opera and you will usually be rewarded with a substantial racket". Robinson goes on to say that Verdi's splendid noisiness is effectively harnessed to such occasions as "parades, rallies and speeches", which during the Risorgimento were heard as Verdi's amplifications of real-life occurrences. (*Aida* [sic] is no exception, with, for example, early in Act II the tremendous ensemble piece "Su del nilo", for several soloists and a mass chorus). (Said 1994: 136)

For Said, the conflict between the ancient Egyptians and Ethiopians dramatised by *Aïda* was at least as much about the tensions in Verdi's own time within Italy and Europe. And these tensions resonate again with the political agitation several decades later as they are portrayed in the Italian chapters of *Aaron's Rod*. In Milan, Aaron witnesses a confrontation between anarchists and soldiers in which "The mob broke as if something had exploded inside it" (*AR* 185), foreshadowing the anarchist bomb in Florence that ultimately smashes his flute. Encouraged by his friend Lilly, Aaron drops the pieces of his broken instrument into the river Arno (*AR* 284), which evokes the river Nile given this passage's references to the biblical Aaron, who was enslaved with his brother Moses in Egypt.[16] Indeed, the novel ends with a final reference to Egypt in Lilly's closing speech about power: "It was that great dark power-urge which kept Egypt so intensely living for so many centuries" (*AR* 297). This reference to Egypt, like others in Lawrence's work, implies that "dead" civilisations may yet retain a seed of redemptive power.[17] For Adorno, in his brief review of *Aïda* written in 1929, the potential to redeem opera from crisis lay in "Aïda's beautiful music and the beautiful singing thereof" (Goehr 2009: 135). Lawrence recognises a similar potential, if not in *Aïda*, then in song itself. His Marchesa saves herself through song reversing the self-sacrifice of Verdi's Ethiopian princess.

Lawrence had already written back to the militarism and imperialism of *Aïda* in his translations of songs of the Egyptian fellaheen, as recorded by the German Egyptologist Heinrich Schäfer in *Die Lieder eines ägytischen Bauern* (*Poems* 696). Begun in December 1910, as his mother Lydia was dying, the poems of Lawrence's "All of Us" took on a new urgency and very different meaning when he returned to them in November 1916: he described them to J.B. Pinker "as a tiny book of poems of the present day … Give it the people as the 'war literature' they are looking for" (*3L* 51). The fellaheen had been recruited not only to the excavations of Egyptian antiquities as described in the base texts but also to imperial military causes since the late nineteenth century.[18] This situation escalated during the First World War when more than one million Egyptian soldiers defended Egypt, the Middle East (Saudi Arabia, Iraq, Jordan, and Palestine) and Europe, and more than half were killed (Al-Youm 2015: n.p.). Lawrence's "All of Us" poems penetrate behind the statistics, however, by focusing on how the war affects "those who are not fighting it: wives and lovers, parents and children, younger siblings", and thereby they "also circumvented the war's sheer size", as noted by Kate McLoughlin (2015: 51–52). These deceptively simple songs enabled Lawrence to focus on the individual tragedies otherwise drowned out in a sea of noise.

No-one was willing to publish "All of Us" and so it languished until 1919, when Lawrence reworked the sequence as "Bits" and sent the poems to Harriet Monroe, who published 12 under the title "War Films" in the After-the-War number of *Poetry* in July 1919 (the same month as his letter to Marsh about the sickening noise of London, with which this chapter began).[19] The poem "Zeppelin Nights" records bombing raids over London, with references to the war in other poems extending from the Western Front in Flanders to the Eastern Front in Mesopotamia, Turkey, and Salonika.[20] A recurrent focus on the tragedy of ordinary lovers separated by war chimes faintly (perhaps ironically) with the tragic love story of Aïda, the Ethiopian princess, and Radames, the Egyptian Captain, while allusions to tombs, graves, holes, and coffins may also recall their final entombment (*Poems* 143, 144, 146). In 1915, Lawrence had written to Cynthia Asquith (the intended dedicatee of "Bits") about his feelings of spending the first five months of the war "in the tomb" (*2L* 267), but he continued to resist the drive towards death that he perceived within the culture that fostered war, not least through his defiant sing-songs with friends (for instance, in Cornwall as discussed in Chap. 5).

Laird astutely observes that Lawrence's description of *Pansies* "could as easily describe 'Bits'" (or "All of Us"): "This little bunch of fragments is offered as a bunch of *pensées*, anglice pansies; a handful of thoughts. Or if you will have the other derivation of pansy, from *panser*, to dress or soothe a wound, these are salves and ointments and caustics, dressings for the mental and emotional wounds of the day" (Laird 1988: 108; *Poems* 667). Lawrence's 34 "tiny poems" do resemble fragments, but they are also constructed according to a looser unity, akin to a Romantic song cycle, that relates to the 134 *Lieder* on which they were based. Lee M. Jenkins writes, in a wide-ranging discussion of the significance of these poems, that "Lawrence found in folk song—both fellaheen and German—a mode of resistance to the deadly technologies of industry and the war, and yet 'All of Us' is also a working model of the way in which the folk tradition evolves in response to modernity" (Jenkins 2016: 37). In part, it is the subversive irreverence of folk song that appealed to Lawrence; something "a bit wicked" that he emulated in "All of Us" (*3L* 221) and that he appreciated in the "Volkslied [folk song]" contained in the edition of the *Minnesingers* he reviewed in January 1912: "A bookful of courtly, medi-aeval love-song soon cloys ... So the inclusion of coarse, harsh folksong among so much sugar-cream of sentiment is welcome" (*IR* 198). These *Lieder* were on his mind again in 1920–1921, when he wrote Part II of *Mr Noon*: Gilbert Noon is "a warbling Minnesinger" who is also transcribing a "book of songs" he finds in the home of his German hosts (*MN* 234–235), with reference perhaps to the *Minnesingers* and/or to Lawrence's own translations of Schäfer's *Lieder* and/or as a way of describing a new way of composing literature. To what extent, then, does Lawrence also bring the fragmentary structure of song books or song cycles to his other collection of war poems, *Bay*, and his opera-resistant novel *Aaron's Rod*?

"After the Opera": Silence and Songs

Akin to the poetry sequence "All of Us", *Bay* constitutes what Lawrence called a "little book ... à propos of the war" (*3L* 233). These 18 poems repurposed several of his unpublished juvenilia and integrated them with new verses written in 1917–1918 to form what Keith Cushman considers "a true sequence" that constitutes "much more than the sum of its parts" (Cushman 1988: 181, 183, 188). His description evokes something of Lawrence's conception, in "Why the Novel Matters", that "The whole is a strange assembly of apparently incongruous parts, slipping past one another" (*STH* 195), and Lawrence's ongoing ethical concern with the relationship between parts and putative whole that he registered in *Women in Love*. Unfortunately, however, *Bay* is rarely read or studied as a self-contained collection, hindered perhaps by Lawrence's reordering and dispersal of the poems within his *Collected Poems* (1928). *Bay* is also "less personal and less grand" than the collection *Look! We Have Come Through!* (1917) that preceded it (Cushman 1988: 188) and lacking in the individual gems of *New Poems* (1918), such as "Piano" and "Seven Seals".[21] In declining to publish "All of Us" and then taking so long to publish *Bay* (Lawrence joked that it would be among his "posthumous works" [*8L* 29]), Cyril Beaumont contributed lastingly, albeit unintentionally, to the neglect of Lawrence as a war poet.[22] But Beaumont's actions—and inactions—have also served to obscure the links between these collections of war poems and Lawrence's manifest interest in folk song and *Lieder* towards the end of the war.

As Cushman observes, the *Bay* poems "are written in Lawrence's early style, making use of traditional rhyme, metre and stanza in a flexible and often awkward manner" (Cushman 1988: 188). Like his early poems (indeed some originated in the same period), their simplicity owes something to the folk songs of his youth (discussed in Chap. 2), but the loose structure of the sequence may also derive from his closer acquaintance with German *Lieder*. Bethan Jones posits a "cyclical, accumulative" process in the imagery of the poems in *Bay*—which "spiral back on themselves as they gather oscillating associations" (Jones 2015: 68)—and which in turn is suggestive of the structuring both of Debussy's music, particularly the *arabesque* discussed in Chap. 4, and of Romantic song cycles from fragments that are yet linked musically.

Above all, the poems of *Bay* circle around a variety of musical genres and forms as if to question what is appropriate for war music. There were many available musical responses to war—encompassing an older tradition of heroic marches, from Handel's *Saul* to Richard Strauss's *Ein Heldenleben*; soldier's songs which were perceived as morale-boosting but varied from the nostalgic ("It's a Long Way to Tipperary") to the mildly satirical ("We Are the Rag-Time Infantry"); and a wave of requiems and memorials which largely followed the peace (see Kennedy 2017)—but in *Bay*, Lawrence critiques all of them. The best-known poem in the sequence, "After the Opera", mocks the predominantly female civilian audience for taking the staged "tragedy so becomingly" (*Poems* 39), seemingly oblivious to the real tragedy taking place almost within earshot across the channel. Opera seems trivial by comparison and the poet declares himself "glad to go back to where I came from" (*Poems* 39)—implicitly to the frontline as in "Going Back", the poem that followed on in the original sequence. These poems reference the void in understanding between combatants and non-combatants, which the poet imaginatively bridges in linking the "Sound of artillery" (*Poems* 127) at the front with the civilian's experience of Zeppelin raids over London (in "Bombardment"). But there is no invocation of the warrior's heroism.

The forms that Lawrence chooses for the poems of *Bay* are anti-heroic, mocking any associations of the title with the hero crowned with bay (Cushman 1988: 188). On the contrary, "On the March" apes the heroic form of the military march using monosyllables to represent a wearily repetitive and seemingly "endless" "tramp / Onward":

> Beat after beat falls sombre and dull.
> The wind is unchanging, not one of us knows
> What will be in the final lull
> When we find the place where this dead road goes. (*Poems* 122)

The beats of the poem also evoke the nostalgic wartime songs that anger Richard Lovat Somers in "The Nightmare" chapter of *Kangaroo*, which is based on Lawrence's personal experience: "This ghastly trailing song, like death itself ... The miserable songs—with their long long ways that ended in sheer lugubriousness: real death-wails! These for battle songs. The wails of a dying humanity" (*K* 229–230). The "long long ways" favoured in the popular songs quoted on these pages—"Tipperary" and "There's a long long trail a-winding"—echo with the "long road" of "On the March", where "Perhaps we shall come to oblivion" (*Poems* 122).[23]

The proximity of "lull" and "dead" in the stanza quoted above, reinforced by the poem's closing metaphor of "going to sleep the sleep with those / That fall forever" (*Poems* 123), suggests a trope of the deathly lullaby, developed throughout the cycle by repetition of the words "slumber" and "sleep" (ten times) and exemplified in "War-Baby" and "Winter-Lull". Lull provides the root of lullaby and bears a similar meaning to "soothe or calm to sleep by sounds or movements", although it also carries the suggestion of deception or delusion and the quietening or intermission in a storm. The irony of this double meaning increases with the juxtaposition of lull with winter, since the harshness of the weather cuts off any hope of soothing or calming, and coldness suggests death rather than the warm comfort of sleep. All sound is cut off too: the word "silence" or "silent" is used five times in a 20-line poem, with additional synonyms of "hushed", "No sound", "Noiselessly", "inaudibly":

> We are folded together, men and the snowy ground
>   Into nullity.
> There is silence, only the silence, never a sound
>   Nor a verity
> To assist us; disastrously silence-bound! (*Poems* 124)

Bay exhibits several parallels with Debussy's response to the war, which was marked by an intensification of the silence that was already a hallmark of his work. He wrote very little in the first year of the war, reflecting in January 1916 that "there's no way of writing war music in wartime. To be honest, there's no such thing as war music" (Lesure and Nichols 1987: 313). He was as critical of the martial music of the "two Richards" (Wagner and Strauss) as he was of the seeming frivolity of *Parade* (Orledge 1982: 176); a fantastic production by Diaghilev's Ballets Russes in 1917, which incorporated Picasso's famously elaborate and impractical costumes and a variety of sound effects, including a typewriter and pistol.[24] Debussy's silence was broken only once in the first year of the war by his *Berceuse Héroïque* (1914), written as part of a tribute from the French nation to the King of Belgium and incorporating an excerpt of the Belgian national anthem, the *Brabaçonne*. Debussy's title translates as *Heroic Lullaby*, although one wonders how a lullaby could ever be heroic.

Four minutes in length and muted in its orchestration, Debussy described his *Berceuse* as a "homage to so much patient suffering": "melancholy and discreet and the *Brabaçonne* doesn't make a racket. If you don't hear enough of the ravaging of Belgium in it, let's say no more" (qtd. Lesure and Nichols 1987: 313). But critics like Lawrence Gilman found it inadequate as "war music", complaining that Debussy "has given us seven pages of music that is amazing for its flatness, its thinness, its vacuity, its triteness" (Gilman 1916: 616). His sombre version of lullaby suggests the more permanent form of sleep into which so many European citizens were falling, as evoked by Lawrence in *Bay*, and in Wilfred Owen's poems "Exposure", "Futility", and "Strange Meeting".[25] All these works respond to the bitterly cold winters of the war—as do Debussy's subsequent *Noël des enfants qui n'ont plus de maisons* (1915) and *En blanc et noir* (1915)—but also the idea of a winter for the whole of humanity. In September 1915, Lawrence wrote that "This is the real winter of the spirit in England. We are just preparing to come to fast grips with the war" (*2L* 393), and in a letter of January 1918 (in which he also tells Cecil Gray that "I'm not writing anything—only sit learning songs"), he announced that "ones self seems to contract more and more from everything, and especially from people. It is a kind of wintering. The only thing to do is let it *be* winter" (*3L* 197). While *Bay* suggests war as "a kind of wintering", this idea becomes central to *Aaron's Rod*, which begins in the darkness of Christmas Eve (close to the winter solstice) and ends with Aaron asking Lilly: "What am I going to do this winter, do you think?" (*AR* 292).

Winter Journeys: Lawrence and Schubert

The conjunction of winter, war, and musical themes in *Aaron's Rod* resonates with Schubert's well-known song cycle, *Winterreise* (*Winter Journey*), his setting of poems by Wilhelm Müller which have the qualities of folk songs and echoes of the political upheavals of post-Napoleonic Europe described in Heine's 1844 satirical verse epic *Deutschland. Ein Wintermärchen* (*Germany. A Winter's Tale*) (Bostridge 2015: 120, 31). Against this backdrop of a political wintertime, Müller's poems depict the wanderings through a hostile world of an unnamed protagonist, who also makes an inward journey that questions his very existence. Like the wanderer protagonist of *Winterreise*, Aaron leaves his house during the night for reasons which are never fully explained and embarks on a journey of exploration which is ultimately inconclusive.[26] He is thus an echo of Romanticism's central figure of the alienated wanderer, who both seeks solitude and suffers from it. *Winterreise* opens with the poet-singer's statement that "I came a stranger, / I depart a stranger" (qtd. Bostridge 2015: 3), which Lawrence echoed in a letter from Baden-Baden where he finished *Aaron's Rod* after a two-year hiatus: "I feel a stranger everywhere and nowhere" (*3L* 726).

In many ways, Müller's wanderer-singer, as described in "Der Wegweiser" (The Signpost), is the epitome of the Romantic artist (qtd. Bostridge 2015: 399):

Why do I avoid the ways
Other wanderers go by?
Seeking out hidden paths
Through snowed-up rocky heights?

He also exhibits the Romantic fascination with death, which for Lawrence was strongly related to the death wish enacted by the First World War (exemplified by Gerald Crich in *Women in Love*, as discussed in Chap. 5). When Müller's protagonist sings "I must go a road / From which none has returned" his words chime uneasily with Lawrence's poem "On the March" that depicts a similar journey "Perhaps ... to oblivion":

If so, let us forge ahead, straight on
If we're going to sleep the sleep with those
That fall forever, knowing none
Of this land whereon the wrong road goes. (*Poems* 123)

The word "road" tolls in the final line of each of the poem's nine stanzas, qualified by various adjectives—"strange" (twice), "long" (twice), "wan", "dead", "old", "last" and finally "wrong". For Lawrence, humanity was unequivocally on the wrong path.

About Schubert, Lawrence was more ambivalent. His early enthusiasm for works such as "Gretchen am Spinnrade" (*1L* 73) and the "Unfinished Symphony" (*1L* 322) turned to disgust in the aftermath of the war: following a concert in Sicily in May 1920, he wrote that "I hated Bach and Schubert and Wagner and Brahms and all the lot of them" (*3L* 514). Nonetheless, Schubert is included in the repertoire of songs described in *Kangaroo*, in which Harriett (a character based on Frieda) plays "Schubert or Schumann or French or English folk songs, whilst Victoria sang", and a rendition of "Larboard Watch" (an old favourite from Lawrence's Haggs Farm days as noted in Chap. 2) gives way to Schubert's "Du bist wie eine Blume" (*K* 43–44). Howard Mills has discerned parallels between the late works of Schubert (namely his last piano sonata) and those of Lawrence (particularly *Sketches of Etruscan Places*), in terms of "the inseparable relationship between two opposed forces", that he identifies as "life and death" (Mills 1999: 157). *Winterreise* is another of Schubert's late works that engages with these themes, while also suggesting a return to the Romantic fragment that counteracts the unity of orchestral forms such as the sonata, thereby providing a possible model for Lawrence's project in *Aaron's Rod*.

As Susan Youens writes of *Winterreise*: "The privileged Romantic status of music as the queen of the arts is still evident in the wanderer's numbed, desperate grasp on it alone as the focal point of existence, but music is no longer a means of transcendence or a way to communicate with another living being. Indeed, it heightens his isolation" (Youens 1991: 70). A similar lack of transcendence is evident in the winter journey of Lawrence's musician-wanderer in *Aaron's Rod*, in which music is no longer perceived as means of providing unity to a shattered world whose cultural forms must now reflect that fragmentation. There are parallels, too, with Ford Madox Ford's technique in his tetralogy *Parade's End* (1924–1928), in which "Music is invoked as a way of coping with an event, but its association with violence during the war means that it cannot be considered a separate, transcendent, or humane realm" (Moss 2017: 60). In describing his experiences under bombardment in terms of Wagnerian opera, Ford draws attention to a relationship between noise and music that, in Josh Epstein's eloquent analysis, "shape[s] the writing of the early twentieth century. Modernists imagined music as a mediation of noise: an effort to interpret, orchestrate, sublimate, amplify, or critique the sounds and the affective shocks of industrialization, urbanization, warfare, publicity, and mechanical reproducibility" (Epstein 2014: xv). For Lawrence, the musical method of Schubert's *Winterreise*, in compiling a loosely unified structure that reflected the fragmentary nature of Müller's poems, suggested one possibility for mediating the gap between music and a noisy world explored in *Aaron's Rod*.

Schubert developed his own version of the song cycle, which was less unified than that of Beethoven, for example, whose *An die ferne Geliebte* was perceived by Alfred Einstein as "fused into a musical and psychological whole ... by means of the unifying accompaniment and the return to the beginning" (qtd. Youens 1991: 73). In *Winterreise*, as Youens describes, the relationships between the songs are "more subterranean" but they do exist; for instance, in "musical emblems of the journey" as "footsteps" and "numerous offbeat accents" which register "mental turmoil ... stumbling footsteps and straying" (Youens 1991: 74–75). In a similar way, Baker perceives that in *Aaron's Rod* "A current of musical symbolism ... draw[s] the many disparate strands together and impos[es] its own distinctive unity upon the novel" (Baker 1983: 67). I would add to this that the novel's episodic nature echoes the loose structure of a song cycle which provides some unity to its fragments. Deborah Stein proposes that:

> when Schubert composed *Winterreise* he returned to the fragment concept to convey the complex, often opposing emotions and conflicts of his wanderer, including the protagonist's ambivalence towards death. Indeed, the poetry set by each song is but a moment in a lengthy, rambling journey, every song a vignette in which the wanderer attempts to cope with his chaotic and conflicting emotions. (Stein 2016: 368)

Aaron's Rod is similarly conflicted and unresolved, not least in terms of a tension between words and music that it also shares with *Winterreise*.

In setting poetry to music, as Youens comments, there is inevitably some antagonism between the two since "Music always insists on its identity as music, whatever representational and expressive text-setting duties it is assigned". In the case of *Winterreise*, "Müller's calculated [verbal] reticences invite fleshing-out in instrumental terms ... After all, the cycle ends with the vision of the mute instrumentalist [the hurdy-gurdy player] to whom only the most minimal of tones remain, a creature beyond the reach of language" (Youens 1991: 108).[27] This provides an interesting context in which to reconsider the silencing of Aaron's flute in the penultimate chapter of *Aaron's Rod* and the final chapter's lengthy meditation on "Words" (after its title). Aaron has been presented as someone whose "mind is music":

> even his deepest *ideas* were not word-ideas, his very thoughts were not composed of words and ideal concepts. They too, his thoughts and his ideas, were dark and invisible, as electric vibrations are invisible no matter how many words they may purport. If I, as a word-user, must translate his deep conscious vibrations into finite words, that is my own business, I do but make a translation of the man. He would speak in music. I speak with words. (*AR* 164)

An intrusive narrator acts as a translator for Aaron—rather as Lawrence acted as a translator of the fellaheen songs and also as a Chladni plate captures the invisible vibrations of musical sound. But is the silencing of his flute a sign that Aaron is muted or that he will find a new way through words rather than music, perhaps with Lilly as his translator? The text is ambiguous. "Driven to bay, and forced to choose", Aaron expresses similar feelings of oblivion as the poems of *Bay* or *Winterreise*: "Forced to choose, and yet, in the world having nothing left to choose" (*AR* 289). He resists Lilly, as he resisted the Marchesa, "silenced for a moment by this flood of words" (*AR* 296). But as a musician, still, "Aaron listened more to the voice than the words. It was more the sound value which entered his soul, the tone, the strange speech-music which sank into him" (*AR* 296–297). Lilly, like Lawrence himself, has no final answer to the problems he has posed in this novel, except to "leave Europe. I begin to feel caged" (*AR* 291).

Schoenberg faced a similar problem in his three-act opera *Moses und Aron* (1932), which remained unfinished: "Only the first two acts of the work are usually performed, although the composer sanctioned the possibility of presenting the final act in spoken form" (Berry 2007: 85). Schoenberg's Moses laments "O word, thou word that I lack!", but as Mark Berry points out his lament is spoken rather than sung and, in this sense, it is song rather than words that he lacks (Berry 2007: 98). In Schoenberg's radical modernism, the unity of music drama is undermined. Lawrence, on the other hand, went on to explore new ways of bringing music drama into other forms in his more overtly religious and musical work of the mid-1920s.

After the completion of *Aaron's Rod*, Lawrence's own wandering intensified. He wrote to Knud Merrild in October 1923 that "I feel as if I should wander over the brink of existence" (*4L* 507). From the twilight of Europe, he turned towards the morning of the new-old world of the Americas, and here he experienced a renewal of language and vision. Remote from the noisy industrialisation of Europe and much of America itself, the wordless rhythms of the Native Americans provided the basis of a world revival through songs and hymns in *The Plumed Serpent* (1926) and inspired the composition of his own music for his final play *David* (1926).

Recommended Listening

Debussy	*Berceuse Héroïque*
Handel	"Honour and Arms", from *Samson*
Mussorgsky	Overture to *Khovanshchina*
Scarlatti	*Cantata Pastorale per la Natività di Nostro Signore Gesù Christo*; "O cessate di piagarmi", from *Il Pompeo*
Schubert	*Winterreise*
Vaughan Williams	*A London Symphony* (particularly the restored 1914 version)
Verdi	"Su del Nilo", from *Aïda*.
Wagner	"Magic Fire Music", from *Die Walküre*.

Notes

1. The poorly understood condition of shell-shock accounted for 10% of British battle casualties during the First World War, although a study conducted by C.S. Myers in 1915–1916 had found that "many shell-shocked soldiers had been nowhere near an explosion but had identical symptoms to those who had" (Jones et al. 2007: 1641).

   The extent to which Lawrence experienced war trauma—resulting from the banning and burning of *The Rainbow*, examinations for military service for which he was repeatedly found "unfit" and his expulsion from Cornwall under the Defence of the Realm Act—is a contested topic. Paul Delany (1979) was one of the first to extrapolate from "The Nightmare" chapter of *Kangaroo*, a thesis that the war was an overwhelming "nightmare" for Lawrence. For a more recent discussion of Lawrence's neurasthenia caused by the war, see Krockel 2011: 65–66, or of Lawrence's "disenchantment" caused by the war, see Frayn 2014: 119–137. For a lucid summary of "wartime neurosis" in *Aaron's Rod*, see also Vine xxviii–xxx.

2. Tennessee Williams also began a dramatisation of Lawrence's experience titled "Night of the Zeppelins", of which a fragment survives (Williams 2015).

3. For further discussion of the part and whole in a musical context, in Lawrence's work compared with Dorothy Richardson, see Reid 2015.

4. Other French songs mentioned are "Trois jeunes tambours", "En passant par la Lorraine", and "Auprès de ma blonde" (*AR* 259), also "Malbrouk" that the Marchesa refuses to sing (*AR* 255). Catherine Carswell recalls that Lawrence had "a little manual of French songs which he carried about everywhere like a Bible" (Carswell 1981: 105). In September 1926, he sent "a book of French songs" to his niece Margaret Needham to help her in learning the language (*5L* 564).

5. Number 13 Guilford Street was the house of Barbara Low (*5L* 329), since replaced by an apartment building, which Lawrence visited briefly on his way to stay with Kot at 5 Acacia Road, St. John's Wood. The Foundling Hospital was extant in 1919. In the 1920s, it was relocated outside London and a property developer demolished the hospital buildings: see https://www.coramsfields.org/who-we-are/our-history/

   Almost a decade later, in Florence, Lawrence noted in a letter that Frieda is "trying to play Handel, the *Messiah*" (*6L* 207).

6. For a recording of "Honour and Arms" visit: https://www.youtube.com/watch?v=VM1RoF_ly8c

7. At their first meeting, Crawford sang Scarlatti's "O cessate di pragarmi" (an aria from the opera *Il Pompeo* of 1683), which she says "became the signature tune of this new friendship", and also that she sang "a lot of Italian folk songs he had never heard and liked very much" before "All too soon he had to rush away to Charing Cross to get a train to Croydon" (Lovat Fraser 1970, 135).

8. Italy had a strong tradition of pastoral Christmas music dating back to at least the sixteenth century, probably originating in folk songs but the genre was also taken up by Baroque composers, including, for example, Scarlatti's Christmas oratorio (*Cantata Pastorale per la natività di Nostro Signore Gesù Christo*) and Corelli's "Pastorale", either of which make a striking contrast with the pomp and circumstance of Handel.

9. Crystal Palace was visible "on fairly clear days" (*1L* 83) from Davidson Road School, Croydon, where Lawrence was employed as a teacher from 1908–1912, but there is no evidence that Lawrence attended any concerts there. For a description of the mass performances of Handel, see, for example: https://www.ram.ac.uk/public/uploads/documents/6c453a_henry-wood-crystal-palace.pdf. "The Handel Centenary Festival of 1859 inaugurated the triennial Handel Festival and, in 1882, a large amateur choir and orchestra was formed as the Handel Society, dedicated to the revival of the composer's less familiar works and the practice and performance of other music"; for example, Sir Henry Wood directed "the Handel Festival, Crystal Palace, June 1926, with a chorus of 3500 and orchestra of 500".

10. Implicitly, the war has numbed the Marchesa into a dormant state. In *Die Walküre*, Brünnhilde disobeys her father Wotan by protecting Sieglinde and her unborn child, who will become the hero Siegfried (who gives his name to the third instalment of the *Ring* cycle). As a punishment, Wotan sends Brünnhilde to sleep on a hillside protected by a magic ring of fire, which can only be penetrated by a hero (namely Siegfried who returns to rescue her). For Alex Aronson, *Aaron's Rod* is an "anti-Wagnerian novel" that "appears to be an unintentional contribution to the dispute (of which Lawrence in all likelihood was unaware) between the Wagnerians and the anti-Wagnerians in literature" (Aronson 1980: 98). However, the evidence presented throughout my study (particularly in Chap. 3) suggests that Lawrence consciously engaged in discourses concerning literary Wagnerism.

11. The original one-hour version, written in 1913, was premiered at Queen's Hall, London, in March 1914. It was revised and cut in 1920, for publication, and again in 1936.

12. For an outline of the dispute between Wells and James regarding form see Dirda 2011: "Wells himself famously disagreed with Henry James about the nature of fiction. While the Master argued that exacting control, a consistent point of view, and close attention to form were essential to true literary artistry, Wells was convinced that we shouldn't allow the novel to be so straitjacketed or constrained. 'Tristram Shandy'—a loose and baggy masterpiece in which almost anything goes—was, significantly, Wells' choice for the greatest English novel. Authorial voice matters, he believed; it gives charm and humanity to a narrative". Lawrence had also been reading Lev Shestov's *All Things Are Possible*; his Foreword to the translation by

his friend S.S. Koteliansky posits that "the real unification lies in the reader's own amusement, not in the author's unbroken logic" (*IR* 7). For further discussion of this, see Park 2001.

13. Steve Taylor, for example, perceives that Lawrence's "attitude is as far removed from the optimistic humanism of his contemporary H.G. Wells as it is possible to be" (Taylor 2004–2005: 65).

14. For parallels with Mozart and *The Magic Flute*, see Reid 2011. There are also a number of references to magic in *Aaron's Rod*, including the reference to "incantation" as discussed above (*AR* 273).

15. *Aïda* had been performed at Covent Garden Opera on the day on which the Austro-Hungarian Empire invaded Serbia, signalling the start of the First World War (Franchi 2014: n.p.). For much of the war the opera house remained closed, but Thomas Beecham's opera company performed in other West End theatres and around Britain.

16. In Exodus 7: 20, Aaron uses his rod to turn the river Nile into blood (killing the fish and making the water unusable) as one of the plagues sent by God to persuade the Egyptians to free the Jews. In Lawrence's novel, it is Aaron's flute that is tainted by blood and its spell is broken, symbolically freeing Aaron to pursue a new path.

17. There are many references to Egypt in *Women in Love*—for example, Birkin "would be night-free, like an Egyptian" (*WL* 319)—and in the imagery of Lawrence's late poem "The Ship of Death".

18. See, for example, the sketch "Registering Fellaheen for the Conscription", by Elizabeth Butler (Alice Meynell's sister) in her *From Sketch Book and Diary* (1909): https://commons.wikimedia.org/wiki/File:Elizabeth_Thompson_registering-fellaheen-for-the-conscription.jpg

19. For the complicated evolution of "All of Us", see Christopher Pollnitz's comprehensive Introduction to *Poems* 696–700.

20. The diversity of locations, as well as voices in these poems makes the title "All of Us" very apt, as Kate McLoughlin notes in her analysis of the sequence as war poems (McLoughlin 2015: 59).

21. The Beaumont edition of *Bay* is available online at http://www.gutenberg.org/ebooks/22734

22. The ill-matched and brightly coloured illustrations by Anne Estelle Rice may also have hindered: Lawrence thought "they're pretty bad: no good at all" (*3L* 366).

23. "Obsequial Ode" is also dirge-like, or "monotonous" to use the word repeated twice in "Rondeau of a Conscientious Objector", in which the evocation of "a dull grey heap in the west" mocks the nostalgic song "There is a little grey home in the west" (*Poems* 125, n.904). This song written in 1911 was popular in the early stages of the First World War. Words by D. Eardley-Wilmot and music by Hermann Lohr; the lyrics and

a recording from 1912 are available here: http://www.firstworldwar.com/audio/littlegreyhomeinthewest.htm. Lawrence also references it in Part I of *Mr Noon* to satirise Emmie's prioritising of domesticity over passion (*MN* 87). Lawrence may have resurrected this early poem in response to John McRae's ubiquitous rondeau "In Flanders Fields" (1915), since *Bay* contradicts its themes of heroic sacrifice. Instead of the glorification of home invoked by wartime songs such as "Keep the home fires burning", the final poem of Lawrence's sequence "Nostalgia" depicts home as a haunted place, "no longer ours" (*Poems* 131).

24. Soon after the start of the war, Debussy abandoned his oriental ballet *No-ja-li* because "I should not like this music to be played until the fate of France is decided, for she can neither laugh nor cry while so many of our people are being heroically mutilated" (qtd. Orledge 1982: 186).
25. Fittingly, Owen's poems were included in Britten's *War Requiem*.
26. Ian Thomson briefly notes some similarities with Schubert's *Winterreise* (Thomson 2018: 176 n.14).
27. The final song of *Winterreise*, "Der Leiermann" (The Hurdy-Gurdy Man), depicts a debased version of the artist, who "grinds away, as best he can", but "No-one wants to hear". The cycle ends with a moment of identification as the singer wonders: "Strange old man, / Should I go with you? / Will you to my songs / Play your hurdy-gurdy?" (qtd. Bostridge 2015: 463).

REFERENCES

Al-Youm, Al-Masry. 2015. Egypt's Army Marks 101 Years Since WWI Participation. *Egypt Independent*, November 11. http://www.egyptindependent.com/egypt-s-army-marks-101-years-wwi-participation/

Arblaster, Anthony. 1987. "A London Symphony" and "Tono-Bungay". *Tempo* 163: 21–25.

Aronson, Alex. 1980. *Music and the Novel: A Study in Twentieth-Century Fiction*. Totowa: Rowman and Littlefield.

Asquith, Cynthia. 1968. *The Diaries of Lady Cynthia Asquith*. Foreword by L.P. Hartley. London: Century.

Baker, Paul G. 1983. *A Reassessment of D.H. Lawrence's "Aaron's Rod"*. Ann Arbor: UMI Research.

Berry, Mark. 2007. Arnold Schoenberg's "Biblical Way": From "Die Jakobsleiter" to "Moses und Aron". *Music & Letters* 89 (1): 84–108.

Bostridge, Ian. 2015. *Schubert's Winter Journey: Anatomy of an Obsession*. London: Faber & Faber.

Carswell, Catherine. 1981. *The Savage Pilgrimage*. Cambridge: Cambridge University Press.

Cushman, Keith. 1978. *D.H. Lawrence at Work: The Emergence of the "Prussian Officer" Stories*. Hassocks: Harvester Press.

———. 1988. *Bay:* The Noncombatant as War Poet. In *The Spirit of D.H. Lawrence,* ed. Gāmini Salgādo and G.K. Das, 181–198. Basingstoke: Macmillan.

Deems Taylor, Joseph. 1920. Review of *Musical Portraits,* by Paul Rosenfeld. *Dial,* September: 313–319.

Delany, Paul. 1979. *D.H. Lawrence's Nightmare: The Writer and His Circle in the Years of the Great War.* Hassocks: Harvester Press.

Dirda, Michael. 2011. Revisiting H.G. Wells's Literary Masterpiece. http://www.salon.com/2011/06/16/tono_bungay_hg_wells

Epstein, Josh. 2014. *Sublime Noise: Musical Culture and the Modernist Writer.* Baltimore: Johns Hopkins University Press.

Ferris, David. 2010. Afterword to The Song Cycle: Journeys Through a Romantic Landscape, by John Daverio. In *German Lieder in the Nineteenth Century,* ed. Rufus Hallmark, 388–394. New York/Abingdon: Routledge.

Franchi, Francesca. 2014. The ROH During World War 1: Suffragettes, Star Names and Shut Doors. http://www.roh.org.uk/news/the-roh-during-world-war-i-suffragettes-star-names-and-shut-doors

Frayn, Andrew. 2014. *Writing Disenchantment: British First World War Prose.* Manchester: Manchester University Press.

Gilman, Lawrence. 1916. Drama and Music. *The North American Review* 203: 613–617.

Goehr, Lydia. 2009. *Aïda* and the Empire of Emotions (Theodor W. Adorno, Edward Said, and Alexander Kluge). *Current Musicology* 87: 133–159.

Jenkins, Lee M. 2016. "A Propos of the War": D.H. Lawrence's "All of Us". *Journal of D.H. Lawrence Studies* 4 (2): 25–46.

Jones, Bethan. 2015. Pivotal Poems: Turning Back to Lawrence's *Bay.* *D.H. Lawrence Review* 40 (2): 54–71.

Jones, Edgar, Nicola T. Fear, and Simon Wessely. 2007. Shell Shock and Mild Traumatic Brain Injury: A Historical Review. *American Journal of Psychiatry* 164: 1641–1645. http://www.simonwessely.com/Downloads/Publications/Military/historical/Jones%202007%20-%20shell%20shock%20mtbi.pdf

Kennedy, Michael. 2002. *The Works of Ralph Vaughan Williams.* Oxford: Clarendon Press.

Kennedy, Kate. 2017. Requiems and Memorial Music. In *The Edinburgh Companion to the First World War and the Arts,* ed. Anne-Marie Einhaus and Katherine Isobel Baxter, 230–241. Edinburgh: Edinburgh University Press.

Kennedy, Kate, and Trudi Tate. 2011. Editorial: Literature and Music of the First World War. *First World War Studies* 2 (1): 1–6.

Krockel, Carl. 2011. *War Trauma and English Modernism: T.S. Eliot and D.H. Lawrence.* Basingstoke: Palgrave Macmillan.

Laird, Holly A. 1988. *Self and Sequence: The Poetry of D.H. Lawrence.* Charlottesville: University Press of Virginia.

Lesure, François, and Roger Nichols, eds. 1987. *Debussy Letters*. Cambridge, MA: Harvard University Press.

Lovat Fraser, Grace. 1970. *In the Days of my Youth*. London: Cassell.

McLoughlin, Kate. 2015. "All of Us": D.H. Lawrence's First World War Poems for the People. *Journal of D.H. Lawrence Studies* 4 (1): 45–66.

Merrild, Knud. 1938. *A Poet and Two Painters: A Memoir of D.H. Lawrence*. London: Routledge.

Mills, Howard. 1999. Trusting Lawrence the Artist in Italy: Etruscan Places—and Schubert. In *D.H. Lawrence in Italy and England*, ed. George Donaldson and Mara Kalnins, 154–175. Basingstoke: Macmillan.

Moss, Gemma. 2017. Music, Noise, and the First World War in Ford Madox Ford's *Parade's End*. *Modernist Cultures* 12 (1): 59–77.

Nehls, Edward. 1957. *D.H. Lawrence: A Composite Biography, Vol. I 1885–1919*. Madison: University of Wisconsin Press.

Orledge, Robert. 1982. *Debussy and the Theatre*. Cambridge: Cambridge University Press.

Park, See-Young. 2001. D.H. Lawrence Unbuttoned: *Aaron's Rod, Kangaroo*, and the Influence of Lev Shestov. In *Writing the Body in D.H. Lawrence: Essays on Language, Representation, and Sexuality*, ed. Paul Poplawski, 79–91. Westport: Greenwood Press.

Reid, Susan. 2011. "The Insidious Mastery of Song": D.H. Lawrence, Music and Modernism. *Journal of D.H. Lawrence Studies* 2 (3): 109–130.

———. 2015. In Parts: Bodies, Feelings, Music in Long Modernist Novels by D.H. Lawrence and Dorothy Richardson. *Pilgrimages: Journal of Dorothy Richardson Studies* 7: 7–29. http://dorothyrichardson.org/journal/issue7/Reid15.pdf

Said, Edward W. 1994. *Culture and Imperialism*. London: Vintage.

Stein, Deborah. 2016. The End of the Road in Schubert's *Winterreise*: The Contradiction of Coherence and Fragmentation. In *Rethinking Schubert*, ed. Lorraine Byrne Bodley and Julian Horton, 355–382. New York: Oxford University Press.

Taylor, Steve. 2004–2005. D.H. Lawrence and the Fall. *Journal of the D.H. Lawrence Society*: 65–82.

Thomson, Ian. 2018. The Flute in *Aaron's Rod*. *Journal of D.H. Lawrence Studies* 5 (1): 163–178.

Vine, Steven. 1995. Introduction: D.H. Lawrence's Exodus. In *Aaron's Rod, by D.H. Lawrence*, ed. Mara Kalnins, xv–xxxvi. Harmondsworth: Penguin.

Williams, Tennessee. 2015. Night of the Zeppelins. *Katherine Mansfield Studies* 7: 161–177.

Youens, Susan. 1991. *Retracing a Winter's Journey: Schubert's "Winterreise"*. Ithaca/London: Cornell University Press.

CHAPTER 7

New World Musicals: *The Plumed Serpent* and *David*

INTRODUCTION

Lawrence wrote from New Mexico, in May 1924, that "the vibration is so different, England is as unreal as a book one read long ago" (*5L* 44). His essay "Indians and Entertainment" (1924), drafted a few weeks earlier, relates this vibration to his experience of Native American song (specifically the "song to make the corn grow"):

> The drum is a heart beating with insistent thuds. And the spirits of the men go out on the ether, vibrating in waves from the hot, dark, intentional blood, seeking the creative presence that hovers forever in the ether, seeking the identification, following on down the mysterious rhythms of the creative pulse, on and on into the germinating quick of the maize that lies under the ground, there, with the throbbing, pulsing, clapping rhythm that comes from the dark, creative blood in man, to stimulate the tremulous, pulsating protoplasm in the seed-germ, till it throws forth its rhythms of creative energy, into rising blades of leaf or stem. (*MM* 63)

These "insistent thuds" are a world away from the "great waves" of musical "silence" of "The Cathedral" chapter of *The Rainbow* (1915), and yet his earlier quest for "rhythmic form" was also expressed in terms of vibrations (in his analogy with the Chladni patterns made by sound waves [*2L* 184]). The rhythmic language deployed in this essay almost a decade

© The Author(s) 2019
S. Reid, *D.H. Lawrence, Music and Modernism*,
Palgrave Studies in Music and Literature,
https://doi.org/10.1007/978-3-030-04999-7_7

later—and which continues in *The Plumed Serpent* (1926) and *David* (1926)—builds on similar techniques of repetition and phrasing as the musical prose in *The Rainbow* (1915) discussed in Chap. 4.

In the passage above, the word "rhythm" occurs three times, reinforced by the measured development of "pulse"/"pulsing"/"pulsating" and a triplet of two-syllable descriptors "throbbing, pulsing, clapping". The rhythm of Native American song is artfully, but seemingly effortlessly, replicated in a flowing sentence of 99 words, divided into shorter clauses that resemble lines to be sung or chanted or spoken to the accompaniment of a beating drum. The most important word here is "creative", repeated four times to emphasise the mystery of "creative energy", and underlined by a continuity established through insistent repetition (ten times) of the present continuous tense. The essay goes on to suggest, "There is, in our sense of the word, no God. But all is Godly" (*MM* 66). The "Godly" is also corporeal, symbolised by the "heart beating" and "pulsing", in an echo of the visceral rhythms of "pulse" and "beat" in the opening paragraphs of *The Rainbow*, which bring poetic language down to earth.

The very different "vibration" of New Mexico influenced a further religio-musical turn in Lawrence's writing that resulted in works which have often struck critics as "unreal".[1] This chapter argues that by departing from the conventions of realism Lawrence arrived at an intermedial form, culminating with the composition of ten pieces of music for his final play *David*, that was quintessentially modernist in its "quest for meaning [which] engages all our senses at once" (Albright 2000: 6–7). However, the publication and reception histories, respectively, of *David* and *The Plumed Serpent* have served to obscure the extent of Lawrence's musical ambitions and achievements, which should stand alongside musico-literary works by his contemporaries, particularly the operas *Le Testament de Villon* (1919–23) by Ezra Pound and *Four Saints in Three Acts* (1927–28) by Gertrude Stein.[2]

Two of Lawrence's songs for *David* were written into the manuscript (see, for example, Fig. 7.1), but they were not included in the text published by Martin Secker in December 1926 or in the play's premiere performance at the Regent Theatre in London on 22 May 1927. Lawrence sent a revised score of nine pieces to William Atkins in October 1926, writing that "It is very simple, needs only a pipe, tambourines, and a tom-tom drum … If only one can get that feeling of primitive religious passion across to a London audience. If not, it's no good" (*5L* 557).[3] But his music was not used: the programme for the "Three Hundred Club

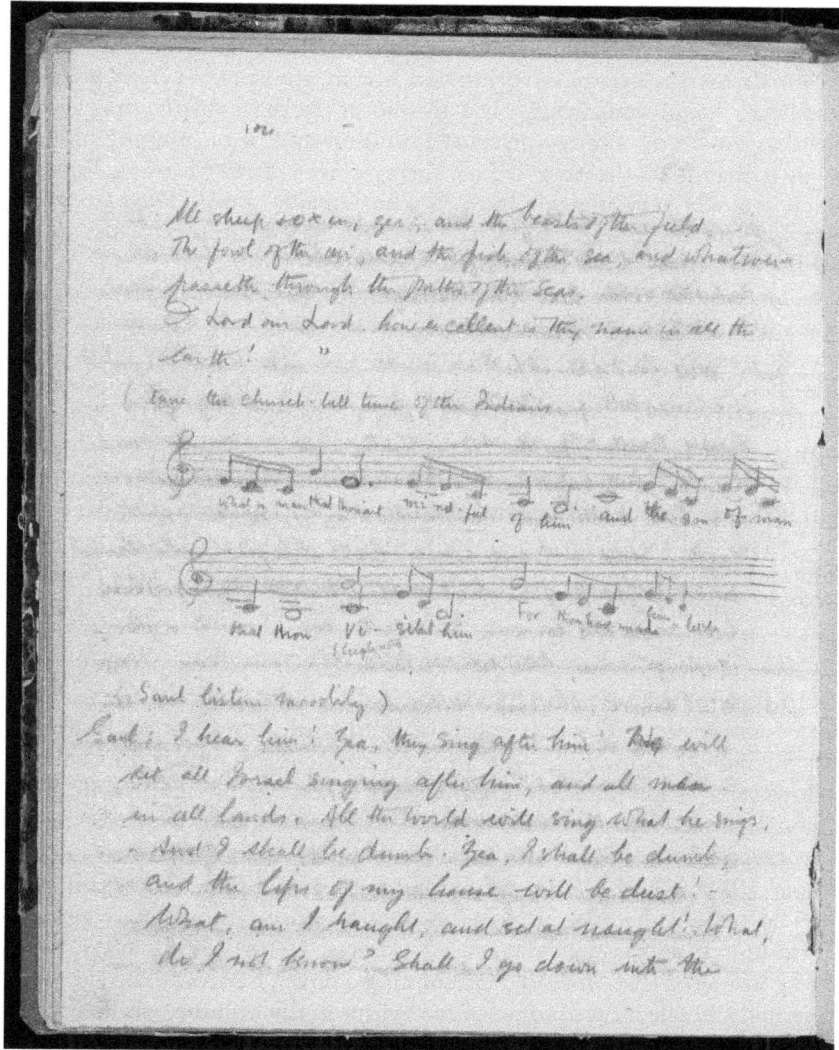

Fig. 7.1 Manuscript of music for *David* (Manuscripts and Special Collections, the University of Nottingham, La Z 1/32/49v)

production, under the direction of Mrs Geoffrey Whitworth" credits Richard Austin as the composer of "Incidental Music" and a single singer, Arthur Gomez.[4] According to Edward Marsh, the results verged on the ridiculous: "Saul was raving on a throne at the back of the stage and David sat down on a settee near the footlights and began singing one of his own psalms to the tune we all know so well from Morning Prayer, which seems a very unlikely cure for the jimjams" (qtd. *Plays* lxxxvii). This was not the soundscape that Lawrence had written into his script and the effect was, as he had feared, "no good".

"The music for *David*" then lay dormant for 70 years: it finally received its world premiere at the University of Nottingham, on 20 April 1996, when it was performed separately from the play.[5] In 1999, the music was published in the Cambridge Edition of *The Plays* in 1999, where it is presented separately from the text of the play in Appendix V. At the time of writing, there has been no full production of *David* as Lawrence intended and it remains a neglected and poorly understood part of his oeuvre.[6] With its large cast of 58 performers, including soloists, choruses, dancers, and instrumentalists, *David* is operatic in scale and should also help us to think differently about the form of the novel that preceded it, *The Plumed Serpent*, which Lawrence's friend Witter Bynner described as "grand opera" (Bynner 1953: 218).

Contemporary reviewers of *The Plumed Serpent* were particularly hostile to the musicality of its language and the unconventional mixture of poetry and prose within the narrative. Katherine Anne Porter observed that the novel's "sound is music", but its phrases were mostly "booming, hollow", like "the high sounding nonsense of a sixteenth-century Spanish mystic; their ecstasy follows the pattern of artificial raptures, self-conscious as a group of Gurdjieff's disciples revolving in a dervish dance" (qtd. Draper 1970: 270–271). Porter further complained that "The hymns of Quetzalcoatl form a broken cycle through the story, curious interruptions to the muscular power of the prose" (Draper 1970: 271), while Edwin Muir considered that, instead of attempting a novel, Lawrence should have presented "a collection of some of the hymns in this volume, with perhaps a few more" (Muir 1926: 719). The editors of Lawrence's *Complete Poems* may have agreed with Muir since they presented 26 "Poems from *The Plumed Serpent*" as a discrete cycle (*CP* 786–813).[7] But extracting the "poems" from the novel ignores their multiple functions as structuring devices, musical manifestos and, above all, passages that were expressly designed to be sung, chanted or spoken aloud to the accompaniment of drums and sometimes flutes. Indeed, in the novel these pieces are called "the Songs and Hymns of Quetzalcoatl" (the Aztec God in the guise of a plumed serpent that gives the novel its title) (*PS* 261). As with the music that Lawrence composed for *David*, the songs and hymns were woven into the text; they augment the musicality of the surrounding prose and convey much of the religious meaning, as more detailed consideration will show in the final sections of this chapter.

For Muir and Porter, as for subsequent critics of *The Plumed Serpent*, the problem was one of literary form—much as it had been for the critics of Lawrence's first overtly musical novel, *The Trespasser* (1912). Muir (1926) found that *The Plumed Serpent* "rarely succeeds in combining the three [genres]"—travelogue, fiction, and gospel—and Porter directed readers back to Lawrence's realist novel, *Sons and Lovers* (1912), in order to "realize the catastrophe that has overtaken Lawrence" (Draper 1970: 271). At the same time, however, Porter recognised the "sheer magnificence of writing" that "rises from the page", conjuring "human beings ... speaking with a ghostly intimacy, as if you were listening to the secret pulse of their veins" (Draper 1970: 270). Porter thus echoes Lawrence's ambition for the novel stated in his essay on "The Novel and the Feelings" (1925)[8]: "If we can't hear the cries far down in our own forests of dark veins, we can look in the real novels, and there listen in. Not listen to the didactic statements of the author, but to the low, calling cries of the characters, as they wander in the dark woods of their destiny" (*STH* 205). As discussed in Chap. 6, Lawrence's series of essays on the novel, written in the 1920s, explodes the narrative conventions of realism, advocating a return to "the little early novels" of the Gospels or Plato's *Dialogues* and lamenting that "philosophy and fiction got split" (*STH* 154).[9] Aptly, then, Muir (1926) compared *The Plumed Serpent* to Nietzsche's *Thus Spake Zarathustra* in its aspirations to be a revisionary gospel. Indeed, Lawrence intended that Native American song would be the means of disseminating his creed.

In "Indians and Entertainment", Lawrence identified the religious impetus for a community based on shared rhythm rather than the melody of "individualised emotion":

Sometimes the song has merely sounds, and a marvellous melody. It is the seal drifting in to shore on the wave, or the seal woman, singing low and secret ...

> This is approaching the Indian song. But even this is pictorial, conceptual far beyond the Indian point ...
>
> The Indian, singing, sings without words or vision ...
>
> ... Hence, to our ears, the absence of melody. Melody is individualised emotion, just as orchestral music is the harmonising again of many separate, individual emotions or experiences. But the real Indian song is non-individual, and without melody. (*MM* 62)

He perceives an exotic otherness shared with "The Seal Woman's Song" (from Marjory Kennedy-Fraser's arrangements of *Songs of the Hebrides*) that had struck him in 1917 as one of "songs of the damned ... songs of those who inhabit an underworld ... The old world must burst, the underworld must be open and whole, new world" (*3L* 180). But now the Native American song suggests a possible means to open up a "whole, new world" through a hybrid of musical forms.[10] As Catherine Carswell wrote of Lawrence, "When I heard him lift up his voice in 'Sun of my soul, thou Saviour dear', I thought he would not be content to die without having written hymns of his own. We have his hymns in *The Plumed Serpent*" (Carswell 2000: 32).

However, in Lawrence's versions of hymns the sun takes on a very different role, as announced by the living Quetzalcoatl:

> The stars and the earth and the sun and the moon and the winds
> Are about to dance the war dance round you, men!
> When I say the word, they will start. (*PS* 242)

In the apocalyptic vein that commenced with Birkin's vision of "a world empty of people" in *Women in Love* (*WL* 127) and culminated in Lawrence's last prose work *Apocalypse* (1930), Quetzalcoatl announces: "Let us have a spring cleaning in the world" (*PS* 242). Lawrence set out to put indigenous music at the centre of his dream of a revitalised Mexico, which would also become the centre of a new world. American composer Reginald de Koven wrote in 1909, "Whoever it was that said. 'Let me write the songs of a nation, and I care not who makes its laws,' enunciated a truth having to do with the effect of distinctively national music upon a nation or people, whose importance can hardly be overlooked" (de Koven 1909: 390). To some extent this seems to have been Lawrence's mission when he came to write of the revolutionary potential of Mexico as it emerged from the turbulence of the Mexican Revolution of 1910–1920. As his Mexican novel proclaims, "in the Songs and the Hymns of Quetzalcoatl, there spoke a new voice, the voice of a master and an authority" (*PS* 261). The novel's authoritarian politics—and violence—raise concerns, although nuanced readings discuss these in their colonial and post-colonial contexts (Booth 2000; Jenkins 2015; Reid 2014; Roberts 2004; Ruderman 2014).[11] For the specific purposes of this study, then, I turn first to situate Lawrence within his musico-historical context, comparing his treatment of the "music of America" with composers such as Dvořák, Copland, and Chávez and the putative "primitivism" of his rhythms with those of Stravinsky. This discussion sets the stage for more detailed consideration of the music of *The Plumed Serpent* and *David*, which in many ways resemble music dramas that are hybrid in form and intermedial in content. *The Plumed Serpent* and *David* are not "wordless music like the Indians have" (*5L* 591) but sung manifestos for a new world.

LAWRENCE AND THE MUSIC OF AMERICA

By the early twentieth century, Native American songs—like those that Lawrence heard "the Indians drumming and yelling at our camp-fire" at the Del Monte Ranch (*5L* 47), at the Taos pueblo, and further afield at Santo Domingo and the Hopi territory of Arizona—were threatened with extinction. Ceremonies such as the Hopi Snake Dance had become tourist attractions for enormous crowds of tourists, including the former US President Theodore Roosevelt (see his account in Roosevelt 1913) and numbering 3000 when Lawrence attended in August 1924.[12] His essay "The Hopi Snake Dance" (1924) expresses an awareness of how the western gaze reduces the ceremony to "a cultured spectacle"—like "a circus turn" or "the Russian ballet" (*MM* 80–81)—and how this strengthened his resolve to convey the religious mystery to a philistine public:

> It is a strange low sound, such as we never hear, and it reveals how deep, how deep the men are in the mystery they are practising, how sunk deep below our world, to the world of snakes, and dark ways in the earth, where are the roots of corn ... They are calling in the deep, almost silent snake-language, to the snakes and the rays of dark emission from the earth's inward "Sun". (*MM* 86)

Lawrence's prose emulates the rhythms of the music, while the word "deep"—which becomes particularly important for the religious conception of *The Plumed Serpent* and *David*—echoes with the final version of his essay on "Fenimore Cooper's Leatherstocking Novels" (1923), which he revised soon after his arrival in New Mexico:

> What did Cooper dream beyond democracy? Why, in his immortal friendship of Chingachgook and Natty Bumppo he dreamed the nucleus of a new society. That is, he dreamed a new human relationship. A stark, stripped human relationship of two men, deeper than the deeps of sex. Deeper than property, deeper than fatherhood, deeper than marriage, deeper than love. So deep that it is loveless. The stark, loveless, wordless unison of two men who have come to the bottom of themselves. This is the new nucleus of a new society, the clue to a new world-epoch. (*SCAL* 58)

This passage anticipates the basis of the religious relationships between men, Ramón and Cipriano in *The Plumed Serpent* and David and Jonathan in *David*, in which their homoerotic bonding is mediated by carefully choreographed rituals and music.[13]

Longfellow's epic poem *Song of Hiawatha* (1855), which Lawrence recited to Jessie Chambers in their youth (Chambers 1980: 95), provides another important intertext, particularly for the emerging music of America. As Michael Pisani relates, *Hiawatha* was "an eminently musical poem: music, song and dance were integral to the Ojibwe history it proposed to relate" (Pisani 2005: 128). Accordingly, there were many musical adaptations, which provide important parallels as "they contributed substantially … to the ways in which native America was imagined" (Pisani 2005: 128), and because they differ significantly from Lawrence's musical re-creations. Robert Stoepel's *Hiawatha: A Romantic Symphony* (1859), for example, was a grand production, played by 50 classical musicians, three vocal soloists and a huge chorus, which evoked "exoticism" through pentatonic harmonies and imaginative use of rhythms, and yet suggested a paradigm for rendering America's pastoral past and wide-open spaces that persisted through to Aaron Copland's *Appalachian Spring* (1944). Copland strenuously resisted Native American themes, and insisted that there were no "Indians" in Martha Graham's ballet production of his work, but as Nina Perlove observes, "Indian musical exoticism may have indeed influenced works such as the Third Symphony, *El Salon Mexico, Rodeo, Billy the Kid*, and the *Duo for Flute and Piano*" (Perlove 2000: 53).

When the Czech composer Antonín Dvořák was recruited to America's newly formed National Conservatory of Music between 1892 and 1895—to help establish "a national American school of composition" (Hamm 1983: 410)—*Hiawatha* was the seminal text for American composers. The Conservatory's founder and director, Jeanette Thurber, suggested *Hiawatha* as the subject for an opera, but instead its influence is manifest in Dvořák's *New World Symphony*, particularly the Scherzo (Pisani 2005: 146–148). But, Pisani asserts, "It is essential not to mistake Dvořák's preoccupation with *Hiawatha* … as reflecting an interest in American Indian musics … Longfellow's classic served principally as a source of poetic folklore" (Pisani 2005: 146). The composer Joseph Horowitz has also noted that "the Scherzo of the New World symphony, with its tom-tom beat, is Dvořák's version of an 'Indian dance'", inspired by the Dance of Pau-Pau Keewis at Hiawatha's Wedding (Horowitz 2005: 19; Longfellow 1893: XI ll. 101–109):

> First he danced a solemn measure
> Treading softly like a panther.
> Then more swiftly and still swifter,
> Whirling, spinning round in circles,
> Leaping o'er the guests assembled,
> Eddying round and round the wigwam,
> Till the leaves went whirling with him,
> Till the dust and wind together
> Swept in eddies round about him.

Michael Beckerman, who has studied Dvořák's copy of the poem and his compositional sketchbook, notes how the music brings out the "Eddying" and "whirling" of lines 107–109 with "an ambling violin countermelody" (Pisani 2005: 147). This classical treatment contrasts with the circling dance motif in *The Plumed Serpent*, described by a writer who had read Longfellow but also witnessed and participated in "the Indian tread dance" (*5L* 67). The following passage of *The Plumed Serpent* is extracted from Kate Leslie's first experience of the new Quetzalcoatl music, as an Irishwoman visiting Mexico:

> The song seemed to take new wild flights, after it had sunk and rustled to a last ebb. It was like waves that rise out of the invisible, and rear up into foam and a flying, disappearing whiteness and a rustle of extinction. And the dancers, after dancing in a circle in a slow, deep absorption, each man

changeless in his own place, treading the same dust with the soft churning of bare feet, slowly, slowly began to revolve, till the circle was slowly revolving round the fire, with always the same soft, down-sinking, churning tread. And the drum kept the changeless living beat, like a heart, and the song rose and soared and fell, ebbed and ebbed to a sort of extinction, then heaved up again. (*PS* 128–129)

The "rustle", "ebb", and "dust" may seem to echo with the Dance of Pau-Pau Keewis, but rather than getting swifter, as in Longfellow's poem, here "the rhythm remained exactly the same to the end", underlined by the drum, which is "like a pulse inside a stone beating". More than a ground bass, then, the drum is the heartbeat of a music (and a people), which is constant, repetitive, and without development and where rhythm predominates over melody and harmony: the very antithesis of western music. Erna Fergusson's near-contemporaneous study of *Indian Ceremonials of New Mexico and Arizona* confirms Lawrence's interpretation: "Efrem Zimbalist, who has studied primitive music in all parts of the world, says that the American Indian's music is the most difficult he knows. Lacking harmony, the Indian achieves his effects entirely by rhythm, often combining several rhythms in one song and always using short intervals and very baffling pauses ... often in the dances one can distinguish as many as four rhythms at once" (Fergusson 1931: xxiv).

There are resonances, too, with the revolutionary primitivism of Stravinsky's *The Rite of Spring* (1913), which Lawrence's reference to the "Russian ballet" in the context of "The Hopi Snake Dance" may acknowledge.[14] Stravinsky's use of pounding and complex rhythms shocked and challenged his contemporary listeners, although, as a reviewer for the *Manchester Guardian* reflected: "for all the boldness and the novelty ... All he does is to enhance rhythm at the expense of melody" (Bonavia 1913). A century later, *The Rite of Spring* is regarded as one of the formative compositions of the twentieth century, and as the composer George Benjamin recognises: "Some of the score's most electrifying moments come when opposed rhythmical strands are piled on top of one another. Such superimpositions amount to a musical collage, creating a form of highly organised chaos. This was the expansion of polyrhythm, one of modern music's most essential innovations, way beyond anything conceived before" (Benjamin 2013). In Stravinsky's case, a huge orchestra provided these cross-rhythms, while the rhythmic effects of *The Plumed Serpent* are simply suggested by drums and flutes, with the important addition of voices.

However, both Stravinsky and Lawrence engage a primitivist influence in music that, as Daniel Albright observes, did not always minimise the darker side of "primitive" life, as primitivism in literature and painting tended to do: "the ritualistic aspect of Primitivism is sometimes transposed into expressions of terror, terror before archaic sexual intensities that are beyond our power to comprehend" (Albright 2004: 235–236). This darker side of "primitive" Mexico is apparent in Lawrence's response to the brooding threat of its landscape, seemingly steeped in darkness and blood:

> Superficially, Mexico might be all right ... Until you were alone with it. And then the undertone was like the low, angry, snarling purring of some jaguar spotted with night. There was a ponderous, down-pressing weight upon the spirit: the great folds of the dragon of the Aztecs, the dragon of the Toltecs winding around one and weighing down the soul. And on the bright sunshine was a dark steam of angry, impotent blood, and the flowers seemed to have their roots in spilt blood. The spirit of place was cruel, down-dragging, destructive. (*PS* 49–50)

This description marks a sharp contrast with Copland's reaction to his visit to Mexico in 1932, which is a more romanticised conceptualisation of "Indian blood" in the tradition of the "noble savage":

> Mexico offers something fresh and pure and wholesome—a quality which is deeply unconventionalized. The source of it is the Indian blood which is so prevalent. I sensed the influence of the Indian background everywhere— even in the landscape. And I must be something of an Indian myself or how else could I explain the sympathetic chord it awakens in me. (Qtd. Perlove 2000: 55)

Copland's *El Salón México* (premiered by the Mexican Symphony Orchestra conducted by Carlos Chávez in 1937) is an orchestral suite that claims to be based on Mexican folk music, though much less recognisably than the compositions of his friend Chávez.

Lawrence's "Songs of Quetzalcoatl", by contrast, express a darker sense of Mexico through an irregular rhythm that aims to unsettle the listener. Sandra Gilbert, for instance, notes that, despite the use of "openly drumming, incantatory repetition" in the "First Song of Huitzilpochtli", "the drumming repetition never becomes droningly regular; rather, it is syncopated in a number of ways" (Gilbert 1972: 237–238). This musical technique of syncopation marks a world of difference from the relentless trochaic tetrameter of Longfellow's epic *Song of Hiawatha* or the "more or less conventional salon pieces" published by the Wa-Wan Press for the promotion of Native American music in 1901–1912.[15] Lawrence's "Songs and Hymns of Quetzalcoatl" are not intended for parlour performance or the concert hall but for the outdoor stage of Mexico—by a lake from whence a new way of life will spread across the globe: "It was as if, from Ramón and Cipriano, from Jamiltepec and the lake region, a new world was unfolding, unrolling, as softly and subtly as twilight falling and removing the clutter of day" (*PS* 359).

LAWRENCE'S "SONGS AND HYMNS OF QUETZALCOATL"

On arriving in Mexico, Lawrence was disappointed to find that "They are terribly un-dancy, these Zapotec and Mixtec Indians" (*5L* 195). There were few performances of the music and ceremonial dances that pre-dated the Spanish conquest in 1519, a situation that José Vasconcelos, the first Secretary of Public Education in post-revolutionary Mexico (1921–1924), sought to address by encouraging a revival of the old traditions and commissioning composers, including Chávez, to produce Mexican music. Although Copland claimed that most of his peers "discovered America in Europe" (qtd. Perlove 2000: 51), he found that:

> Chávez' music is above all profoundly non-European. To me it possesses an Indian quality that is at the same time curiously contemporary in spirit. Sometimes it strikes me as the most truly contemporary music I know, not in the superficial sense, but in the sense that it comes closest to expressing the fundamental reality of modern man after he has been stripped of the accumulations of centuries of aesthetic experiences. (Qtd. Perlove 2000: 72)

This idea of stripping away aestheticism—which resonates with Lawrence's perception of the "stripped human relationship" (*SCAL* 58)—is perhaps most evident in later compositions by Chávez that use Aztec instruments (flutes and percussion), such as *Xochipilli* (1940), although he also wrote Aztec ballets *El fuego nuevo* (*New Fire*) (1921) and *Los cuatro soles* (*Four Suns*) (1926).[16]

Lawrence, however, probably learned about Aztec music from sources such as Lewis Spence's *The Gods of Mexico* (1923), which claims the absolute centrality of music and dance to the religion of the Aztecs who followed the Quetzalcoatl cult:

> In several of these [Aztec] chants we assuredly arrive at the whole signifi-
> cance of Mexican religion, which in its essence, and as seen at the Conquest
> period, was nothing more than a vastly elaborated rain-cult, similar in its
> general tendency to that still prevalent among the Pueblo tribes of New
> Mexico and Arizona, yet broader in outlook, of a higher complexity and
> productive of a theology and an ethical system of greater sophistication and
> scope. The religion of the Pueblo peoples is, indeed, the poor and degener-
> ate descendant of the bizarre and picturesque ritual of the Mexicans, or,
> more probably, had a common origin with it. (Spence 1923: 11)

Since this was essentially a rain-cult akin to the Hopi Snake Dance that
Lawrence had witnessed, he took this as a model for his revitalised Mexican
songs of religion. As he admits in *The Plumed Serpent*: "It was really the
music of the old American Indian ... it was hardly music" (*PS* 126).
Lawrence therefore communicates his revival of the cult of Quetzalcoatl
through a series of "chants"—the text of which also bears some resemblance to the Aztec hymns set out in Spence's book (*PS* 462 n. 119:8).
For example, Lawrence's "The Coming of Quetzalcoatl" (*PS* 119–120)
seems to build from a fragment quoted in Spence (1923: 189):

> Out of the land of the rain and the mist
> I, Xochiquetzal, come.
> Out of Tamoanchan,
> The pious Piltzintecutli weeps;
> He seeks Xochiquetzal.
> To the land of corruption I must go.

Ramón's Fourth Hymn, "What Quetzalcoatl saw in Mexico" (*PS*
256–260), elaborates at length on Mexico as a "land of corruption" cor-
rupted by greedy foreigners.

Importantly, Lawrence's "chants" are sung to the accompaniment of
drums and flutes or sometimes spoken "to echo the vanished barking of
the drum" (*PS* 122). This is an alien experience to Kate as she hears this
music through western ears for the first time:

> There was a rippling and a pulse-like thudding of the drum, strangely arrest-
> ing on the night air, then the long note of a flute playing a sort of wild,
> unemotional melody, with the drum for a syncopated rhythm. Kate, who had
> listened to the drums and the wild singing of the Red Indians in Arizona and

> New Mexico, instantly felt that timeless, primeval passion of the prehistoric races, with their intense and complicated religious significance, spreading on the air.
>   She looked enquiringly at Juana, and Juana's black eyes glanced back at her furtively.
>   "What is it?" said Kate.
>   "Musicians, singers," said Juana evasively.
>   "But it's *different*," said Kate. (*PS* 117)

Difference is very much the point here. This is not western-style art music: Lawrence pointedly chooses to recreate pre-Columbian music (or his version of it) rather than translate its spirit into a western format that would be more readily intelligible to a western audience. In the drafting of the novel,[17] the guitar and mouth-organ of contemporary Mexico (Q150–151) gave way to the traditional drums, introduced late in the first draft—during Ramón's Fourth Hymn, as "a sound which is strange, frightening, and at the same time familiar from past ages in the blood of all men: the rapid, savage beating of drums, the vibration of tom-toms" (Q 226)—whereas the music has a "religious significance" from early on in *The Plumed Serpent* (*PS* 117). At the same time, however, the rhythms and particularly the words of the songs owe something to the Moody and Sankey hymn-books and biblical texts of Lawrence's Congregationalist upbringing (Wright 2000: 203; Bricout 2014: 82–98), and perhaps also to Longfellow's *A Psalm of Life* that he quoted while in Mexico (*4L* 521).[18]

The music affects Kate before she becomes conscious of the words. Indeed, it is only in the redrafting of the novel that the hymns are written down (Martz 1995: xvi); in the first draft, followers must learn by listening and they are less sure of the words ("We don't know many. We only know the first one, all of it. But Francisco knows the second" [Q150]). Given the considerable length of some of the songs published in the final version of the novel—"Quetzalcoatl looks down on Mexico" is the longest at 98 lines—these are not intended to form part of an oral tradition. And yet the songs remain interwoven in the text, together with long passages of prose poetry, so that it is hard to determine the musical boundaries. As Holly Laird summarises, the effect of these blurred transitions between poetry and prose is "to evoke a smooth, ritualistic flow of song" (Laird 1988: 160).

The First Hymn is followed by a long passage of poetic prose spoken aloud "in a slow, clear, far-off voice, that seemed strangely to echo the vanished barking of the drum: 'Listen to me, men! Listen to me, women of these men!'" (*PS* 122). This speech culminates in a greeting to Quetzalcoatl and a farewell to Christianity, repeated as a chanted refrain by the listening crowd: "*Bienvenido! Bienvenido! Adios! Adios!*" (*PS* 126). Then, when the music resumes, "The words did not matter. Any verse, any words, no words, the song remained the same: a strong, deep wind rushing from the caverns of the breast, from the everlasting soul!" (*PS* 127). From this point, the tension between words and music dissolves in a "wild, blind song" that accompanies a circle dance, which finally overcomes Kate's western inhibitions in oceanic terms:

> The slow, vast, soft-touching revolution of ocean above upon ocean below, with no vestige of rustling or foam. Only the pure sliding conjunction …
>
> How strange, to be merged in desire beyond desire, to be gone in the body beyond the individualism of the body, with the spark of contact lingering like a morning star between her and the man, her woman's greater self, and the greater self of man. Even of the two men next to her. What a beautiful slow wheel of dance, two great streams streaming in contact, in opposite directions. (*PS* 131)

The oceanic qualities of music evoked here are reinforced by the imagery of the songs and hymns, in which Quetzalcoatl arises from "the stillness where waters are born" (*PS* 119) and "strength wells up in [him] like water in hot springs" (*PS* 339).

Although the text depends on words, music loosens this dependence and there is a constant struggle in *The Plumed Serpent* to escape the constraints of language. Michael Bell astutely points to Lawrence's "radical frustration with language in *The Plumed Serpent*" but notes that "wordlessness is not an option in fiction; not, at least, for the author" (Bell 1992: 179, 167). It strikes me that Lawrence does indeed attempt, in passages such as the one quoted above, through the rhythms of music and bodily movement, to evoke a state of wordlessness in his characters. But this is a different conception than the endless melody of Wagnerian harmonies in which the individual is subsumed within the universal, as exemplified in *The Trespasser* (1912). In order to retain individuality, Lawrence takes what Marianna Torgovnick recognises as an "unusual" step "in retaining gender in his version of the oceanic" (Torgovnick 1990: 165).[19] For Lawrence, she asserts, "primitives hold the key to sexual harmony and harmony with nature" (Torgovnick 1990: 169), but in musical terms— and in line with Lawrence's vocabulary—rhythm seems a more appropriate term than harmony. The "opposite directions" of Lawrence's circle dance represent opposing rhythms and a preservation of the boundary between self and other that would be elided by harmony.

By the end of the novel, the Quetzalcoatl music shapes the rhythm of daily life, replacing the clock and the church bells for telling the time (see also Clark 1964: 75):

> But the world was somehow different: all different. No jangle of bells from the church, no striking of the clock. The clock was taken away.
> And instead, the drums. At dawn, the heavy drum rolling its sound on the air. Then the sound of the Dawn-Verse chanted from the tower, in a strong man's voice:
> The dark is dividing, the sun is coming past the wall.
> Day is at hand. (*PS* 357–358)

Time becomes spatialised and the physical properties of music—and life—are restored. The staging of life in all its dimensions is thus an important part of Lawrence's project in *The Plumed Serpent* which chimes with a corporeal turn in modernist music.

Lawrence's Music Dramas

Soon after arriving in New Mexico, Lawrence felt that he had arrived in the midst of a "comic opera played with solemn intensity ... here am I, a lone lorn Englishman, tumbled out of the known world of the British Empire on to this stage: for it persists in seeming like a stage to me, and not like the proper world" (*MM* 113).[20] The theatre continued to preoccupy him as he reflected on how Native Americans appeared to have no abstract sense of entertainment: "There is none of the hardness of representation. They are not representing something, not even playing. It is a soft, subtle *being* something" (*MM* 65). Meeting the actress Ida Rauh strengthened Lawrence's resolve to write another play and—after discarding the fragments of *Altitude* and *Noah's Flood*—he began work on *David*, which like *The Plumed Serpent* was conceived in Mexico but drew on the religious spirit and music of the Native Americans of Arizona and New Mexico (see also Moran 2015: 134). Indeed, as he completed *The Plumed Serpent*, he wrote to Rauh: "I could take a wonderful play out of it, if I dared. *I dare do all that may become a man*, said somebody [*Macbeth* I vii l. 46]. It's the becoming—But I shall not forget that play. It's rankling somewhere" (*5L* 199).

The staginess of *The Plumed Serpent* contributes to the critical debate about its form. Laird perceives that "this novel is book *and* stage, something to be watched and watched warily" (Laird 1988: 166). For Louis Greiff, it is "stunningly cinematic" (Greiff 2001: 222), while for Hugh Stevens the beautifully handmade costumes suggest "something of the catwalk" (Stevens 2000: 220). But Bynner's perception of a "grand opera" (Bynner 1953: 218) is perhaps the most useful way to analyse the mixture of prose and poetry in the novel, which resembles the alternation between aria and recitative in opera. This notion would also situate *The Plumed Serpent* within a long tradition of "Aztec" operas, from Purcell's unfinished *Indian Queen* (based on Dryden) to Chávez's above-mentioned Aztec ballets of the 1920s.[21]

It is important in Lawrence's new world that the gods take physical form, and this is accomplished with a prominent display of male flesh in both *The Plumed Serpent* and *David*. In the former, Kate's first experience of the musicians sets the scene:

> The drum was in the centre of the clearing, the drummer standing facing the crowd. He was naked from the waist up, wore snow-white cotton drawers, very full, held round the waist by a red sash, and bound at the ankles with red cords. Round his uncovered head was a red cord, with three straight scarlet feathers rising from the back of his head, and on his forehead, a turquoise ornament, a circle of blue with a round blue stone in the centre. The flute player was also naked to the waist, but over his shoulder was folded a fine white sarape with blue-and-dark edges, and fringe. Among the crowd, men with naked shoulders were giving little leaflets to the onlookers. And all the time, high and pure, the queer clay flute was repeating a savage, rather difficult melody, and the drum was giving the blood-rhythm. (*PS* 118)

The emphasis on the physical appearance of the musicians resonates strongly with the stage instructions for Harry Partch's *Delusion of Fury* (premiered in 1969), in which the American composer sought to foreground his musicians as part of the performance:

> The musicians must of course be in costume, and I have a singularly clear idea as to what the costumes should be like as to detail and what they should convey: a sense of magic, of an olden time, but never of a precise olden time. They should certainly not suggest anything that is either Japanese or Ethiopian.
>
> The basic garment of the musicians should be a huge pair of pantaloons, wrapping around the waist in East-Indian fashion. In Act I they should also wear a poncho-like garment—a single, full piece of cloth with a neckhole. It

must be completely unadorned, without collages or beads or anything that tinkles in the light. The poncho is discarded at the end of Act I. During Act II the musicians are naked from the waist up.

To compensate for this very simple costume each musician will wear a fantastic headpiece. Each will be different, or frequently different. (Qtd. Blackburn 2008: 9)

The details of the costumes are uncannily similar—white drawers and ponchos—although the physical onstage presence of the musicians and their baring of flesh are the most striking and unusual parallels. Partch may not have read *The Plumed Serpent*, but he quoted approvingly from Lawrence's "Introduction to These Paintings" (1929) in his book *Genesis of a Music* (1949).

Contemporary visual art, and attitudes toward it, which arouse explosive resentment in D.H. Lawrence, in many ways parallel this situation in "serious" music. In viewing paintings, he maintains, we "are only undergoing cerebral excitation … The deeper responses, down in the intuitive and instinctive body, are not touched. They cannot be, because they are dead. A dead intuitive body stands there and gazes at the corpse of beauty: and usually it is completely and honestly bored".

And intuition died, declares Lawrence, because "Man came to have his own body in horror". We are afraid of the "procreative body" and its "warm flow of intuitional awareness", and fear is "poison to the human psyche". (Qtd. Albright 2004: 36)

Daniel Albright suggests that the "corporealism" that Partch recognised in Lawrence is best exemplified in his final novel *Lady Chatterley's Lover* (1928), but since he also acknowledges that "Music plays little role in this novel" (Albright 2015: 229), I suggest that *David* provides a stronger parallel. In his final play, Lawrence's corporealism demands to be seen and heard. He wanted his play to be performed rather than published as "literature", in the hope of reaching a less cerebral audience: "Playgoing isn't the same as reading. Reading in itself is highbrow. But give the 'populace' in the theatre something with a bit of sincere good-feeling in it, and they'll respond. If you do it properly" (*5L* 274).

It is striking, then, that Lawrence's idea of doing theatre "properly" involved music and, again, Partch provides an instructive parallel. As Andrew Granade explains in his biography of Partch, the composer had a high regard for the Greek conception of "perfect *melos*" in which "drama was not only spoken but sung and danced to instrumental accompaniment" (Granade 2014: 31). In Partch's view, "composers had gone astray by throwing away the acoustic basis of music, and by ceasing to build music on the expressive ability of human speech". He therefore believed that "Of all the tonal ingredients a creative man can put into his music his voice is at once the most dramatically potent and the most intimate" (qtd. Granade 2014: 31). To what extent is Lawrence's *David* informed by similar principles?

DAVID: LAWRENCE AS COMPOSER

In Gilbert of *Mr Noon* and Ramón of *The Plumed Serpent*, Lawrence cast himself as a composer, but in *David* (his namesake) he became one. The scores for two songs were written into the manuscript of his most intermedial work (as shown in Figs. 7.1 and 7.2), a further two pieces were added in the typescript, and six more were drafted for the play's premiere, making a total of ten songs; although, as noted above, his music for *David* was not performed until 1996. In addition, there are stage directions throughout that describe music (and sounds), mostly performed by singers and musicians onstage. With at least one of the pieces (the setting of Psalm 8 in Scene 11), he sought the advice of Arthur Gair Wilkinson and his wife Lilian (his neighbours in Scandicci, Italy), who recorded in her diary that "we were able to find a good many mistakes and A[rthur] did a great deal of neat scratching out for him" (qtd. *Plays* 587).[22] This brief collaboration over the score points to what Lawrence might have achieved if he had the opportunity to work with a director and composer on a full staging.

A parallel is suggested by Pound's opera *Le Testament de Villon* (composed 1919–1923), which was scored with the assistance of the avant-garde composer George Antheil (best-known for his score for the 1924 film *Ballet Mécanique*, a landmark in inter-arts modernism). Pound—who had long regarded the troubadour as "the ideal poet ... simultaneously writer and composer"—set texts by Villon in an attempt to create "an art that takes place in the limbo between speech and music" (Albright 2004: 25–26). Like Lawrence, Pound was more concerned with rhythms than with melody and he was not a trained composer. Margaret Fisher describes *Le Testament* as "the musical composition of a modernist poet who taught himself to compose in order to master rhythm ... The experiments of th[e] 1923 score warrant comparison with other experiments of the time—Stravinsky's rhythmic unorthodoxy, Charles Ives's eclectic collage

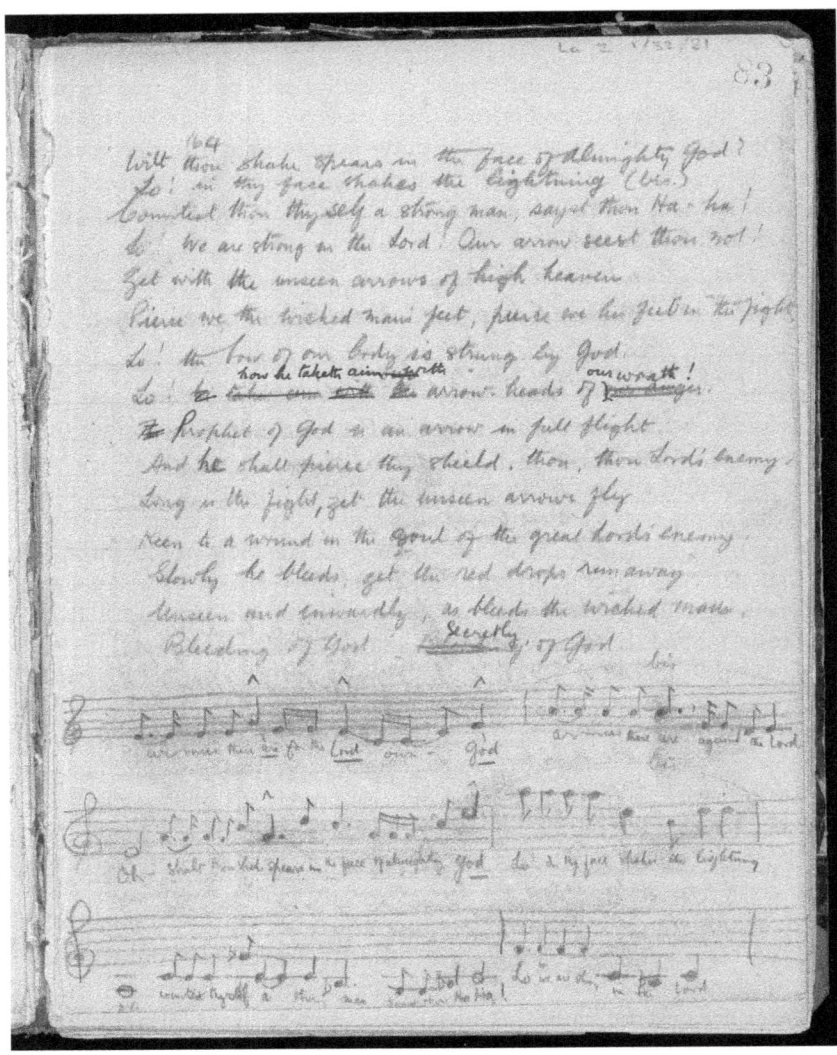

Fig. 7.2 Manuscript of music for *David* (Manuscripts and Special Collections, the University of Nottingham, La Z 1/32/81r)

of musical materials, and Henry Cowell's advocacy of polyrhythms" (Fisher 2006: 139). *Le Testament* received its premiere at the Salle Pleyel in Paris in 1926, the year before *David*, also in a reduced version; the first fully staged performance of the 1923 score was performed in 1971, but "at least half a dozen" have followed (Fisher 2006: 139–144).[23]

In terms of scale and content, however, a closer comparison is Handel's oratorio *Saul*; indeed, at one stage Lawrence wanted to change his title (in line with his apparent sympathies) to Saul (*Plays* n. 435:1). As Virginia Hyde writes:

> Some of the most noteworthy features of Lawrence's drama may result from his likely knowledge of G. F. Handel's *Saul* (1739) … Like Lawrence, the composer makes Saul the central character and puts his lively daughter Michal, David's wife, in prominent focus. In addition, the sixteen scenes of the play, in an unusual tableau-style arrangement, recall the shifting scenes of the *Saul* oratorio, and a chorus is an important feature of both Lawrence's and Handel's works. (Hyde 1992: 59)

Lawrence registered his disapproval of the funeral march from *Saul* in his first essay "Art and the Individual" (1908) and although his casting and content (based closely on the second half of the First Book of Samuel) is similar, the musical styles are very different. Handel's music is scored for a full western orchestra, while the instrumentation Lawrence calls for is "very simple, needs only a pipe, tambourines, and a tom-tom drum" (*5L* 557) and he left the arrangements to the performers. Tambourines—or "timbrels"—are referenced in the Bible, but the tom-tom drum is clearly influenced by his experiences of Native American music, while the pipe, as in *The Plumed Serpent*, may be a clay-pipe such as the Aztecs used (*PS* n. 117:34). This hybrid musical ensemble bears no resemblance to Handel's stately baroque music, which Lawrence had specifically repudiated when Kai Götzsche and Knud Merrild performed the "Largo" (from Handel's *Xerxes*) at a musical evening at the Del Monte Ranch. Merrild records how "With great emphasis, Lawrence burst forth, 'How perfectly awful! Of all things, why did you have to play that?'", and that although "The evening was soon repeated[,] We did not, however, play any more classical music; not because we thought it hurt Lawrence's fine musical ear—he was not such a connoisseur of music. He didn't care for or appreciate most classical music, even when played by symphony orchestras" (Merrild 1938: 132–133).

A more immediate influence than Handel may have been provided by Meta Lehmann, an artist who "knew both the Lawrences" and the Danes. Lehmann was also "a friend of the Indian and a student of his life and customs" who "wrote songs and put them to music" (Merrild 1938: 148). With her, Native Americans were more spontaneous and did not feel the need to perform as Merrild felt they did for Mabel Luhan: "Meta would play the piano, or they [the Indians] would beat the drum, or both, and sing and dance without being asked" (Merrild 1938: 149). As already noted, the drum was an important component in Lawrence's music for *David*, the performance of which was left to the spontaneity of the musicians and director.

Lawrence's scores are only for the vocal line, which for him, as for Partch, was clearly the most important component. Philip Blackburn describes how Partch "gave voice the primary role and constructed the necessary instruments to support it" (Blackburn 2008: 4), which has some parallels with Lawrence's expectation that the instrumentation would follow the score of his vocal line. In Lawrence's play, David is repeatedly described as a singer, although in the biblical account his instrument is the harp, with which he attempts to soothe Saul's temper. Accordingly, Lawrence's text alludes to "the harp-strings of the king's ears [being] unstrung" (*Plays* 457), but David himself is frequently associated with birdsong—Saul calls him "Thou bird of the pert whistle!" and Goliath "thou whistling bird!" (*Plays* 456, 469)—a cerebral trope in Lawrence's oeuvre, which, as Hyde observes, aligns him with Christ's "spiritual faculty" and against the "old dispensation of the flesh now represented by Saul" (Hyde 1992: 57).[24] Or, in Nietzschean terms, as Lawrence Gamache points out, this illustrates "the movement away from a Dionysian, primitive, passionate religious impulse ... to a more Apollonian era under David" (Gamache 1982: 240)—a movement which the play postpones by leaving the conflict between Saul and David unresolved.

As regards Lawrence's score, Bethan Jones acknowledges that it is "in places problematic ... with the vocal line ranging over three octaves, which is unrealistic given the usual range of the human voice" (Jones 2012: 163). But since Lawrence was a keen recreational singer, who was able to read music, Jones suggests that "he was deliberately forcing the voice to extremes in places, with the intention of creating a sound that was strained and rough; ecstatic and rhapsodic" (Jones 2012: 163). For example, she notes that "It is no accident that the highest-pitched vocal line occurs on the words 'Lo in thy face strikes the lightning', while the lowest pitched falls on 'slowly he bleeds yet the red drops run away' ... He is purposely highlighting the contrast between different kinds of utterance—one declamatory and the other 'inward'" (Jones 2012: 163). I would add that he also uses male and female vocals for contrasting purposes. The first three pieces are sung by women (Saul's daughters Merab and Michal, and their maidens), who also play tambourines and dance, and these are joyful celebrations of victories over the Amalekites (Scene 1) and the Philistines (Scene 9), and of the love of Jonathan and David (Scene 10). These songs are also playful, perhaps mischievous, as the behaviour of the women repeatedly foreshadows trouble for Saul. Male voices dominate the later scenes—David's Psalm in Scene 11 and the Chorus of Prophets in Scene 15—and, by contrast, these songs deal with religious messages. The music of the prophets is partly inspired by S.S. Koteliansky's rendition of a Hebrew version of Psalm 33, as disclosed when he wrote to his friend: "Wonder if you'll recognise the prophets singing Ranané Sadikim. But it won't sound the same" (*5L* 557). The sound world, like the scenery, has been transposed to the new world.

In Scene 1, as Michal dances and her "ornaments clink", Jonathan warns her not to draw the attention of Samuel, and Saul instructs the women: "Go to the house and hide your spoil, for if this prophet of prophets find the Treasure of the Amalekite upon you, he will tear it away, and curse your youth" (*Plays* 437). The song's announcement that "Saul came home with the spoil of the Amalekite!" sets the scene for Saul's downfall, as he was instructed by God to destroy the Amalekite, but instead he has taken King Agag captive and allowed his people to bring back the spoils of war. The song's five-time refrain "Amalekite" on a descending cadence, slightly varied, thus undercuts the joy of the victory. In Scene 10, Saul hears his daughters and maidens continuing a song of celebration over the Philistines that constitutes Scene 9 and his jealousy is inflamed: "They have ascribed to David ten thousands, and to me they have ascribed but thousands. And what can he have more, but the kingdom?" (*Plays* 481).

Although Lawrence did not compose songs between the opening of Scene 1 and Scene 9, the intervening text contains much of musical interest that cumulatively, as Laird wrote of *The Plumed Serpent*, "evoke[s] a smooth, ritualistic flow of song" (Laird 1988: 160). The biblical rhythms of longer passages of speech often imitate music, intensifying techniques of repetition and punctuated pauses that I have analysed in previous chapters. In Scene 1, when Samuel enters to remonstrate with Saul, his series of questions suggest a rising cadence which contrasts with the repetition of the word "deep" (a word that is often used in the Psalms as noted by Wright 2000: 210). These lines demand to be chanted to the beating of a drum:

> What meaneth this bleating of the sheep in my ears,
> And the lowing of the oxen which I hear?
> …
> Stay, and I will tell thee what I have heard
> Out of the inner darkness, this night.
> …
> When thou wast little in thine own sight,
> Wast thou made chieftain of the tribes of Israel,
> And the Deep poured his power over thee,
> To anoint thee king?
> And the voice out of the deeps
> Sent thee on a journey …
> Why then did you not obey the voice …? (*Plays* 438)

Samuel thus underlines the importance of listening to "the voice out of the deeps" rather than the "voice of the people"—and, by implication, the songs that will torment Saul as the play progresses and, as he descends into madness, the "other voices hear I in the night—other voices—!" (*Plays* 439, 487).

Scene 2 is a long monologue by Samuel: a prose poem that resembles passages in *The Plumed Serpent* and uses similarly cosmic language:

> Speak to me out of the whirlwind,
> Come to me from behind the sun,
> Listen to me where the winds are hastening.— (*Plays* 442)

The periodic use of dashes to break up long passages of poetic prose, here and throughout the play, gives the impression of verses or bar lines in music. The metaphor of "the deeps" becomes extended water imagery, which again echoes parts of *The Plumed Serpent*:

> Nothing is good for me but God.
> Like waters he moves through the world,
> Like a fish I swim in the flood of God Himself.—
> Answer me, mover of the waters,
> Speak to me as waves speak,
> Without mouths. (*Plays* 442)

Samuel's speech also suggests the rhythmic patterns of sound waves—waves that "speak"—a more organic concept of music that displaces the fiddle-bow and sandbox of the Chladni experiments that informed Lawrence's idea of "rhythmic form" a decade earlier (*2L* 184).

Scene 6 begins with another long monologue: "Michal, *with tambourine, singing, or talking to herself*" (*Plays* 461). The repetition of words, notable in Samuel's monologue, features here as musical refrains, similar to the techniques of hymns and folk songs discussed in Chap. 2. Michal begins: "As for me, I am sad. I am sad, I am sad, and why should I not be sad?" The next three sentences each contain the word "gone", followed by three clauses piling up negatives: "never", "No-one", "no", and then returns to "I am sad, I am sad, my life is useless to me". This highly patterned, rhythmic repetition is sustained over 40 lines, which to David Ellis seems "driven laboriously along with a series of exclamations and rhetorical questions … a nightmare for any actress" (Ellis 1998: 246). However, Ellis makes no such complaint about Saul's first long speech (38 lines) in Scene 7, a moving lament about his loss of power redolent of Lawrence's own "loss of sexual potency" (Ellis 1998: 261):

> This is a day to make songs for.—But not in the name of Saul. Whom will the maidens sing to? … To that ruddy-faced fair youth, with a young beard on his mouth.— … Ah the blithe thing! Ah the blithe boy! Ah God! God! was I not blithe? Where is it gone? Yea, where!—Blitheness in a man is the Lord in his body. (*Plays* 471)

The music composed for Scene 9—a celebration of David's victory over the Philistines—is a simple and repetitive song, in which Merab and Michal alternately sing solos and together with their maidens, and all sing together the joyful refrain "A-li-lu-lu!" (*Plays* 591)—which sounds like a version of "Allelujah" and/or ululations, such as the cries of Native Americans. In Scene 10, the maidens are "still singing outside" as Merab and Michal enter "running round Saul with their tambourines" (*Plays* 481). Their song modulates first into a reflection of the friendship of David and Jonathan—"Jonathan and David! Lu-lu-lu-a! / Here they come, the loving two-a!"—and then Michal's taunting of her sister Merab who has been promised to David without "bride-money": "Empty-handed David came! / Merab saw him full of shame! / Lu-li-lu-lu! Lu-li-lu-lu-lu! / A-li-lu-lu!" (*Plays* 482–484).

In Scene 11, the music becomes a male affair. Jonathan and David "make music together, so the women listen … And men and women listen diligently, to learn as it droppeth from his mouth. And Jonathan for very love writes it down" (*Plays* 487). David is thus presented as a composer, as well as a singer. Then "*A man is heard in the courtyard, singing loud and manly, from Psalm 8*". Saul, we are told, "*listens moodily*": "He will set all Israel singing after him, and all men in all lands. All the world will sing what he sings". David sings Psalm 8 for Saul, which only inflames him further. Saul reneges on his promise to marry David to Merab and Scene 12 begins with a taunting tune (sung by herdsmen): "Ya! David missed her. / Let him get her sister" (*Plays* 493). This announces David's wooing of Michal, which draws on the religious eroticism of the "Song of Songs" (discussed in Chap. 4), in comparing "my wanting of this maiden is next to my wanting thee [Lord]" and references to the pomegranate and rose of Sharon (*Plays* 496–498). At the beginning of Scene 13, David's prayer is set out like free verse, in which he asserts his own voice, asking that the Lord "Hearken unto the voice of my cry" (*Plays* 501). His prayers are not fully answered in Lawrence's version, in which he flees the murderous wrath of Saul in a quasi-farcical scene.

The penultimate scene (15) contains more than half the music that Lawrence wrote for the play, performed by a Chorus of Prophets: "*Some have harps, psalteries, pipes and tabrels. There is wild music and rough, ragged chanting*" (*Plays* 514).[25] Jones writes that "The combination here of monologue and underlying tune has extraordinary dramatic potential … Unlike the isolated instances of David's Psalm tune and the snatches of female melody alluded to above, the music of Scene 15 is fully integrated with the action and provides a continuous backdrop to the entire dramatic sequence" (Jones 2012: 162). However, as I have explained throughout this discussion, there is potential for music to be integrated throughout the play. It is fitting, though, that the music here heightens this climactic clash between the Apollonian and Dionysian. The combination of soldiers and prophets is reminiscent of the final scene of Wagner's *Parsifal*, but rather than ascending into spirituality, there is a final assertion of the flesh by Saul, who throws off first his coat and then his shirt, to stand "naked and nameless" in an echo, too, of Shakespeare's "Edgar, I nothing am!" (*King Lear* II.3.21): "Shall a soldier be more blessed than I? Lo! I am not dead, thou Almighty! My flesh is still flame, still steady flame. Flame to flame calleth, and that which is dead is cast away! (*Flings off his shirt: is seen, a dark-skinned man in leathern loin-girdle.*)" (*Plays* 519).

By comparison, the final scene of *David* is anti-climactic and the play finishes in medias res. It seems that Lawrence cannot bear to kill off Saul (unlike Handel whose oratorio ends with elegies for Saul and Jonathan), or to portray David's triumph. Instead, Jonathan reflects: "I would not see thy new day, David. For thy wisdom is the wisdom of the subtle, and behind thy passion lies prudence. And naked thou wilt not wilt not go into the fire.— ... Yea, the flame dies not, though the sun's red dies!—And I must get me to the city—(*Rises and departs hastily.*)" (*Plays* 524–525). In Lawrence's final novel *Lady Chatterley's Lover* (1928), the flame passes ultimately to Oliver Mellors and Connie Chatterley, whose love creates a "Pentecost, a forked flame" (*LCL* 301).

CODA

Lawrence's work of the American period has often been dismissed as a phase from which he retreated to the English setting of *Lady Chatterley's Lover*, but he remained committed to the music of Native Americans as the basis of a new society. He made a somewhat rueful disclosure to the readers of Compton McKenzie's *Gramophone* magazine (December 1926) that his favourite singer was "a Red Indian singing to the drum, which sounds pretty stupid" (*5L* 570)—certainly his choice stood out among more conventional choices of Feodor Chaliapin, Jenny Lind and Nelly Melba.[26] His correspondence with Rolf Gardiner suggests how "we might possibly slowly evolve a new rhythm of life: learn to make the creative pauses, and learn to dance and to sing together", "dances from all the world ... mass music, and canons, and wordless music like the Indians have" (*5L* 552–553, 591).[27] Lawrence came to disagree with Gardiner's vision of communal life, but it was, as Ellis remarks, "much like the one Mellors advocates in the final version of *Lady Chatterley's Lover*" (Ellis 1998: 401). The problem Lawrence sought to address throughout the 1920s was a lack of vitality in the modern world, of which a mechanical response to music was a telling symptom. As Connie Chatterley reflects on hearing schoolchildren grinding through a singing lesson: "What could possibly become of such a people, a people in whom the living intuitive faculty was dead as nails, and only queer mechanical yells and uncanny will-power remained?" (*LCL* 152).

In Lawrence's final novel, tellingly, there is not much play with music, which has become mechanised through the media of gramophone and radio rather than live performance. However, the sexual renewal experienced by Connie and Oliver Mellors is accompanied by a rain-dance, which may owe something to the rain-cults of Quetzalcoatl and Native Americans. But Connie's strange blending of "eurythmic dance-movements" and "wild obeisance" also draws on similar currents of "primitivism" that motivated Stravinsky and the Ballets Russes in *The Rite of Spring* (1913). Even as Lawrence criticised the superficiality of some of these cultural appropriations, he participated in a similar stream of inter-arts modernism that sought meaning "beyond the sound of words" (*WL* 250).

RECOMMENDED LISTENING

Native American music	Hopi Snake Dance
Chávez	*Xochipilli*
Copland	*Appalachian Spring*
Dvořák	*New World Symphony*
Handel	Funeral March from *Saul*; Largo from *Xerxes*
Partch	*Delusion of Fury*
Pound (with Antheil)	*Le Testament de Villon*

NOTES

1. Michael Bell also detects "the culmination of lines of thought which had been developing since the composition of *The Rainbow* and *Women in Love*", although he perceives *The Plumed Serpent* as "an effective mirror image of *The Rainbow*: it is both an inverted and an illusory version of the real thing" (Bell 1992: 165–168).

2. As discussed later, Pound wrote the music for *Le Testament*. Virgil Thomson wrote the music for Stein's *Four Saints*, but it is Stein's language that is musically interesting to Brad Bucknell (2001: 165). Extracts of both works are available on YouTube. For James Moran, *David* is "proto-Brechtian" (Moran 2015: 134).

3. For some unknown reason, the music for the opening scene was omitted from the letter to Atkins (*Plays* 587).

4. University of Nottingham, Manuscripts and Special Collections, La Z 10/1/2.

5. A recording of the premiere performance of "Music for David" is in the archives of the University of Nottingham Manuscripts and Special Collections (uncatalogued as at June 2018). Introduced and narrated by

John Worthen, Bethan Jones explains how, in the absence of instrumental scoring by Lawrence, she and the musicians attempted to follow the lead of the vocal line in providing an appropriate accompaniment.

6. For the performance history of *David*, see *Plays* lxxix–lxxxix. Two scenes were cut at its premiere at Regent Theatre. It was staged in Cambridge on 23–28 October 1933 (with one scene cut) and again on 4–6 February 1958 with the complete text. In addition, there was an outdoor performance on 12 May 1938 at the Hillside Theater, Occidental College, Los Angeles, attended by Frieda Lawrence, Aldous Huxley, Gerald Heard, Dudley Nichols, John Spewack, Helen Gahagan, Melvin Douglas (see Squires 1991: 174 n. 1, 176). This was directed by Kurt Baer von Weisslingen, assisted by Kathy Shirley Herbig, a junior music major. As the manuscript was on display, and this contained music for two of the songs, it is possible that at least some of the music was performed.

7. Christopher Pollnitz, editor of the Cambridge Edition of *The Poems*, has elected not to include Lawrence's poems from *The Plumed Serpent* or other prose works.

8. A fuller discussion of listening to Lawrence's texts is given in my chapter on Lawrence in the forthcoming *Edinburgh Companion to Literature and Music* (Reid 2020).

9. This quotation is from "The Future of the Novel [Surgery for the Novel—or a Bomb]", one of eight essays on the novel that Lawrence published in 1923–1928 (collected in *STH*).

10. Catherine Carswell recalls that Lawrence "had some Hebridean numbers which he howled in what he ingenuously supposed to be the Gaelic, at the same time endeavouring to imitate the noise made by a seal!" (Carswell 2000: 90–91).

11. The recent application of post-colonial critique has also informed understandings of western Others in musicology: for instance, as cited here, Perlove 2000 and Pisani 2005.

12. For a film of the Hopi Snake Dance from 1924, the same year that Lawrence attended, see https://www.youtube.com/watch?v=DKc6Bxif8Zg

13. Marianna Torgovnick was among the first to analyse a turn in Lawrence's perception of the "primitive" as "feminine" in *Women in Love* to "masculine" in *The Plumed Serpent* (Torgovnick 1990: 160). For further discussion of homoeroticism in *The Plumed Serpent*, see Stevens 2000, and for a discussion commencing with the Fenimore Cooper essay see Reid 2009.

14. Susan Jones notes that Lawrence's essay coincided with reviews of a revival of *The Rite* (Jones 2013: 113). See also her interesting analysis of similarities between his story "The Woman Who Rode Away" and *The Rite* (2013: 113–117).

15. Arthur Farwell fashioned the tribal songs recorded by scholars like Alice C. Fletcher into pieces to be played on the piano, while in orchestral pieces evoking indigenous music, such as Edward MacDowell's *Indian Suite* (1896), "lush chromatic harmonies and rich scoring ... obscure[d] the fact that the melodic material is drawn from another culture" (Hamm 1983: 415).

16. For a discussion of the influences of Native American music in Copland's work, see Perlove 2000.

17. A first draft called *Quetzalcoatl* was written during Lawrence's first visit to Mexico in 1923; it was substantially revised on his second visit and completed in February 1925. For synopses of the novel's evolution, see *PS* xxiii–xli and *Q* ix–xxxi.

18. For example, the more conventional four-line stanza scheme of "Jesus' Farewell" (*PS* 279–280) may owe something to the format of Longfellow's "A Psalm of Life" (available online at https://www.poetryfoundation. org/poems/44644/a-psalm-of-life).

19. As Torgovnick notes, this results in a paradox that the novel cannot resolve since the oceanic "recognizes no such coherent boundaries" (Torgovnick 1990: 170).

20. Lawrence began writing what became "Indians and an Englishman" (*Dial*, February 1923) on 18 or 19 September 1922 (*MM* xiii).

21. Notably, these Aztec operas often had a political agenda: Purcell's was anti-Spanish propaganda while Chávez aimed to raise national consciousness.

22. Lawrence inscribed a copy of *David* "To Arthur G. Wilkinson / from / D.H. Lawrence / Christmas 1926", Nottingham MSS La/15. The Wilkinsons were artists, whose children had musical leanings, and they shared many musical evenings with the Lawrences. For more about Lawrence's relationship with the Wilkinsons, see Sagar 2011.

23. A version was broadcast by the BBC in 1931, a concert version at the Salle Pleyel in Paris in 1926, with the first fully staged production following in 1971 and "at least a half dozen" since then (Fisher 2006: 139–144). A live recording of the 1980 performance by the AKSO Ensemble is available on YouTube: https://www.youtube.com/watch?v=h87wzHikkwc

24. Virginia Hyde notes that the association of David with a dove and Saul with an eagle probably derives from Lawrence's reading of Jenner's *Christian Symbolism* and traces his shifting view of David through to *Sketches of Etruscan Places* (Hyde 1992: 56–58).

25. As noted in Chap. 2, the poet W.B. Yeats liked to hear his poems recited to the accompaniment of a psaltery (Nehls 1957: 131).

26. The December 1926 number of *The Gramophone* included a "Symposium" of 27 "distinguished men and women", who had been asked to name their favourite song, composer, tune, and singer. D.H. Lawrence supplied the following details to the editor Compton Mackenzie, which were printed

verbatim: "My favourite song is, I think, 'Kishmul's Galley', from the Hebridean Songs, and my favourite composer, if one must be so selective, Mozart; and singer, a Red Indian singing to the drum, which sounds pretty stupid" (*5L* 570). Feodor Chaliapin—famous for his rendition of the Volga Boat Song—was the most frequently named singer (five times), with mentions of other well-known figures such as Nellie Melba and Jenny Lind. Of the 27 contributors, 9 (one-third) chose Mozart, with Bach in second place with 6 votes, closely followed by Wagner with 5. The song choices, however, were more diverse and the contributors admitted that they found making a clear decision much more difficult: Schubert is perhaps the predictable winner though only marginally with five votes followed closely by various Mozart arias (confirming an operatic bias overall) and various Scottish songs, like "Kishmul's Galley", with four a piece.

27. Rolf Gardiner (1902–1971) was a pioneer of Land Service Camps for Youth in northern Europe after the First World War, including the Musikheim at Frankfort-on-Oder, a centre of social therapy through music, art, and husbandry and the Springhead estate for students and the unemployed (Nehls 1957: 666). Initially, a disciple of Lawrence (see Ellis 1998: 308), Gardiner differed in approach, writing that "wise though much of Lady Chatterley was, it was weak in so far as Lawrence damn-well … wanted to have his revenge" (qtd. Nehls 1957: 667).

References

Albright, Daniel, ed. 2000. *Untwisting the Serpent: Modernism in Music, Literature, and Other Arts*. Chicago: Chicago University Press.

———, ed. 2004. *Modernism and Music: An Anthology of Sources*. Chicago: University of Chicago Press.

———, ed. 2015. Corporealism. In *Putting Modernism Together: Literature, Music and Painting, 1872–1927*, 211–232. Baltimore: John Hopkins University.

Bell, Michael. 1992. *D.H. Lawrence: Language and Being*. Cambridge: Cambridge University Press.

Benjamin, George. 2013. How Stravinsky's *Rite of Spring* Has Shaped 100 Years of Music. *Guardian*, May 29. https://www.theguardian.com/music/2013/may/29/stravinsky-rite-of-spring

Blackburn, Philip. 2008. *Delusion* 2.0: Harry Partch and the Philosopher's Tone. *Hyperion* III (1): 1–20. http://www.nietzschecircle.com/Philosophers_tone.pdf

Bonavia, Ferrucio. 1913. New Orchestral Suite by Stravinsky. *Manchester Guardian*, September 5. https://www.theguardian.com/music/2016/apr/12/from-the-archive-stravinsky-firebird-suite-review-1913

Booth, Howard J. 2000. Lawrence in Doubt: A Theory of the 'Other' and Its Collapse. In *Modernism and Empire*, ed. Howard J. Booth and Nigel Rigby, 197–223. Manchester/New York: Manchester University Press.

Bricout, Shirley. 2014. *Politics and the Bible in D.H. Lawrence's Leadership Novels*. Montpellier: Presses Universitaires de la Méditerranée.

Bucknell, Brad. 2001. *Literary Modernism and Musical Aesthetics: Pater, Pound, Joyce and Stein*. Cambridge: Cambridge University Press.

Bynner, Witter. 1953. *Journey with Genius: Recollections and Reflections concerning the D.H. Lawrences*. London: Peter Nevill.

Carswell, Catherine. 2000. *The Savage Pilgrimage*. Cambridge: Cambridge University Press.

Chambers, Jessie (E.T.). 1980. *D.H. Lawrence: A Personal Record*. Cambridge: Cambridge University Press.

Clark, L.D. 1964. *Dark Night of the Body: D.H. Lawrence's "The Plumed Serpent"*. Austin: University of Texas Press.

De Koven, Reginald. 1909. Nationalism in Music. *The North American Review* 189.640 (March): 386–396.

Draper, R.P., ed. 1970. *D.H. Lawrence: The Critical Heritage*. London/New York: Routledge & Kegan Paul.

Ellis, David. 1998. *D.H. Lawrence: Dying Game 1922–1930*. Cambridge: Cambridge University Press.

Fergusson, Erna. 1931. *Dancing Gods: Indian Ceremonials of New Mexico and Arizona*. Albuquerque: University of New Mexico Press.

Fisher, Margaret. 2006. The Music of Ezra Pound. *The Yale University Library Gazette* 80 (3/4): 139–160.

Gamache, Lawrence. 1982. Lawrence's *David*: Its Religious Impulse and Its Theatricality. *D.H. Lawrence Review* 15: 235–248.

Gilbert, Sandra M. 1972. *Acts of Attention: The Poems of D.H. Lawrence*. Ithaca/London: Cornell University Press.

Granade, S. Andrew. 2014. *Harry Partch, Hobo Composer*. Rochester: University of Rochester Press.

Greiff, Louis K. 2001. *D.H. Lawrence: Fifty Years on Film*. Carbondale/Edwardsville: Southern Illinois University Press.

Hamm, Charles. 1983. *Music in the New World*. New York/London: W.W. Norton.

Horowitz, Joseph. 2005. Dvořák and the Teaching of American History. *The Magazine of History* 19 (4): 17–19.

Hyde, Virginia. 1992. *The Risen Adam: D.H. Lawrence's Revisionist Typology*. University Park: Pennsylvania State University Press.

Jenkins, Lee M. 2015. *The American Lawrence*. Gainesville: University of Florida Press.

Jones, Bethan. 2012. D.H. Lawrence and the "Insidious Mastery of Song". *D.H. Lawrence Studies (Korea)* 20 (2): 155–175.

Jones, Susan. 2013. *Literature, Modernism and Dance*. Oxford: Oxford University Press.

Laird, Holly A. 1988. *Self and Sequence: The Poetry of D.H. Lawrence*. Charlottesville: University Press of Virginia.

Longfellow, Henry Wadsworth. 1893. The Song of Hiawatha. In *Complete Poetical Works*, ed. Horace E. Scudder. New York/Boston: Houghton, Mifflin & Co. Bartleby.com 2011. http://www.bartleby.com/356/99.html

Martz, Louis L. 1995. Introduction. In *Quetzalcoatl*, ed. Louis L. Martz, ix–xxxi. New York: New Directions.

Merrild, Knud. 1938. *A Poet and Two Painters: A Memoir of D.H. Lawrence*. London: George Routledge & Sons.

Moran, James. 2015. *The Theatre of D.H. Lawrence*. London: Bloomsbury.

Muir, Edwin. 1926. Review of *The Plumed Serpent*. *The Nation* & *The Athenaeum*, 719.

Nehls, Edward. 1957. *D.H. Lawrence: A Composite Biography, Volume One 1885–1919*. Madison: University of Wisconsin Press.

Perlove, Nina. 2000. Inherited Sound Images: Native American Exoticism in Aaron Copland's *Duo for Flute and Piano*. *American Music* 18 (1): 50–77.

Pisani, Michael V. 2005. *Imagining Native America in Music*. New Haven/London: Yale University Press.

Reid, Susan. 2009. Idylls of Masculinity: D.H. Lawrence's Subversive Pastoral. In *New Versions of Pastoral*, ed. David James and Philip Tew, 95–106. Cranbury: Fairleigh Dickinson.

———. 2014. Decolonizing Time: The Mexican Temporalities of D.H. Lawrence, Aldous Huxley and Carlos Fuentes. *Journal of Postcolonial Writing* 50 (6): 717–729.

———. 2020, forthcoming. Listening in to D.H. Lawrence: Music, Body, Feelings. In *Edinburgh Companion to Literature and Music*, ed. Delia da Sousa Correa Edinburgh: Edinburgh University Press.

Roberts, Neil. 2004. *D.H. Lawrence, Travel and Cultural Difference*. Basingstoke: Palgrave Macmillan.

Roosevelt, Theodor. 1913. The Hopi Snake Dance. *Outlook*, October 18: 365–375. http://www.theodore-roosevelt.com/images/research/treditorials/o196.pdf

Ruderman, Judith. 2014. *Race and Identity in D.H. Lawrence: Indians, Gypsies, and Jews*. Basingstoke: Macmillan.

Sagar, Keith. 2011. Lawrence and the Wilkinsons. In *"Art for Life's Sake": Essays on D.H. Lawrence*, 44–60. Nottingham: CCCP.

Spence, Lewis. 1923. *The Gods of Mexico*. London: T. Fisher Unwin.

Squires, Michael, ed. 1991. *D.H. Lawrence's Manuscripts: The Correspondence of Frieda Lawrence, Jake Zeitlin and Others*. Basingstoke: Macmillan.
Stevens, Hugh. 2000. *The Plumed Serpent* and the Erotics of Primitive Masculinity. In *Modernist Sexualities*, ed. Hugh Stevens and Caroline Howlett, 219–238. Manchester: Manchester University Press.
Torgovnick, Marianna. 1990. *Gone Primitive: Savage Intellects, Modern Lives*. Chicago: University Press of Chicago.
Wright, T.R. 2000. *D.H. Lawrence and the Bible*. Cambridge: Cambridge University Press.

CHAPTER 8

Conclusion: Aspiring to the Condition of Song

Given Lawrence's sustained engagement with music throughout his life and work evidenced throughout this study, it is difficult to understand why this aspect of his art has not attracted more critical attention. Personal memoirs about Lawrence emphasised his love of music and early critics frequently commented on the musicality of his work, but certain of his contemporaries had an undue influence on his literary heritage. In his Introduction to *The Letters of D.H. Lawrence* (1932), Aldous Huxley moulded a lasting view of the type of artist that Lawrence was, including the idea that "In music, for example, he liked the folk-song, because it was a slight thing, born of immediate impulse. The symphony oppressed him; it was too big, too elaborate, too carefully and consciously worked out" (Huxley 1932: xvii). In some ways, this juxtaposition of folk song versus symphony is borne out by my own study, but in other ways Huxley's binary is too simplistic, not least in its emphasis on method rather than meaning: for Lawrence, these were inseparable.

Huxley also helped to sediment the importance of form as a marker of musico-literary modernism, which would prevail for at least the rest of the twentieth century. When Werner Wolf (1999) looked back at the history of *The Musicalization of Fiction*—a term he borrowed from Huxley's novel *Point Counter Point* (1928)—he grounded his study in a triumvirate of modernist writers who overtly experimented with musical structures: Huxley's use of counterpoint standing alongside James Joyce's fugal

© The Author(s) 2019
S. Reid, *D.H. Lawrence, Music and Modernism*,
Palgrave Studies in Music and Literature,
https://doi.org/10.1007/978-3-030-04999-7_8

construction of the "Sirens" chapter in *Ulysses* (1922) and Virginia Woolf's shaping of experience through music in "The String Quartet" (1921). All three are perceived to follow models of orchestral music. Although Lawrence was demonstrably engaged with the intermediality of words and music throughout his career, he plays no part in Wolf's account and is rarely mentioned alongside these musical modernists.

For Huxley, there was a triumvirate of composers—Bach, Mozart, and Beethoven—who featured in his writing more than any others (Allis 2014: 138). These were the same "great masters" (*AR* 167–168) that Lawrence ostensibly turned against in the 1920s, although in 1926 he declared in *Gramophone* magazine that Mozart was his favourite composer (*5L* 570) and in 1927 he was sufficiently interested in Beethoven to read his *Letters* (*6L* 213). In *Point Counter Point*, Huxley satirised Lawrence's response to Beethoven through a thinly veiled pen portrait of his friend as Mark Rampion:

> Slowly, slowly, the melody unfolded itself. The archaic Lydian harmonies hung on the air. It was an unimpassioned music, transparent, pure and crystalline, like a tropical sea, an Alpine lake ...
> "Lovely, lovely," said Rampion, when the record was finished. "You're quite right. It *is* heaven, it *is* the life of the soul. It's the most perfect spiritual abstraction from reality I've ever known. But why should he have wanted to make that abstraction? Why couldn't he be content to be a man and not an abstract soul?" (Huxley 2004: 564–566)

In effect this is a debate about absolute music, which Rampion finds wanting as a mode of artistic expression: "Rampion had refused to be convinced. Was the proof, after all, no proof? Did the music refer to nothing outside itself and the idiosyncrasies of its inventor?" (Huxley 2004: 566). For Huxley, however, music was "just music", as he wrote in his 1922 review "Literary Music": "A large amount of the supreme music of the world is not merely written around any external literary subject; it is not even expressive of any particular emotion; it is, as we have said of Beethoven's latest work, just music" (qtd. Witen 2018: 52). Huxley's idea of literature followed a similar model and, accordingly, Lawrence disliked *Point Counter Point*, not for its method, but for its world view characterised as "a phantasmal boredom ... inertia, inertia, inertia and final atrophy of the feelings" (*6L* 600). Such inertia is the target of his cultural critique in *Lady Chatterley's Lover* (1928), published in the same year as Huxley's novel.

However, Lawrence also refused to make their differences personal: "I say there are many men in a man, and the Aldous that wrote the *CounterPoint* ... is only one of the Aldouses, and perhaps by no means the best or most important" (*7L* 170). Lawrence's idea of multiplicity is also evident in his writing, which often holds several positions at once, which conflict and shift over time. There were several voices—or several Lawrences—in any text, which contributed to the polyphonic qualities that David Lodge identified (Lodge 1985). For Lawrence, polyphony was a means of celebrating differences and therefore served an ethical purpose. In this sense, at least, Huxley was right to emphasise Lawrence's "prodigious power of rendering the immediately experienced otherness in terms of literary art" (Huxley 1932: xii), even as he disagreed with his friend's rejection of absolutes—including "absolute music"—that made this relativity possible.

While Huxley's version of polyphony in *Point Counter Point* also incorporates multiple voices these are, as Wolf recognises, implicitly "structural analogies" that "justify and foreground the specifically aesthetic quality of the new manner of narrative organization" (Wolf 1999: 181). In Lawrence's post-war writing, the individual parts are more important than any putative aesthetic whole, which is why he prefers "Plato's Dialogues" (*STH* 154) to the long modernist novels of James Joyce, Dorothy Richardson, and Marcel Proust (*STH* 151)—or the song to the symphony.

The emphasis on symphonic form in studies of music and literary modernism has also contributed to the relative neglect of other writers, such as E.M. Forster, whose *Howards End* earns only an honourable mention by Wolf "for containing important specimens of verbal music" (Wolf 1999: 126). Wolf defines "verbal music" as "a form of covert musical presence in literature ... but above all by making extensive use of the mode of musical imitation" (Wolf 1999: 64). This "mode of musical imitation" is evident in much of Lawrence's prose writing, too, as the contents of this book have demonstrated. But what constitutes a higher level of musicalisation of fiction for Wolf is the intensity with which Joyce and Anthony Burgess (in his 1974 novel *Napoleon Symphony*) "create a piece of verbal music that continually reminds the reader of the musical pretext and keeps the impression alive that here indeed 'verbal narrative' is given 'symphonic shape'" (Wolf 1999: 207). Since, from the very start of his career, Lawrence doubted the ability of the symphony to say anything at all, or its usefulness to the writer, his model of modernist musicality differed from his peers conceptually even though it was similar at the level of language.

Burgess, a prolific composer-cum-writer, knew more than most about the twin arts of music and literature and showed a rare appreciation for the musicality of Lawrence's writing. Burgess compared "Laurentian noise and fire" with "Mahlerian consummation" (Burgess 1985: 99)—with all that comparison implies for putting a whole universe into an epic construction (to paraphrase Mahler)—and measured the achievements of Lawrence's short life against those of "Mozart, Schubert, Purcell and Pergolesi" (Burgess 1985: 199), composers whose music Lawrence had enjoyed. Burgess noticed that while Lawrence was professing to spurn "art music", he featured it prominently, not least in *Mr Noon* (1984) in which he cast himself as a composer: "a highly skilled one, apparently, since he is working on a violin concerto and, in Part II, is assembling the materials for a symphony" (Burgess 1985: 34). But, just as Gilbert Noon turns from his symphony to a "book of songs" (*MN* 234), Burgess also discards symphonic criteria in setting Lawrence alongside James Joyce, concluding that "The modernism of Lawrence's fiction lies, as with Joyce's, in the narrowing of the gap between poetic and prose statements, the forcing on the critic of the novel an approach previously reserved to the lyric poem" (Burgess 1985: 207). His ultimate tribute was to set four of Lawrence's poems in a song cycle, *Man Who Has Come Through* (1985), which was performed at the Lawrence Centenary Festival and subsequently forgotten by Lawrence scholars (details are therefore provided in the Afterword).

Forster had already recognised Lawrence's ability to blur boundaries as "the only living novelist in whom the song predominates, who has the rapt bardic quality" (Forster 1990: 116), positing a tradition of Balder and Blake, which I would extend to include the poets Yeats and Pound. Daniel Karlin perceives that the figure of the singer "is still strong in the late nineteenth and early twentieth centuries—in Whitman, Swinburne, Hardy, Yeats, Stevens, and Pound—and then gradually lessens in importance" (Karlin 2013: 3). These are all figures that have featured in this study of Lawrence and music, and might also encompass Joyce, who shared Lawrence's passion for song. A book on literary modernism and song has yet to be written, but this could bring together a more diverse constellation of musical writers, that would narrow the gap between absolute music and song.

RECOMMENDED LISTENING

Beethoven   String Quartet No.15, third movement "Heiliger Dankgesang"

REFERENCES

Allis, Michael. 2014. Contemporary Music in Huxley's Music Criticisms. *Aldous Huxley Annual* 14: 137–162.

Burgess, Anthony. 1985. *Flame into Being: The Life and Work of D.H. Lawrence.* London: William Heinemann.

Forster, E.M. 1990. *Aspects of the Novel.* Harmondsworth: Penguin.

Huxley, Aldous. 1932. Introduction. In *The Letters of D.H. Lawrence,* ix–xxxiv. London: William Heinemann.

———. 2004. *Point Counter Point.* London: Vintage.

Karlin, Daniel. 2013. *The Figure of the Singer.* Oxford: Oxford University Press.

Lodge, David. 1985. Lawrence, Dostoevsky, Bakhtin: D.H. Lawrence and Dialogic Fiction. *Renaissance and Modern Studies* 29 (1): 16–32.

Witen, Michelle. 2018. *James Joyce and Absolute Music.* London: Bloomsbury.

Wolf, Werner. 1999. *The Musicalization of Fiction: A Study in the Theory and History of Intermediality.* Amsterdam/Atlanta: Rodopi.

CHAPTER 9

Afterword: Anthony Burgess's D.H. Lawrence Suite

Anthony Burgess completed his settings of four Lawrence poems titled *Man Who Has Come Through* in Monaco in April 1984. Then 67, Burgess was the author of some 28 novels, but also a prolific composer of more than 100 works, including three symphonies (Burgess 1982: 36–40).[1] Although he "wish[ed] people would think of [him] as a musician who writes novels, instead of a novelist who writes music on the side" (qtd. Phillips 2010: 3), most of his music was not performed during his lifetime. Hearing his Symphony No. 3 in C in 1975 was, Burgess wrote, "the truly great artistic moment" of his life (qtd. Phillips 2010: 3). Burgess took music seriously and it was also a means by which he "expressed his deepest affinity for the writers he loved the most" (Philips 2009: 13), including Shakespeare, Hopkins, Joyce, Eliot and, belatedly, Lawrence.

At around 35 minutes, *Man Who Has Come Through* was Burgess's longest song cycle to date, similar in length to his symphonies; a point to which I will return later. The songs also provide a commentary on Lawrence's life—a sort of musical biography—that complements his prose volume *Flame into Being: The Life and Work of D.H. Lawrence* (1985; also serialised in the *Sunday Times*) and four-part documentary series for London Weekend Television titled *The Rage of D.H. Lawrence*.[2] In some respects, Burgess regarded Lawrence as a fellow outsider and wanderer, who was insufficiently appreciated in his home land: "The Bloomsbury group that for so long ruled English taste disliked him intensely. He was a

© The Author(s) 2019
S. Reid, *D.H. Lawrence, Music and Modernism*,
Palgrave Studies in Music and Literature,
https://doi.org/10.1007/978-3-030-04999-7_9

working man who had not been to Oxford or Cambridge: what right had he to turn himself into one of England's most important novelists and poets?" (Burgess 1998: 303). The title of Burgess's song cycle is taken from Lawrence's autobiographical "Song of a Man Who Has Come Through", but it defiantly speaks of both its subject and the composer, whose music was largely ignored.

In *Flame into Being*, Burgess notes "a certain piquancy in the chance concelebration of the birth of a great German composer who became British [Handel, born in 1685] and that of a great British writer who, marrying a German, abandoned Britain" (Burgess 1985: xi). But he also discerns a similarity in their rendering of British people and landscape, comparing "'Here the ploughman near at hand/Whistles o'er the furrowed land', from Handel's setting of Milton's L'Allegro" with Lawrence's novels *The White Peacock, Sons and Lovers* and *The Rainbow*. Handel's oratorio *L'Allegro, il Penseroso ed il Moderato (The Cheerful, the Thoughtful, and the Moderate Man)* (1740) sets Milton's two poems with a third by Charles Jennens to represent three humours of man, and so suggests an interesting context for Burgess's D.H. Lawrence Suite which depicts the poet in a variety of moods.

Man Who Has Come Through consists of an optional prelude/postlude and the following poems, set for tenor voice, flute, oboe, cello, and piano:

End of Another Home Holiday (1909)	10 mins	Moderato a piacere
Song of a Man Who Has Come Through (1914)	3 mins	Allegro molto vivace
Snake (1920–1921)	14 mins	Very freely
Bavarian Gentians (1929)	6 mins	Andantino

PERFORMANCE HISTORY

The premiere performance was held at the Congregational Centre, Castle Gate, Nottingham, on Sunday, 22 September 1985, as part of the D.H. Lawrence Centenary Festival. The programme, which included other music from Lawrence's time, was as follows:

Warlock	Songs
Debussy	Syrinx for solo flute
Franck	Prelude, Chorale and Fugue
Scriabin	Two Poems for Piano, Op. 32
Burgess	D.H. Lawrence Suite

The programme also notes that "The writings of [Scriabin's] friend Merezhovsky have been called a prototype of D.H. Lawrence's mystique of the flesh".[3]

Burgess was not present at the premiere, but the conductor Peter Palmer wrote to thank him for "Bravely entrusting us with your DHL Suite. Curious how the one self-commissioned centenary piece should be (in my opinion) the most substantial of the lot. It gave my colleagues great pleasure to prepare it: we are only sorry the composer was not there to take a bow" (qtd. Phillips 2010: 283). A second performance by the same musicians, at the Nottingham University Music Society on 23 January 1986, was sponsored and broadcast by Radio Trent.[4]

Following Burgess's death in 1993, extracts of *Man Who Has Come Through* were included in a tribute, "An Airful of Burgess", broadcast by BBC Radio Scotland on 21 August 1994.[5] There was another full performance at the Third International Symposium of the Anthony Burgess Centre at the University of Angers in 2006, although unfortunately without the cellist who was taken ill (Jeannin 2010: 6). This conference also gave rise to an edited collection of essays on Burgess and music (Jeannin 2009).

Burgess's D.H. Lawrence Suite has gained a place in Burgess studies but has left few traces in Lawrence scholarship or more generally. I have been unable to find any reviews of the premiere performance in the archives of either the D.H. Lawrence Centre at the University of Nottingham or the Anthony Burgess Foundation in Manchester. However, the Foundation holds an unpublished lecture by James Sparling (2003) that discusses a performance (unspecified) and a recording (also unspecified).

The extensive programme for the Lawrence Centenary Festival programme included more musical tributes to Lawrence than we might expect now.[6] A performance by the Royal Philharmonic Orchestra of "Music for Lawrence" featured music from the year of Lawrence's birth: Glinka's Overture to Russian and Ludmilla, Grieg's Piano Concerto, and Tchaikovsky's *Manfred Symphony*. There was an opera based on the short story "Fanny and Annie", a musical version of "The Ass" and from the Cantamus Girls Choir "Shall We Sing Thee Summat", which included settings of seven Lawrence poems by Nigel Osborne (see the Appendix for further details). There were more songs, too, performed by the Derby Opera Workshop, the Eastwood Collieries Male Voice Choir and, at the Old Vic Tavern in Nottingham, "A cavalcade of songs, poems and sawn-off stories aimed at bringing down governments and raising merry hell!"

The Poems and Settings

The four poems selected by Burgess span Lawrence's poetic career and are presented chronologically, suggesting phases of his life. These are the same four poems anthologised in *The Faber Book of Modern Verse* (Roberts 1943) that Burgess owned, and the song texts correspond with this edition.[7] So, although Burgess owned several volumes of Lawrence's poems and dedicated two chapters of *Flame into Being* to the poetry, his selection seems to have been determined by the anthology.

The first, less well-known poem "End of Another Home Holiday" deals with the poet's guilt about leaving his home and his mother, depicting a first struggle into independent manhood. The second deals with what Lawrence described in the Foreword to *Look! We Have Come Through!* (1917) as "the intrinsic experience of a man during the crisis of manhood, when he marries and comes into himself" (*CP* 191). "Snake" is more representative of Milton's "thoughtful man" seeking his place in nature, but also questioning anew his manhood: "If you were a man/You would take a stick and break him now" (*Poems* 303). Echoing a passage in *Macbeth*, where Lady Macbeth berates her husband's cowardice and questions his manhood, "When you durst do it, then you wert a man" (I. vii. 39–57), Amit Chaudhuri notes how Lawrence's words sound like "a sexual gibe" (Chaudhuri 2003: 14). Finally, "Bavarian Gentians" describes the experience of man's "slow, sad" descent into the immaterial realm of death, where the poet "is but a voice/or a darkness invisible enfolded in the deeper dark" (*Poems* 611). In this respect, Burgess pays tribute to the poet by giving him a voice and his settings are also respectful of Lawrence's texts. As Sparling observes, Burgess sets "word for word what Lawrence wrote—no more, no less" and refrains from "word painting" (Sparling 2003: 35). He seems intent on underlining the verbal music of Lawrence's poems rather than his own music and, indeed, the Anthony Burgess Foundation holds a recording of Burgess reading the poems aloud as if to understand their rhythms and stresses.

The settings reflect a range of musical influences, including composers from Lawrence's own time. As noted by Paul Phillips, these include Max Reger and Alban Berg, also: "Strauss, Mahler, Schoenberg, and Stravinsky, whose music from around 1910 straddles the line between tonality and atonality" (Phillips 2010: 284). There are also echoes of Debussy in the optional prelude and/or postlude, as well as the contours of "Snake"; a tribute perhaps to *Prélude a l'après-midi d'un faune*, which spellbound Burgess as a child, with its "quite incredible flute solo, sinuous, exotic, erotic" (Burgess 1982: 17). Rather than the English tradition of Holst, Delius, and Elgar that he aspired to continue (Burgess 1982: 158), Burgess's settings reflect the broader movements in European music which influenced Lawrence's development as a writer.

The choice of male voice differs from other song cycles of Lawrence's poems, including Nigel Osborne's *For a Moment* (1985), commissioned and performed by the Cantamus Girls Choir, or William Neil's *Waters Are Shaking the Moon* (1996), for mezzo soprano. Other precedents, however, include Benjamin Britten, such as his Serenade for tenor, horn, and strings (Op. 31), as well as Burgess's previous settings of Shakespeare, Hardy, Eliot, and Joyce for tenor and piano. There are also some resonances with Michael Tippett, who wrote all his songs for men and particularly with his late, playful *Songs for Dov*, which similarly tell of a man's struggle to come to terms with his world.

The optional prelude and/or postlude is brief at only 14 bars, scored as lento and pianissimo. Otherwise, the first song starts almost without an introduction. Phillips notes that its "highly chromatic setting, though it begins and ends in A minor, modulates restlessly, often on the brink of atonality" (Phillips 2010: 284). The setting thus underlines the poet's mixed feelings about asserting his independence from his mother. The song begins nostalgically—"When shall I see the half-moon sink again/ Behind the black sycamore at the end of the garden?" (*Poems* 31)—but is punctuated by more urgent passages. The sound words and rhythms of the poem are imitated by the instruments: the "midnight bell", "the sharp clean trot of a pony down the road", and "sharp little sounds dropping into silence" (*Poems* 31).

"Song of a Man Who Has Come Through" is brief at less than three minutes; played as "Allegro Molto Vivace" the effect is urgent and emphatic. Again, the instruments mimic the sounds of the poem, particularly the wind and the knocking of angels at the door. Although this might call to mind the more famous sound of Fate knocking at the door in Beethoven's Fifth Symphony—an important referent for modernist composers and writers— Burgess avoids the potential for heavy drama. The knocking is suggested by triplets played on flute, oboe, and cello preceding unaccompanied voice. Then all instruments join for a joyful resolution "No, no, it is the three strange angels. / Admit them, admit them" (*Poems* 205).

"Snake" is long and languorous, extending over 13 minutes, with sparse instrumental passages and a more pronounced parlando style. Marc Jeannin has noted that this piece seems to be in "slow motion" (Jeannin 2010: 10).

Certainly, there are long passages which evoke "the intense still noon", and the slowness of the snake "as if thrice adream" (*Poems* 304). This setting begins and ends with long slow instrumental passages. The intro lasts more than a minute and here the flute particularly recalls the sinuous music of Debussy's *L'après-midi d'un faune*. The languor is punctuated by clamorous moments of doubt about the poet's manhood—"If you were a man" (*Poems* 303)—and whether he should kill or revere the snake. The poet's inner conflict is a theme running through these poems and which Burgess mimics in his music, with the parlando style here contrasting with the sinuous movement of the snake.

"Bavarian Gentians" was written a few months before Lawrence's death, in the same period as the "Ship of Death". Like Persephone, the poet is fading and though Lawrence seems to be affirming death, the music underlines an ambivalence. While the poem descends "down the darker and darker stairs" (*Poems* 611), the music ascends, finishing on a long high note. The ascent could be interpreted as a triumph—a final coming through perhaps—although it also suggests an interrogative tone.

Overall, the modernist music of Burgess's settings complements the modernism of Lawrence's poetry, while the song cycle also emphasises different phases of his life and a sense of development. In this sense, the Suite seems symphonic. It is probably no coincidence that its duration approximates to his Third Symphony, since Burgess's compositional method was to decide how long a piece of music would last: "A symphony was, before Sibelius's Seventh, expected to last at least 30 minutes. I foreheard mine as lasting between thirty-five and forty [minutes], with this duration parcelled as follows: first movement, about twelve minutes; second (scherzo), five; slow movement, eight; finale, ten or more" (1982: 52). This compares closely with the timings of *Man Who Has Come Through*, in which the songs last ten, three, fourteen, and six minutes, with "Snake", the third song, standing out as a doubly extended slow movement.

Burgess's *Napoleon Symphony: A Novel in Four Movements* (1974), which followed the structure of Beethoven's *Eroica Symphony*, took its title not from the key but from the book's subject. I would argue that Burgess also proposes a unity for his Suite in its title, *Man Who Has Come Through*. The significance of the symphonic structure, then, is to underscore the key theme that unites the four poems and, more broadly, what Burgess perceives as a keynote of Lawrence's oeuvre: the struggle to become a man in all his relationships—with mother, with wife, with the living world, and finally, with death.

NOTES

1. A more complete list is offered in Phillips 2010: Appendix 1.
2. Available on YouTube.
3. University of Nottingham, Manuscripts and Special Collections La S 1/4/11.
4. University of Nottingham, Manuscripts and Special Collections La Z 10/1/13/1.
5. Recording held at the Anthony Burgess Foundation, Manchester.
6. University of Nottingham, Manuscripts and Special Collections La S 1/4/5.
7. My thanks to Andrew Biswell for pointing this out.

REFERENCES

Burgess, Anthony. 1982. *This Man and Music*. London: Hutchinson.

———. 1985. *Flame into Being: The Life and Work of D.H. Lawrence*. London: William Heinemann.

———. 1998. Lorenzo. In *One Man's Chorus*, 299–303. New York: Carrol & Graf.

Chaudhuri, Amit. 2003. *D.H. Lawrence and "Difference"*. Oxford: Oxford University Press.

Jeannin, Marc, ed. 2009. *Anthony Burgess: Music in Literature and Literature in Music*. Newcastle upon Tyne: Cambridge Scholars Publishing.

———, ed. 2010. *Anthony Burgess: Selected Songs/Chansons Choisies*. Angers: Presses de l'Université d'Angers.

Phillips, Paul. 2009. That Man and Music: Ten Reasons Why Anthony Burgess's Music Matters. In *Anthony Burgess: Music in Literature and Literature in Music*, ed. Marc Jeannin, 7–19. Newcastle: Cambridge Scholars.

———. 2010. *A Clockwork Counterpoint: The Music and Literature of Anthony Burgess*. Manchester/New York: Manchester University Press.

Roberts, Michael, ed. 1943. *The Faber Book of Modern Verse*. London: Faber & Faber.

Sparling, James. 2003. *The Fusion of Two Art Forms in the Work of Anthony Burgess*. Unpublished Lecture from 1986, Updated 2003. Archives of the Anthony Burgess Foundation, Manchester.

Appendix: D.H. Lawrence Set to Music

The following is a chronological list, by no means exhaustive, of some musical settings of Lawrence's work, with references to sources and further information where applicable.

1914	**Peter Warlock** (1894–1930). Red o'er the moon (lost). Setting of D.H. Lawrence poem. Cited in Stephen Banfield. 1985. *Sensibility and English Song: Critical Studies of the Early Twentieth Century*. Cambridge: Cambridge University Press, 525.
1916	**Arthur Walter Kramer** (1890–1969). Green. Setting of poem by D.H. Lawrence. Cited in the British Library Catalogue and in Warren Roberts and Paul Poplawski, eds. 2001. *A Bibliography of D.H. Lawrence*, 3rd ed. Cambridge: Cambridge University Press, 458.
1932	**Adolph Weiss** (1891–1971). *Sketches for "David"*. "An opera in rhythmic declaration, about D.H. Lawrence" (unfinished). Cited in James Karman, ed. 2011. *The Collected Letters of Robinson Jeffers: Volume Two 1931–1939*. Stanford, CA: Stanford University Press.

(continued)

© The Author(s) 2019
S. Reid, *D.H. Lawrence, Music and Modernism*,
Palgrave Studies in Music and Literature,
https://doi.org/10.1007/978-3-030-04999-7

(continued)

1933–1934	**Elizabeth Lutyens** (1906–1983). *Four Songs, for tenor and piano.* 1. Stanzas, by Emily Brontë 2. Thief in the Night, by D.H. Lawrence 3. Nonentity, by D.H. Lawrence 4. Feste's Song, by William Shakespeare Reviewed in the *Times* as "incompletely incubated and inconsequential" (23 July 1934). Cited in Rhiannon Matthias. 2012. *Lutyens, Maconchy, Williams and Twentieth-Century British Music: A Blest Trio of Sirens.* Abingdon: Ashgate, 49.
1940–1942	**Peter Racine Fricker** (1920–1990). Five Songs 1. Giorno dei Morti, by D.H. Lawrence 2. Southern Pastoral, by Yetza Gillsespie 3. Serenade, by Sacheverell Sitwell 4. Tchirek Song, trans. Arthur Waley 5. Egypt's Might Is Tumbled Down, by Mary Coleridge https://www.library.ucsb.edu/special-collections/performing-arts/pamss17c
1941	**Benjamin Britten** (1913–1976). Music for D.H. Lawrence's *The Rocking Horse Winner* adapted by W.H. Auden and James Stern. Cited in Mervyn Cooke, ed. 1999. *The Cambridge Companion to Benjamin Britten.* Cambridge: Cambridge University Press.
Late 1940s	**James McAuley** (1917–1976). Green. Poem by D.H. Lawrence. Cited: http://www.fabermusic.com/repertoire/small-town-941
1954	**Peggy Glanville-Hicks** (1912–1990). *Etruscan Concerto.* For piano and chamber orchestra. Includes quotations from *Sketches of Etruscan Places* by D.H. Lawrence. "Each movement is an evocation of these quotes". Website: www.australianmusiccentre.com.au/work/glanville-hicks-peggy-etruscan-concerto
1958	**Peter Sculthorpe** (1929–2014). *Sun.* For voice and piano. Song cycle of three D.H. Lawrence poems. 1. Sun in Me 2. Tropic 3. Desire Goes Down into the Sea
1961	*Irkanda IV.* For solo violin, strings and percussion. Reprises the setting of "Sun in me".
1963	*The Fifth Continent.* Radiophonic work for speaker, orchestra, and recorded sound (didjeridu and wind). Quotes from Lawrence's novel *Kangaroo* and structures a narrative around his time in Australia.
1965	*Sun Music* I. For brass and strings. "Lawrence … and also the Mexican sun, the Australian sun and my own sun are ever present in it" (Sculthorpe, qtd. Richards 2014: 41)

(continued)

(continued)

1976	*Small Town.* For small orchestra. Reworks the third movement of *The Fifth Continent* Website: www.petersculthorpe.com.au/worklist.htm "Lawrence runs like a vein of ore through Sculthorpe's music": Fiona Richards. 2014. D.H. Lawrence and Peter Sculthorpe. *Journal of D.H. Lawrence Studies* 3.3: 33–50.

1960	**Vittorio Rieti** (1898–1994). *Four D.H. Lawrence Songs.* New York: General Music Publishing and London: Novello.
	    1. Aware
	    2. Thomas Earp
	    3. December Night
	    4. Quite Forsaken
	Cited in Warren Roberts and Paul Poplawski, eds. 2001. *A Bibliography of D.H. Lawrence*, 3rd edn. Cambridge: Cambridge University Press, 288.

1963	**Arnold Cooke** (1906–2005). Nocturnes. A cycle of five songs for soprano, horn, and piano.
	    1. The Moon, by P.B. Shelley
	    2. Returning, We Hear the Larks, by Isaac Rosenberg
	    3. River Roses, by D.H. Lawrence
	    4. The Owl, by A.L. Tennyson
	    5. Boat Song, by John Davidson
	http://www.worldcat.org/title/nocturnes-a-cycle-of-five-songs-for-soprano-horn-and-piano/oclc/741195381?referer=di&ht=edition

1966	**Christopher Rathbone** (b. 1947). Hibiscus and Salvia Flowers. Cantata for tenor and bass soloists, treble choir, six wind soloists, strings, percussion. Website: http://www.rathbonemusic.co.uk

1966	**Dennis Riley** (1943–1999). Cantata I (Op. 8). For mezzo soprano, tenor saxophone, vibraphone, cello, and piano. Setting two texts by D.H. Lawrence:
	    1. Those That Go Searching For Love
	    2. If There Were Not an Utter and Absolute Dark of Silence
	Cited in Kenneth Sheldon Klaus. 1994. *Chamber Music for Solo Voice and Instruments, 1960–1989: An Annotated Guide.* Berkeley, CA: Fallen Leaf Press, 123.

1969	**Will Ogdon** (1921–2013). River Roses. For soprano, flute, and double bass. Setting of D.H. Lawrence poem. Website: www.newworldrecords.org/uploads/fileENjA1.pdf
1971	**Herbert Elwell** (1898–1974). Service of All the Dead. Setting of D.H. Lawrence's poem. http://www.newworldrecords.org/uploads/fileWlmrW.pdf
1977	**Ruth Schönthal** (1924–2006). Poor Bit of a Wench. For voice and piano. www.pytheasmusic.org

(*continued*)

(continued)

1979	**Phillip Rhodes** (b. 1940). *Visions of Remembrance*. For two sopranos and twelve instruments.

    1. Flashback, by Douglas Worth
    2. Grown-Up Relatives, by Anna Jean Rhodes
    3. My Grandmother's Love Letters, by Hart Crane
    4. Piano, by D.H. Lawrence
    Epilogue
Website: www.prhodescomposer.com/chamber.html
Cited by Bethan Jones. 2012. Setting Lawrence. *D.H. Lawrence Studies (Korea)* 20: 164–174.

1980   **Thea Musgrave** (b. 1928). *The Last Twilight*. For chorus and orchestra. Based on *Twilight in Italy*. Commissioned by Anthony Branch and New Mexico D.H. Lawrence Festival: http://www.musicsalesclassical.com/composer/work/1098/11659

1985   **Anthony Burgess** (1917–1993). *Man Who Has Come Through*. D.H. Lawrence song cycle for tenor, flute, oboe, violoncello, and piano. Optional prelude and/or postlude
    1. End of Another Home Holiday
    2. Song of a Man Who Has Come Through
    3. Snake
    4. Bavarian Gentians
See above: Chapter 9 "Anthony Burgess's D.H. Lawrence Suite".

1985   **Andrew Downes** (b. 1950). Piano (Op. 32). A setting of D.H. Lawrence's poem for high voices with piano. www.andrewdownes.com

1985   **Nigel Osborne** (b. 1948). *For a Moment*. Song cycle for female choir, violoncello, and Kandyan drum.
    1. The Dawn Verse
    2. For a Moment
    3. Tarantella
    4. What Is Man Without an Income?
    5. The Drained Cup
Commissioned and first performed by the Cantamus choir, conducted by Pamela Cook, at the D.H. Lawrence Centenary Festival.
Bethan Jones. 2012. Setting Lawrence. *D.H. Lawrence Studies (Korea)* 20: 164–174.

1985   **Mike Westbrook** (b. 1936). *The Ass*. A theatrical setting of Lawrence's poem, including "Lu Me Scecca", a traditional Sicilian song, with English lyrics by Kate Westbrook.
Website: www.westbrookjazz.co.uk/katewestbrook/asscd.shtml

(*continued*)

(continued)

1985	**John Joubert** (b. 1927). Autumn Rain (Op. 105). Setting for choir and piano, commissioned by Cantamus for the D.H. Lawrence Centenary Festival.
1987	The Instant Moment (Op. 110). Five settings from D.H. Lawrence's Look! We Have Come Through! For baritone and string orchestra. 1. Bei Hennef 2. Loggerheads 3. And Oh—That the Man I Am Might Cease To Be 4. December Night 5. Moonrise https://www.johnjoubert.org.uk
1987	**Hans Gefors** (b. 1952). Whales Weep Not. For mixed choir a capella. http://www.musiquecontemporaine.fr/record/oai:cimu-aloes:0095677?language=fr
c. 1987	**James Simmons** (1933–2001). An Irish poet who set poems "mainly by Yeats, but also by Emily Dickinson, D.H. Lawrence, Emily Bronte, Edward Thomas and Blake". Cited in A.S. Knowland. 1992. The Thoughtful Poetry of James Simmons. In *Contemporary Irish Poetry: A Collection of Critical Essays*, ed. Elmer Andrews, 264–285. Basingstoke: Palgrave Macmillan, 265.
1988	**Joanne Forman** (b. 1934). *Nottingham Spleen: Song Cycle for Tenor and Piano.* Includes four poems from *Pansies.* "Stand Up!", "Things Men Have Made", "The Mosquito Knows", and "Start a Revolution". https://archiveshub.jisc.ac.uk/search/archives/df2e7790-1e3f-3970-b0a7-60f1f707ab15
1991	**Gary Bachlund** (b. 1947). To Women As Far As I'm Concerned. For tenor and piano. http://www.bachlund.org/To_Women_As_Far_As_I%27m_Concerned.htm
1993–1996	**Evan Hause** (b. 1967). The Ship of Death (Symphony No. 1). For soprano, contralto, tenor, baritone and large chorus and orchestra. www.evanhause.com
1996	**Carol Barnett** (b. 1949). Piano (after D.H. Lawrence). For solo piano. http://www.carolbarnett.net
1988–1989	**David Matthews** (b. 1943). The Ship of Death. For eight mixed voices.
1994	*Skies Now Are Skies.* For tenor and string quartet. Setting of words by e.e. cummings, D.H. Lawrence, and from The Song of Solomon (see also 2013). Cited: http://www.david-matthews.co.uk/works
c. 1995	*Moments of Vision.* Settings of texts by D.H. Lawrence for mixed voices.
1992	**Ollie Kortekangas** (b. 1955). Amores: Three Songs to Poems by D.H. Lawrence. For mezzo soprano and strings.
1995	Three Romances. Settings of texts by D.H. Lawrence for mixed choir. www.olliekortekangas.com

(*continued*)

(continued)

1998	**Hugh Wood** (b. 1932). *D.H. Lawrence Songs: For High Voice and Piano* (Op. 14). Setting five poems: 1. Dog Tired 2. Gloire de Dijon 3. Kisses in the Train 4. River Roses 5. Roses on the Breakfast Table Cited in Edward Venn. 2016. *The Music of Hugh Wood.* London and New York: Routledge, 244.
1998	**Geoff Palmer.** *Snatches of Lovely Oblivion.* Four songs to D.H. Lawrence poems, for chamber choir and string quartet. 1. Shadows 2. Dog Tired 3. Trust 4. A White Blossom and Piano (simultaneous setting) Website: https://www.geoffpalmercomposer.com/music/snatches-of-lovely-oblivion-four-songs-to-poems-by-d-h-lawrence/
1996	**William Neil** (b. 1954). *The Waters Are Shaking the Moon.* For mezzo soprano and piano. 1. The Hostile Sun 2. Twilight 3. Mystery 4. Love Message 5. Piano 6. Tease 7. Reach Over 8. There Is Rain in Me 9. Baby Songs 10. Shades 11. White Blossom 12. To a Certain Young Lady Website: http://williamneil.net/robot/vocal-music/classical-3/ Bethan Jones. 2012. Setting Lawrence. *D.H. Lawrence Studies (Korea)* 20: 164–174. Nick Ceramella. 2013. Singing Lawrence's Poetry: Interview with Charlotte Stoppelenburg. In *Lake Garda: Gateway to D.H. Lawrence's Voyage to the Sun,* ed. Nick Ceramella, 331–335. Newcastle: Cambridge Scholars. William Neil. 2013. Musical Voyage to the Sun. In *Lake Garda: Gateway to D.H. Lawrence's Voyage to the Sun,* ed. Nick Ceramella, 325–330. Newcastle: Cambridge Scholars.

(continued)

(continued)

2008	**Howard Skempton** (b. 1947). *The Moon Is Flashing*. For tenor and full orchestra. 1. The Moon Is Flashing, by Howard Skempton 2. A Day in Three Wipes, by Chris Newman 3. Snake, by D.H. Lawrence Details at https://global.oup.com/academic/product/the-moon-is-flashing-9780193359758?cc=us&lang=en&#
2012	**Phillip Cooke** (b. 1980). *Three Partsongs*. For choir and organ. 1. I Stood on a Tower, by Tennyson 2. Green, by D.H. Lawrence 3. How Clear, How Lovely, by A.E. Housman. Website: www.phillipcooke.com/list-of-works
2013	**David Matthews** (b. 1932). *Skies Now Are Skies*. For tenor and chamber orchestra. Setting of words by e.e. cummings and D.H. Lawrence (see also 1994). Website: www.david-matthews.co.uk/works/
2013	**Helen Grime** (b. 1981). *Near Midnight*. Orchestral work inspired by D.H. Lawrence's poem "Weeknight Service". Premiered at Bridgewater Hall, Manchester. Website: www.musicsalesclassical.com/composer/work/3953/48311
2014	**Andrew Downes** (b. 1950). Butterfly. Commission for Cantamus Choir. www.andrewdownes.com
2014	**Nick Mulvey** (b. 1984). Cucurucu. Song adaptation of D.H. Lawrence's "Piano". Reached number 26 in the UK Singles Chart. Website: www.songfacts.com/detail.php?id=32613
2015	**Richard Hundley** (b. 1930). Are They Shadows and Other Songs. Ten song settings for voice and piano, including D.H. Lawrence's poem "The Elephant Is Slow to Mate". https://www.sheetmusicplus.com/title/are-they-shadows-and-other-songs-sheet-music/20149194
2016	Music by **Gareth Williams**, libretto by **Anna Chatterton**. *Rocking Horse Winner*. A Tapestry Opera production, based on the short story by D.H. Lawrence. Website: www.tapestryopera.com/rocking
2017	**Fabio Furio**. Sea and Sardinia. Theatrical performance of text by D.H. Lawrence, with videos and narration, music for bandoneon, violin, piano, and double bass. London premiere at Steiner Hall, 14 January 2017. https://www.eventbrite.co.uk/e/sea-and-sardinia-novafonic-quartet-with-simeone-latininarratordirector-tickets-29767172414#
2017	**Howard Skempton** (b. 1947). Man and Bat. Setting of D.H. Lawrence poem for baritone, five strings, and piano. World premiere at Upper Chapel, Sheffield, on 20 July 2017. Website: https://global.oup.com/academic/product/man-and-bat

Index[1]

---

[1] Note: Page numbers followed by 'n' refer to notes.

© The Author(s) 2019
S. Reid, *D.H. Lawrence, Music and Modernism*,
Palgrave Studies in Music and Literature,
https://doi.org/10.1007/978-3-030-04999-7

Lightning Source UK Ltd.
Milton Keynes UK
UKHW020306130219
337169UK00009B/679/P